Scripta Series in Geography

Series Editors:

Richard E. Lonsdale, University of Nebraska
Antony R. Orme, University of California
Theodore Shabad, Columbia University
James O. Wheeler, University of Georgia

In preparation:

Klee, G. A.: World Systems of Traditional Resource Management
Yeates, M. H.: North American Urban Patterns
Brunn, S. D./Wheeler, J. O.: The American Metropolitan Systems
Earney, F. C. F.: Petroleum and Hard Minerals from the Sea
Bourne, L. S.: The Geography of Housing
Jackson, R. H.: Land Use in America

The Geography of Famine

William A. Dando

A HALSTED PRESS BOOK

 V. H. Winston & Sons

John Wiley & Sons
New York

Copyright © V. H. Winston & Sons 1980
First published 1980 by
Edward Arnold (Publishers) Ltd.,
41 Bedford Square, London WC1B 3DQ
and published simultaneously in the United States of America by Halsted Press, a division of
John Wiley & Sons Inc.

British Library Cataloguing in Publication Data

Dando, William A
    The geography of famine, (Scripta series in geography).
    1. Famines
    I. Title
    361.5'5   HC79.F3

    ISBN 0-7131-6295-3

Library of Congress Cataloging in Publication Data

Dando, William A
    Geography of famine.

    (Scripta series in geography)
    Includes bibliographical references and index.
    1. Famines.   2. Food supply.   I. Title.
    II. Series.
    HC79.F3D36   338.1'9   80-11145

    ISBN 0-470-26956-1

To Pap Dando who taught me to love the land and to
Mom Dando who instilled in me the true significance of bread

Typeset in the United States of America by
Marie Maddalena of V. H. Winston & Sons
Printed in Great Britain by
Richard Clay (The Chaucer Press) Ltd,
Bungay, Suffolk

Contents

Acknowledgements

This book had its origin in my discovery of numerous articles and references to droughts producing famines in Imperial Russia and the Soviet Union, while researching data for my Ph.D. thesis in the Library of Congress. Drought and famine were synonymous to many writers, and I began to record citations on the margins of my notes with the intent to test this correlation some day. A Faculty Research Grant some years later from the University of Maryland enabled me to work in the Hoover Library, Stanford University, and my working hypothesis was, "droughts cause famines." What I learned at Stanford troubled me deeply. Searching for solutions to many questions raised and so few answered, I turned to L. Schuyler Fonaroff—a noted medical geographer. We discussed my research on drought and famine, and with his encouragement I wrote an article entitled, "Man-Made Famines: Some Geographical Insights from an Exploratory Study of a Millennium of Russian Famines," which was published in the *Ecology of Food and Nutrition*. This article stimulated a great deal of discussion and I received over three hundred requests for reprints. A Fulbright-Hays Research Grant offered me the opportunity to study wheat-drought-famine in Romania, other grants permitted me to study at various national and international libraries and a University of North Dakota Faculty Research Grant assisted me in developing a computer data bank. This data bank now contains information from over 8000 famines that have occurred in the past 6000 years. A friend, Richard Lonsdale, suggested that I amalgamate the essence of numerous articles and professional papers into a book on famine. I hesitated at first because the topic carries emotional overtones and few professional geographers have written on famines. However, Victor Winston convinced me that a book on the spatial and temporal aspects of famine would be a contribution to the literature. When the book was written I still had doubts, for I had learned a great deal and had more questions in my mind than answers on paper. John Borchert advised me to submit the manuscript for publication, contending that he believed I had employed a scholarly approach to the topic. I fully realize this book is not an exhaustive or learned treatise: any one chapter could easily have been expanded to fill a volume. Although dealing with an extraordinarily complex subject, my basic theme at the onset and at the end remained, "natural factors cause crop failures, but humans cause famines," famines are man-made.

In spite of a steady increasing interest in world food problems, there is no standard definition for famine, research remains lax and few attempts have been made to study famines in a systematic and unbiased manner. The literature on the subject, with some exceptions, is polemical and emotional rather than constructive; negative rather than positive. Most existing works confine their investigations to describing a single famine, to proving that climatic perturbations trigger famines while neglecting the broader aspects which confront decision-makers or to enhancing a most uncompromising attitude. What I have attempted is primarily to supply in an elementary form a systematic introduction to the study of the problem, endeavoring to discard all *a priori* presumptions. At the same time, an effort has been made to give unity to the various speculations by viewing them all steadily in the light of one philosophical conception. Any claim this book may have to originality must be based on the rearrangement and combination of thousands of observations recorded in the past 6000 years, rather than on the invention of anything new.

The writer of a book of this type owes so much to so many people that it would be impossible to name them all. To a few whose contributions were great, thanks may be given by name. Fred Schneider and Sigrid Khera, anthropoligists, and Alan Fusoni, an historian at the National Agricultural Library, read and commented on the Introduction and Chapter 2; R. D. Mower, Director of the University of North Dakota Institute for Remote Sensing, examined Chapter 1; Rames Toma, a nutritionist, reviewed parts of Chapter 3; Kang-tsung Chang, geographer, gave helpful advice on Chapter 5; participants and colleagues at the Midwestern Conference on Food and Social Policy provided helpful suggestions for Chapter 6; Tom Howard, historian, read Chapter 7; S. M. Bhardwaj, geographer, suggested modifications for Chapter 8 and Douglas Munski, geographer, read and commented on the entire text. The errors, omissions, shortcomings, inaccuracies or expressions of opinions in this book remain solely mine. Joseph Wiedel, Donn Baker, Howard Sage and Brad Ellison did most of the diagrams and maps. Gail Krueger, Marcie Leavy and Tina Moe typed the manuscript. Inestimable thanks go to my wife, Caroline, for patience, for encouragement and for editing every page. Finally, I would like to acknowledge a special debt of gratitude to Gabriel Betz and John Borchert for their constant support, and to the University of North Dakota for providing an academic atmosphere where dreams may be converted into realities.

William A. Dando
Department of Geography
University of North Dakota

Introduction

Since the beginning of time those who have inhabited the earth have experienced hunger, starvation and famine. Epidemic starvation or famine was a severe but temporary setback in homo sapien's long struggle to make food supplies available to a given population. Food resources and supplies which had been adequate for one generation would not suffice for a new generation with many additional mouths to feed. Food shortages threatened the very existence of isolated civilizations thousands of years ago, and food maldistribution in the last quarter of the 20th century threatens man's interdependent world civilization. Potential for the first world famine seems unbelievable, for publicized accounts of science successfully applied to farming had all but dispelled theories that population would increase until it exceeded food supplies. Then a series of events occurred, some triggered by natural forces and most intensified by political, economic and cultural factors, which led numbers of prominent demographers, human ecologists and economists to contend that the balance between people and food is more precarious today than in any period of recorded history.[1] Any analysis of human evolution and population growth must concern itself with the different ways men have supplied themselves with sustenance. All homo sapiens must ingest food which must come from animal and vegetable life. Earliest people lived by scavenging, hunting animals, catching fish and gathering wild berries, grubs, roots, honey and anything which by trial and error they found to be edible. This primitive means of gaining a livelihood, a hunting and gathering economy, fostered a life of hardship and scarcity. Winter was a season of acute shortage for animals migrated, berries shriveled and food plants died. Not surprisingly, many primitive hunters and gatherers perished from starvation every winter or spring. It has been estimated that 100,000 years before our era there were only about 5 million people in the world, for hunters and gatherers needed vast areas of land to collect sufficient food for survival.

Continuous experimentation with alternate foods and new foods led to the discovery that not only could seeds and fruits be consumed during the harvest season, but also stored for use in winter. Additionally, it was found that if the seeds of selected plants were scattered over the earth, crops of the seed or grass grew and could be harvested to provide sustenance for another winter. Unwanted plants were cleared away from selected fertile sites and replaced with domesticated varieties to be used for food. Wandering groups became more sedentary and found time to tame animals, develop herds and flocks and keep these animate food sources as "living larders" along with grain, dried fruits or nuts. Animals could be slaughtered in winter or as required and families could eat meat and other foods regularly instead of only at harvest periods or after successful hunting trips. Milk from animals was found to be a nourishing drink and provided a reason for keeping more female than male animals and for retaining only those males whose offspring were docile, meatier and provided more milk. Skins and hides were found to be useful for making food containers, clothing and household utensils. Man hoarded the treasure of his knowledge and technical skill increased from generation to generation, in spite of occasional periods of retrogression.

Food production by simple agriculture exceeded that secured from hunting and gathering. Larger numbers of people were able to survive in areas where agriculture was practiced. They soon learned to till the ground and to train animals to assist in field tasks. Hard work, inventions and innovations provided them with security and winters were no longer feared as they were in the past. The development of simple agriculture and then a division of labor between pastoralism and vegetable-grain agriculture about ten to twelve thousand years ago was by far the most important revolution in human history, for the growth in human population stems from this fundamental change in the method of obtaining food.[2]

Homo sapiens came at last to the knowledge of their mastery over growing things. They calculated the seasons, discovered the virtue of sun and rain and were able to distinguish good soil from bad. However, everyone did not grow the same crops, tend the same animals or favor similar diets. Great variations in world climates, soil types and food production potentials induced groups to develop distinct food preferences. Variations were not confined to food basics such as meats, rice, wheat, corn, rye, barley or potatoes, but applied to a whole array of foods and this later became important for trade.

In a number of definite localities, mostly confined to the muddy deltas or flood plains of large rivers, favored agricultural societies were able to provide more than adequate food in good years for their people and to store reserves for bad years. Each society had its own character and strengths and each supported nonagricultural specialists who produced no food themselves. As nonagricultural specialization developed and as the productivity of farmers increased, more and more people were able to be supported from less and less land.[3] The first specialists were craftsmen who produced useful tools and weapons; closely following if not preceding them were chiefs, war leaders and priests. Three or four millennia before the birth of Christ certain centers of high civilization had already arisen. While the rest of the world was content to languish in the conditions of prehistory, these favored spots were embarked upon the sea of history proper.

A few hundred years ago societies which nurtured, through their agricultural surpluses, large numbers of specialists divided into two types. The first, called the "vegetable civilizations," produced writers, teachers, doctors, lawyers and traders, but few specialists in manufacturing. The second type, the "machine civilization," produced not only the specialists of vegetable civilization but elaborated the manufacturing segment of its economy, utilizing inanimate power extensively. Whole communities were created in which all or almost all of the inhabitants were involved with nonagricultural employment. In these highly specialized segments of machine societies, most of the people were and are physically divorced from the agricultural resources needed to sustain their life—yet tied to basic food supplies by critical transportation-communication networks.[4]

Commercial food suppliers for machine societies quickly identified regions on earth where specialty crops or animal products could be produced most inexpensively and transported most easily to urban markets. They delimited international and national trade areas where cultural or physical restrictions influenced consumptive patterns, crops grown or animals produced for market, and created new markets for various foods which have shifted geographically in time. Agriculture, one of the most respected of all economic activities throughout human history, slowly became the stepchild of machine civilizations. Still, the present distribution of people in the world is closely related to areas of food surplus. All advanced societies, including those classified as machine civilizations, are based on agriculture. People live on parts of the earth where they should live; the distribution of population is in essence an indicator of where humans can secure food for survival.[5]

Yet famines have occurred in the world's best agricultural regions, in all natural zones and have not been restricted to one cultural area or one racial group. They have been a recurrent but predictable scourge throughout the inhabited world, and have varied in severity, location and frequency. In most instances a famine was triggered by crop failure in food surplus areas or the restriction of food imports to deficit areas. The primary natural factors creating a crop failure have been drought, floods, frost, disease and insects; the primary human factors creating a famine have been war, political decisions, internal disruption, cultural restraints, poor communications and inadequate transportation. Specific and general locations of high frequency famine regions have shifted as civilizations or nations emerged, flourished and declined, and as food demands in certain places exceeded food production.[6] Constantly topical as long as society has existed, man-environment-food relationships and problems associated with acute, temporary food shortages are approached and resolved in different ways at every stage of human development.[7]

The world, midway between the end of the Second World War and the beginning of the 21st century, accepted as a way-of-life a stable world economic system and continuous spreading prosperity. New nations emerged from old orders confident of uninterrupted economic and social growth. Technical innovations, communication breakthroughs, transportation network expansion and industrial growth gave rise to expectations of steady improvements in the levels of living of all people. But despite these impressive technical accomplishments and energetic endeavors, there has been a general failure to adequately provide food and sustenance to hundreds of millions of people added to our world since 1945. In the 17th century it is estimated that at least 2 million people died of starvation, 10 million in the 18th century and 25 million plus in the 19th century. Predictions abound of starvation on such a scale that more people will die of famine in the 20th century than in any other century in history. In 1972, grain production declined for the first time in decades and the world was made ominously conscious of man's bond with nature and dependence upon others. World food reserves dropped from an 80 day reserve to a 20 day supply in a few years. The world became cognant of its dependence on the surplus food production of a few nations. North America was identified as the only region of the world that produced significantly more food than it consumed.[8] Primary food production had continued to grow more rapidly than had human population, but the increases in food production had not occurred where the population was growing most rapidly. The food scarcity which emerged in the mid-1970s did not prove temporary as most assumed, it became more or less chronic and even worsened. The cruel, eternal problem of hunger, starvation and famine has been recognized, redefined in 20th century terms, spatially analyzed and projections made. Increasing rates of population growth, food and energy consumption, accelerated resource utilization and depletion, widening gaps between the level of living of developed and developing nations, plus climatic changes, all combined within the finite dimensions of a small planet are producing acute alimentary stress. The catastrophic end product of this stress is famine.

NOTES

[1]P. Erlich, "Looking Backward from 2000 A.D.," in *The Crisis of Survival*, E. Odum et al. (Madison: The Progressive Inc. and by Scott, Foresman & Co., 1970), pp. 238–245; N. Greenwood and J. Edwards, *Human Environments and Natural Systems* (North Scituate, Mass.: Duxbury Press, 1973), pp. 98–102; and T. Poleman, "World Food: A Perspective," *Science*, 188 (May 9, 1975), pp. 510–518.

[2]N. Borlaug, *The Green Revolution Peace and Humanity* (Washington, D.C.: Nobel Foundation and Population Reference Bureau, 1971), pp. 1–18; and A. McKenzie, *The Hungry World* (London: Faber & Faber, 1969), pp. 13–17.

[3]E. Deevey, Jr., "The Human Population," *Scientific American* (Sept., 1960), p. 198.

[4]K. Haselden, "The Social and Ethical Setting of the World Food Situation," in *Alternatives for Balancing World Food Production Needs* (Ames, Iowa: The Iowa State University Press, 1967), pp. 19–23.

[5]J. Howe and J. Sewell, "What is Morally Right?", *War on Hunger*, IX (June, 1975), pp. 1–5.

[6]J. Mayer, "Coping with Famine," *Foreign Affairs*, Vol. 53 (1974), pp. 99–101.

[7]W. Dando, "Man-Made Famines: Russia's Past and the Developing World's Future," *Proceedings of the Association of American Geographers*, Vol. 7 (1975), pp. 60–63.

[8]H. Kissinger, "The Global Community and the Struggle Against Famine," Conference, Rome, *Department of State Bulletin*, LXXI, No. 1851 (Dec. 16, 1974), p. 821.

Part I

Man's bond with the Earth

Chapter 1

Parameters for food production

All living things must consume food at short intervals of time. Without food all living things die. Any substance which provides a human with energy and nutrients is food. Energy is needed as fuel for conscious actions and for growth and replacement of body tissues. Nutrients supply the chemical building blocks for tissue growth and replacement, and construct molecules which regulate and coordinate all body activities. Not everyone has the same nutritional requirements, but normal growth and renewal of body tissue are impossible if any essential components are absent from the diet. Human beings eat animals, plants and animal and plant products.[1] Many different foods may be combined to provide the chemicals a human body needs. People must eat both energy-producing foods (carbohydrates and fats) and a balance of other nutrients (proteins, vitamins, minerals and water). Nutritionists maintain that people should consume each day foods from the four "basic food groups": milk and dairy products; meat, fish, and meat products; breads and cereals; and fruits and vegetables. Exactly what a human eats depends on what is available as food, what his parents and companions eat and have eaten, what skills he has to procure and prepare food and other cultural factors.

Plants, however, are the primary producers in all food chains. They manufacture energy-rich organic substances by converting radiant energy from the sun into chemical energy. Plant productivity is dependent upon the energy conversion process, photosynthesis, but in order to perform photosynthesis and other metabolic processes, land plants must extract water and minerals from the soil.[2] Plant agriculture for food and livestock production in any part of the

3

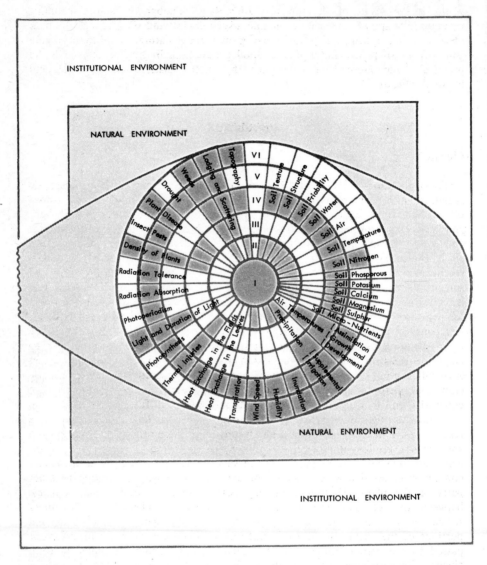

Fig. 1. This diagram illustrates the physical factors considered by the engineer chief while supervising a wheat crop on Dragalina I.A.S. All factors are equally important to the plant, but vary in significance according to changes within the plant as it passes through its life cycle, as indicated by the shaded patterns. Dragalina I.A.S. (state agricultural enterprise) is located in Southeastern Romania.

Ring I	Advanced planning [all]	Ring IV	Sowing procedure
Ring II	Preliminary agrotechniques	Ring V	Plant management
Ring III	Seed selection	Ring VI	Harvest planning

world is the result of the interplay of a large number of factors including geographic or spatial, physical, economic, psychological and social. Since the bulk of the world's agricultural products are grown under natural conditions, climate and soil are of prime importance in food production. In general, climate is the principal basic factor that influences the spatial distribution of crops and livestock (Figure 1).

PHYSICAL

Climate

From the sun, planet earth receives a constant stream of electromagnetic radiation. The electromagnetic spectrum consists of gamma rays, x-rays, ultraviolet, visible light, infrared light (heat rays) and radio waves. Visible light and heat rays profoundly affect the rates at which plants can photosynthesize and grow. Transparency of the atmosphere, cloud cover, position of the plant on earth (latitude) and time of year determine the amount of radiation which reaches a plant on the earth's surface. The angle at which vertical rays from the sun hit the earth determines the intensity of solar radiation at a place. This angle is determined primarily by latitude and by seasons. Constant positive temperatures in the tropics, annually changing temperature in the mid latitudes and constant negative temperature in the polar regions are a direct consequence of radiation regimes. Solar radiation strikes the surface in polar regions at a sharp angle, whereas incoming solar radiation strikes the equatorial regions almost perpendicularly. Incoming solar radiation must penetrate more atmospheric equivalent before reaching the surface of the earth in polar regions than equatorial, and more radiation is scattered, absorbed or diffused.[3]

Plants, through photosynthesis, use solar energy to link atoms together, a reaction wherein sunlight, water and carbon dioxide are utilized to form glucose and oxygen. Photosynthesis occurs primarily in the leaves of green plants. Plant leaves are thin and flat to maximize the surface area that receives sunlight, and contain veins so that water can be brought in and sugar transported to other parts of the plant. Thousands of tiny pores, stomates, regulate gas exchange between the leaf and the atmosphere. Chloroplasts, cells nearest the upper surface of the leaf, contain chlorophyll which absorbs light in the blue and red portions of the visible spectrum. Transformed radiant energy in chemical form is passed to the carbon atoms of carbon dioxide, and carbons are linked to form glucose. Glucose is converted to sucrose or starch. Plant cells use the products of photosynthesis as a source of energy and to build organic molecules. Nonphotosynthetic cells within the plant use this energy for biochemical reactions, to transport substances or to take up minerals from the soil.

Plant growth is determined by many environmental variables, but the factors that influence the rate of photosynthesis are light, temperature and water. Both the number of daylight hours and the intensity of light are important. The greater the daylight period, the greater the number of hours a plant can carry on photosynthesis. Intensity of light affects photosynthetic rates and light intensity required for maximum photosynthesis differs from species to species. Temperature also has a profound effect on plants for it influences the rate of plant growth. Photosynthesis and plant growth proceed slowly at temperatures below 7°C and increase as temperature rises. Optimal temperatures for growth and development of most plants are between 20°C and 35°C. High temperatures, from 45°C to 50°C, are detrimental to the growth of most food plants. Accelerated respiration at high temperatures burns up the products of photosynthesis and plant growth is reduced. Most food plants grow and produce better with alternating day temperature regimes, i.e., high daytime temperatures and low nighttime temperatures. High nighttime temperatures stimulate respiration but with no photosynthesis, sugar made during the light period of the day is consumed by the plant.[4] Many food crops which must synthesize a vast amount of carbohydrate in a limited time cannot be grown in regions with high night temperatures in summer. Food plant growth in the tropics is limited by the imbalance between photosynthesis and respiration as a result of high night temperatures.

Moisture

Water, within the plant and available in the soil, also affects the photosynthesis process. Photosynthesis requires CO_2 and can only occur if leaf pores are open. Open stomates permit water vapor to escape from the interior of the leaf. Water is present in intercellular spaces to maintain internal plant temperatures for a leaf absorbs more energy than it uses. Excessive heat energy must be dissipated or cells will be destroyed. A plant utilizes water as a coolant but must replenish expended leaf cell water supplies. Leaf cells seek water from conductive tissues, and the conductive tissues from the soil via the roots. The loss of water from the leaves of plants as a result of evaporation of cellular water and the movement of water vapor through the stomates is known as *transpiration*. During the night, when pores are closed and transpiration ceases, plants take up water until completely rehydrated. If plants cannot replenish water lost by transpiration, the leaves will wilt and stomates close. Many agricultural plants of significance to human survival utilize large amounts of water. However, water is also lost by evaporation from the surface of the soil. Solar radiation striking the soil, heats the soil surface and converts some soil water to water vapor. Water loss from the soil by transpiration and direct evaporation is described as *evapotranspiration*. Total crop plant productivity at a place is closely related to the amount of water lost each agricultural year by evapotranspiration. Crop plants differ in water requirements, and variations in plant water needs often determine where these plants can be grown.

Soils

Soils supply moisture and nutrients to plants, and crop plants supply nutrients to all organisms whose lives depend on plants. Recognized as mankind's most valuable natural resource, soils are a dynamic natural body on the surface of the earth in which plants grow. Along with providing the foothold for the plants needed for human survival, the most important characteristic of any soil is its fertility. Fertility of a particular soil is a resultant of many variable factors such as texture, structure and tilth, temperature, depth and permeability, aeration and moisture, mineral composition, microorganisms and age.[5] *Texture* is the fineness or coarseness of particles which make up a soil. Commonly, four main textural grades are recognized—gravel, sand, silt and clay. The water holding quality of a soil is governed by texture. Gravelly and sandy soils tend to drain too quickly; clayey soils have drainage problems; a mixture of sand, silt and clay is best for most agricultural purposes. *Structure* refers to the arrangement of soil grains into physical aggregates. Soils possess various structures and react differently to tillage. The principal forms of soil structure are platy, prismatic, columnar, blocky and granular. Although color of soil does not indicate fertility, it bears a reliable relation to soil temperature. Light colored soils react differently to solar radiation than dark colored soils. Some soils are classified as warm soils and others cold, are ready for tillage earlier in the growing season and radiate heat differently at night. Soils vary in depth from a few centimeters to meters. Thin soils mantling underlying bedrock hinder tillage and cultivation; impermeable soils inhibit plant root penetration and growth. Indurated subsoils or compacted layers can reduce the amounts of air and water in a soil. Air is necessary in a soil for seed germination and plant development. Water, absolutely essential for plant life, is present on soil grains, in capillary fillings of spaces between grains and in various chemical bonds within and around soil aggregates. Both air and water partially control fertility and are dependent upon soil texture, structure and depth of water table. Soils are made up of relatively insoluble mineral materials, soluble mineral materials and organic matter. Soluble mineral materials, calcium, potassium, magnesium, etc., comprise the majority of nutrients necessary for plant life. Organic matter, composed chiefly of dead and partially decomposed plant life, is useful for plants only if it is broken down and releases nitrogen and phosphorus into inorganic form. A physical aggregate of mineral particles, chemical plant foods and dead organic matter does not in itself produce a fertile environment for plant roots. Release of the nutrient elements requires the destruction by microorganisms of organic matter from past crops or that of the native soil. Other beneficial properties of organic matter include the capacity to hold nutrient elements such as potassium, calcium and magnesium in combination to increase mellowness and friability, and to retain soil moisture. Finally, the age of a soil is important in determining fertility and desirable qualities for food plant growth. Soils exhibit distinctly different characteristics at each state in their evolutionary life cycle. Usefulness of a soil for agricultural purposes varies according to slope, drainage, geographical location (relative position and accessibility) and economic need.[6]

Growth of an annual seed plant is in four stages: seed germination, vegetative development, reproductive processes and seed maturation. A mature seed contains a living embryo, a quiescent plant, that starts to grow when the proper combination of moisture, temperature and oxygen exist. Germination is complete

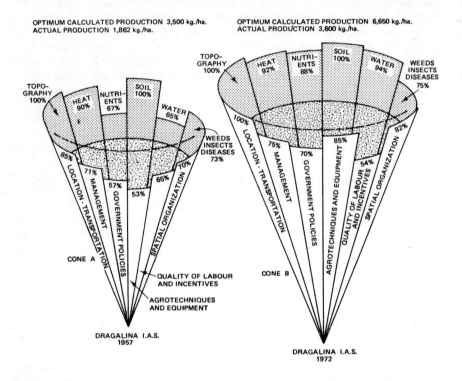

OPTIMUM CALCULATED PRODUCTION 3,500 kg./ha.
ACTUAL PRODUCTION 1,862 kg./ha.

OPTIMUM CALCULATED PRODUCTION 6,650 kg./ha.
ACTUAL PRODUCTION 3,600 kg./ha.

Fig. 2. These cones (A and B) illustrate the principle of limiting institutional and natural factors in agricultural production. Plant growth is dependent upon favorable combinations of all factors and one of these factors out of balance with the others can reduce production. "Agrotechniques and equipment" is the critical limiting factor in Cone A; other factors are present in more adequate amounts but wheat yields are restricted and can be no greater than that permitted by the quantity and quality of agrotechniques and equipment. However, when adequate agrotechniques were applied and more equipment provided the yields of wheat were raised until "quality of labor and incentives" now limit productivity in Cone B. Progressive agriculture is constantly in flux for each step made towards optimum production makes other forward steps possible, including what is considered optimum production; and the most efficient and productive methods of farm management are in essence combinations of time-tested agrotechniques fitted into unique natural and institutional environments in ways which maximize the benefits of the many dependent interactions among what may seem to be separate processes.

Note: The source of data for this analysis of institutional and natural parameters for wheat production on a single state agricultural enterprise was from interviews of 68 employees of Dragalina (Southeastern Romania), 28 employees of state and collective farms which surround Dragalina, and the files of the chief engineer.

when the embryo plant has developed the capability of independent life without dependence on nourishment stored in the seed. Absorption of water from the soil is the first stage of germination and the rate at which the seed absorbs water depends mainly on moisture available, compactness of the soil around the seed and the condition of the seed covering. Seeds absorb moisture faster from warm soils than from cold soils. Once a seed secures adequate water, translocations occur within the embryo and the first shoot and root emerge. As the young shoot pushes its way upward through the soil, mechanical work is done by thrusting soil particles aside and breaking the soil surface crust. The emerged seedling continues life and growth by making and using its own food supply through the photosynthetic process. Vegetative development (change in form, shape and state of complexity) is the period of growth (irreversible increase in size) following seedling emergence onto flowering. A plant increases in size as the cells increase in number or magnitude or both. Increase in size of a cell means that work was done and energy utilized. Temperature of the air, light and concentration of carbon dioxide around a plant have a direct effect upon cell growth.[7] Growth is largely dependent upon the formation of new protoplasm. The nitrogen supply in the soil regulates the ability of the plant to make the proteins that are vital to the formulation of new protoplasms. Inadequate supplies of nitrogen in soils limit crop plant growth, development and yields. All 13 or so major and minor mineral nutrients essential for the growth and function of plants plus water, the medium that disperses protoplasm in the cell, are taken up from the soil by the root.

The vegetative growth of a plant is thus the resultant of a complex interrelationship of a large number of environmental factors. Many agriculturalists have no economic interest beyond the vegetative phase of plant growth for a large number of plants. Other agriculturalists want something more from a plant besides stems and leaves. When a plant reaches a stage in its life cycle and when proper environmental conditions prevail, specific cells in the growing points initiate development of certain tissues that become flower parts. Maturation of seeds is largely influenced by the previous vegetative status of the plant, weather conditions and soil moisture.[8] Yields of crop plants are determined by their inherent capabilities to grow within the limitations imposed by environmental conditions. In general, an agriculturalist can do relatively little to improve the weather conditions prevailing on his fields, but a farmer can have a major impact on the environment of the living roots of a crop plant through soil management (Figure 2).

Drought

An agricultural region classified by a specific crop or definite crop combinations represents human response in time and space to a range of physical factors influencing food plant growth and development, plus a complex of socioeconomic factors. Those who were involved in agriculture at a place for extended periods of time learned to adjust to a places's or a region's physical constraints. Those who were involved in agriculture within traditional agricultural

Fig. 3. Rajastan, India, February 1966. In this state more than 6 million people in 24 districts were affected by the ramifications of droughts (FAO photo).

regions and migrated to new lands along the margins of recognized food plant growth areas experienced dissimilar and cyclic vagaries of weather and climate, that reduced stable yields of the crops they planted. In many instances the land they moved onto was not settled earlier because of acute recurring water or temperature problems, i.e., drought. Drought has erroneously been called the precursor of famine. Droughts occur in most agricultural regions, start at any time, last a week, a month, or years and attain various degrees of severity. A drought's impact ranges from slight personal inconvenience to endangering cultural groups or a nation's ability to survive within a particular region (Figure 3).

Drought has been defined in as many ways as moisture impacts upon human activities. Definitions range from the very general to those specifically stated in terms of the effects on vegetation or on economic and social conditions. All illustrate the "contingent" nature of the drought phenomenon—whether it is viewed from an *atmospheric* perspective, as a period of strong wind, low precipitation, high temperatures and unusually low relative humidity,[9] or from a user perspective, as a condition or rainfall deficiency with respect to crop production.[10]

Drought is defined in *The Glossary of Meteorology* as "A period of abnormally dry weather sufficiently prolonged for the lack of water to cause a serious hydrologic imbalance (i.e., crop damage, water supply shortage, etc.) in the affected area. Drought severity depends upon the degree of moisture deficiency, the duration, and (to a lesser extent) the size of the affected area. In general, the term should be reserved for periods of moisture deficiency that are relatively extensive in both space and time."[11] The major difficulty in preparing a quantitative definition of drought stems from drought being a "non-event" as opposed to such a distinct event as a flood. There is no sharply defined onset to drought. Drought becomes recognizable only after some period of time has elapsed. Even the period of time required for the appearance of drought is difficult to specify since it depends on a large number of physical and biological variables.

A number of attempts have been made to define drought in quantitative terms. Thornthwaite considered that permanent drought exists where the potential evapotranspiration exceeds precipitation throughout the year.[12] Palmer developed an index of drought conditions, and addresses drought as a meteorological anomaly—a deviation from normal weather characterized by prolonged and abnormal moisture deficiency.[13] The severity of drought is measured in Palmer's index by duration and magnitude of that abnormal moisture deficiency. Palmer used Thornthwaite's method of estimating the water demand factor in his index, but other methods can be used for that purpose. It has been suggested that the frequency of dry-day sequences can serve as a measure of agricultural drought, if used in combination with a knowledge of water content, water holding capacity of the soil and water-use patterns of the crops. Palmer and Denny[14] have published an extensive and thorough *Drought Bibliography* with references indicating drought definitions, the nature and severity of droughts which have occurred throughout the world, drought impact, as well as remedial measures.

Tannehill, in his classic study of droughts,[15] wrote that famine, war and disease are the three deadly enemies of the human race. He stated that the three are so intertwined that they cannot be clearly separated and:

> History shows that drought lies at the bottom of most famines. Men who have studied the famines of India say that there is no doubt that these famines have been caused directly by failure of the annual rains. In China there are many famines that are due almost solely to natural causes, chiefly droughts, but some of them are due to heavy rains and flooding of the fields surrounding the shifting beds of China's rivers. There are many contributing factors, but failure of the rains is the principal cause in China and India. The same has been true of Europe.

Droughts do not lie at the bottom of most famines. Droughts can cause a crop failure, but man, by withholding life-supporting food from his fellow man causes famine. Humans have a physical bond to the earth for they secure their sustenance from plants that derive life support from the mineral earth and its atmosphere. However, famine is a cultural hazard—not a physical hazard. There exists definite physical parameters for food production, but there are also more insidious cultural factors in all famine occurrences. A famine is a temporary acute food imbalance at a place in time and can be managed by supplying food from areas not experiencing food shortages.

CULTURAL

There are great physical similarities and dissimilarities between places and regions on the surface of the earth, and there are great variations in the way people have used and are using similar environments for food production. Each organized, cultural group with a system of beliefs, social institutions, skills and tools and material possessions views places and regions differently; each group selected nourishing plants and animals from a range of opportunities, and some succeeded in surviving. Choices made in plant and animal foods and land use were guided and restrained by mental and social constraints and levels of technology. Culture, the total way of life of a people at a place in time, played a very important role in what people saw in their surroundings and what they thought would aid them in survival. Human needs and developed skills determined what was useful. There was a cultural appraisal of what in the physical environment had value. At first, homo sapiens were part of nature. They did not dominate the natural landscape nor mold it; they conformed to natural law. However, as a group's culture and technology became more complicated and sophisticated, they became an agent in changing the face of the earth. Food needs, food habits and food production emerged from a long time process involving the changing relations between man and his physical milieu. Humans in their struggle for survival produced a cultural environment and sequent occupants by different cultures at a place have left their mark on food acceptance and food avoidances.[16]

Historically, the quest for a stable food supply has been the most important factor in the evolution of human society.[17] Humans are distinguished from other animals by their unique brain, speech and hands. They probably were scavengers at one time for humans have no sharp claws or beaks, no powerful hooves or sharp horns and no source of massive strength to crush prey. Their brains enabled people to search for things, and solve problems, remember what was found, accumulate bits of knowledge, synthesize experiences to better chances for survival and pass accumulated experiences to others. Using his brain, speech and hands, homo sapiens were able to select plants and animals, devise tools and develop a technology which made them capable to wrest from the earth a more plentiful and more stable food supply. There was no single source of food or type of food used by all primitive people. Food consumed was related to a complex of physiogeographic conditions, i.e., climate, soils, landforms, location and spatial constraints. They were herbivorous, carnivorous and omnivorous.

Parents transmitted, through power of speech, to their children the results of efforts proven effective for survival including how to get and use food. Plant selection for food use and cultivation, and animal selection for food and companionship took place gradually over a period of 40,000 to 50,000 plus years. The origin of agriculture was not an instant chance discovery. People over tens of thousands of years observed their physical environment, performed experiments of varying sophistication and gained knowledge so that they could produce a more stable food supply by controlling plants and animals at a place.[18]

Control of fire was a great step in emancipating humans from constraints found in the physical environment. Humans are distinguished from other animals by their general preference for cooked food. Heat secured from burning embers made it possible for humans to migrate into climates other than those in which they originated. Humans used fire as a tool to break from total dependence on nature.

Homo sapiens began to produce rather than hunt and gather food at the close of the last Ice Age.[19] Climatic changes at this time were followed by changes in plant and animal life. Humans adjusted to the new conditions and began the slow mastery of the changed physical environment in order to feed themselves. There is adequate researched and published scientific data to suggest that the cultivation of plants and the domestication of animals began at different places. By 6000 B.C., advanced societies on the African, Asian and South American continents had passed from hunting and gathering to raising and breeding animals and cultivating food plants. Cultures with fully efficient, cultivated and domesticated food sources, cities, formal political states, a sense of religious or moral order, social classes and hierarchies, standardized writing and art and unifying transportation networks emerged in ancient Mesopotamia, Egypt and in Mesoamerica. By approximately 4000 B.C., agricultural specialization by occupation had begun and regional-temple-central places were spatially distributed in regions where the agricultural revolution had changed the old relationships between people, places and food sources.[20]

The inhabitants of the earth at this time had many characteristics in common, particularly the continuous quest for stable food sources and the lack of diverse types of food producing plants and animals. Differences in food sources were striking. Some of the differences in foods and food sources can be attributed to the physical environment. Early peoples, driven by hunger, tried any and all resources within a particular physical environment that could contribute to their food needs. Cultivation of plants and domestication of animals enabled humans to secure much more food from a given area to support more people per area, and to insure a supply of food that was more reliable than that gained from hunting, gathering and fishing. Conditions necessary for cultivation of plants and domestication of animals include individuals familiar with local plants and their usefulness for food, a favorable climate without danger of frost or drought and a source of malleable wild flora and fauna. Fortuitous selection and common sense led to plant improvement from season to season and selective breeding. Someone also had to be aware of the improvements and be willing to continue the process of identification and development. In general, regional evolution from weeds to crops and from wildlife to livestock and the emergence of regional food sources and regional food preferences can be explained by: (1) independent discovery, development or invention; (2) diffusion by trade, wars or migration and (3) acculturation, i.e., diffusion by borrowing or imitation.

Most independent discoveries, developments and inventions revolved around a few basic ideas. Many basic ideas in food sources were thought-up independently at different places at similar and dissimilar times. Innovations in food sources and crop cultivation initially spread slowly among cultural groups for there were few people, travel was difficult and language differences impeded communications. At times, one cultural group was reluctant to pass along ideas or to inform another cultural group of inventions. Survival of a way of life and security of a place led to the development of defense mechanisms and war. Concern for group safety led to hoarding of new food ideas and warfare to control areas where staple foods were secured. Yet warfare to retain independent discoveries, inventions or food sources became an early means for spreading ideas about food. Armies must be fed and the food consumed must be acceptable by those who fight. Means were devised to preserve, transport and store food from the homeland for use in a foreign area. In some instances, captives from cultural groups of higher technological achievement became teachers of their captors; conversely, captives from cultural groups of lower technological development absorbed or learned from their captors and took back to their places of origin ideas about foods. Food technology was diffused without complete language mastery or direct language similarity. Introduction of ideas from one group to another—from without, not independent discoveries, development or inventions—brought about most cultural changes in food choices and food acceptances.[21]

Spread of food plants and animals, food technology and food habits was by direct contact or indirect transmission. Direct contact with an originator and acceptance of an innovation is merely the circulation of ideas. Indirect contact, spread, or acceptance of an idea regarding food by a number of people far from the originator or originating group without face-to-face contact is diffusion. If the new plant, animal or food dish was acceptable to a group, if it filled a need and if it solved a problem without disrupting group attitudes and ways, it became part of the group's culture and was developed further. If the new food source or agricultural technique did not fit within the pattern of life that had already evolved, it was rejected. Some cultural groups were unable to adopt a circulated or diffused innovation for their level of technology was not developed to the degree that the innovation could be implemented or maintained. Other groups discovered that the adoption of a new food source proved unfeasible for physical environmental reasons. Rejections or acceptance of new foods or new techniques to produce stable foods were not immediate in most cases. Some groups adopted an idea that contributed to survival, but had not the desire or ability to evolve it further or to improve it. Generally the more specialized, the more complex and the more highly developed a food or food production trait is in an area, the closer this area is to the point of origin. Acculturation is a continuous interaction process between two cultural groups or societies in which the food sources or food habits of the subordinate society is drastically changed or modified to conform with the foods of the dominant group or society. Complete cultural assimilations leading to food conformity are rare and mankind has profited from diversity in food habits and food sources.

NOTES

[1] J. Anderson, "The State of World Food Production," in *Man, Food, and Nutrition*, M. Rechcigl, ed., (Cleveland: CRC Press, 1975), pp. 35–54.

[2] F. Deatherage, *Food for Life* (New York: Plenum Press, 1975), pp. 31–65; *Climate and Food* (Washington, D.C.: Printing and Publishing Office, National Academy of Science, 1976), pp. 3–4.

[3] J. Oliver, *Climate and Man's Environment* (New York: John Wiley & Sons, 1973), pp. 249–258; H. Critchfield, *General Climatology* (Prentice-Hall, 1974), pp. 15–18.

[4] J. Mather, *Climatology: Fundamentals and Applications* (New York: McGraw-Hill, 1974), pp. 157–179; J. Davis, "The Leaf Energy Budget Equation, A Review of the Literature," in *Geographical Horizons*, J. Odland and R. Taffe (Dubuque: Kendal/Hunt, 1977), pp. 218–247.

[5] S. Hendricks and L. Alexander, "The Basis of Fertility," in *Soils, the 1957 Yearbook of Agriculture* (Washington, D.C.: United States Government Printing Office, 1957), pp. 11–16; C. Thornthwaite, "Climate and Moisture Conservation," *Annals of the Association of American Geographers*, Vol. 37, No. 2 (1947), 87–100; C. Thornthwaite, "An Approach Toward a Rational Classification of Climate," *Geographical Review*, 38 (1948), pp. 55–94.

[6] D. Stelia, *The Geography of Soils* (Englewood Cliffs: Prentice-Hall, 1976).

[7] J. Janick, C. Noller, and C. Rhykerd, "The Cycles of Plant and Animal Nutrition," *Scientific American*, 235 (Sept., 1976), pp. 75–86.

[8] J. Martin and W. Leonard, *Principles of Field Crop Production* (New York: Macmillan, 1964), pp. 51–81.

[9] W. Palmer, *Meteorological Drought* (Washington, D.C.: U.S. Department of Commerce, Weather Bureau Research Paper 45, 1965).

[10] G. Barger and H. Thom, "A Method of Characterizing Drought Intensity in Iowa," *Agronomy Journal*, 41 (1949), pp. 13–19.

[11] R. Huschke, ed., *Glossary of Meteorology* (Boston: American Meteorological Society, 1959).

[12] C. Thornthwaite, "An Approach Toward a Rational Classification of Climate," *Geographical Review*, 38 (1948), pp. 55–94.

[13] W. Palmer, "Climatic Variability and Crop Production," *Weather and Our Food Supply* (Ames: Iowa State University Press, CAED Report, 1964), pp. 173–178.

[14] W. Palmer and L. Denny, *Drought Bibliography* (Washington, D.C.: U.S. Department of Commerce, NOAA Environmental Data Service, 1971), 236 pp.

[15] I. Tannehill, *Drought: Its Causes and Effects* (Princeton: Princeton University Press, 1947), pp. 23–24.

[16] F. Simoons, *Eat Not This Flesh* (Madison: University of Wisconsin Press, 1967), pp. 3–6.

[17] H. Brown, *The Challenge of Man's Future* (New York: Viking Press, 1954), pp. 3–45.

[18] J. Harlan, "The Plants and Animals that Nourish Man," *Scientific American*, Vol. 235, No. 3 (1976), pp. 88–97.

[19] K. Narr, "Early Food-producing Populations," in W. Thomas, Jr., ed., *Man's Role in Changing the Face of the Earth* (Chicago: University of Chicago Press, 1960), pp. 134–151.

[20] R. Braidwood, "The Agricultural Revolution," reprinted from *Scientific American* (Sept., 1960), pp. 1–10.

[21] R. Harris, "New Light on Plant Domestication and the Origins of Agriculture: A Review," Vol. 57 (1967), pp. 90–107.

Chapter 2

Crops and Man: An evolution in food sources and food preferences

Food production is a recent phenomenon. Hunters and gatherers, using tools, have survived the rigors of pristine physical environments for millions of years. Food producers have survived the rigors of the physical environment and the capriciousness of other humans for only ten or so thousand years. The consequences of the change in emphasis from food procurement to food production and the resultant human manipulation of food resources have had a profound effect upon all aspects of human culture. For millennia, gathering and hunting was carried out in conjunction with cultivation and herding. Few cultural groups or societies would risk concentrating all activities on a limited number of cultivated crops or domesticated animals, for a crop failure might lead to starvation and famine. As people began to manipulate plants and animals and move them out of their natural habitats, they were able to concentrate food resources into a manageable area and select for specific nutritional characteristics that were not conducive for survival under natural conditions. An amalgamation of cultural decisions affecting physical attributes of selected plants and animals eventually increased the carrying capacity of places. Human interference in the natural process of food plant and animal development extended the area in which a high population carrying capacity was feasible. Expanded and relatively stable food supplies, at places as a direct result of human activities, stimulated increased population and fostered permanent settlement. Famine is a characteristic of crop and livestock agriculture, and was not a facet of preagricultural systems.

THE AGRICULTURAL REVOLUTION

Climatic changes associated with the Ice Age altered the hunter and gatherer's food resources. In order to insure survival, the human response to a changing physical environment and reduced carrying capacity was food production. Changes in physical parameters for plant and animal life varied at places. Most significant were the modifications in long-term climatic patterns. Segments of the earth where once hunters and gatherers had little difficulty securing animals and plants for food became increasingly dessicated. Wild animals withdrew to the banks of lakes, rivers or waterholes. Periodic and permanent drought killed many traditional food plants. Humans sought stabilized water sources, and man and beast were brought into more intimate contact. Eventually some animals were domesticated and selected plants known to be useful for survival were nurtured, then cultivated. Also, ramifications of climatic change, diastrophism and tectonic processes induced variations in sea levels, river base levels and associated aquatic food sources. Humans in their quest for food sources discovered favored sites where fish and other aquatic resources could be secured with limited difficulty. Fresh water forager-fishing groups in tropical areas had less difficulty in keeping fed and had more time to experiment with different food sources. Likewise, changes in climate also influenced the life of hunting and gathering groups in the hilly or mountainous areas of the tropics and subtropics. Here terrain diversity and climatic zones determined by altitude produced great variations in animal habitat and edible plant types within short distances. Diversity in terrain, climate, soils, plants and animals within a limited area enabled humans to settle into more or less permanent places and develop the arts of cultivation and domestication without the pressures from growing or chronic shortages of food. Throughout the world in selected areas, human beings began the agricultural revolution. Hunters and gatherers were compelled by climatic change, population pressures, reduction in carrying capacities or a combination of all three, to find means for securing more food. Individual and group response was dissimilar in diverse physiographic regions. Manifestations of their response was different plant food cultivars and different domesticated food producing animals.[1]

FOOD CROP ORIGINS

The origins of crop agriculture postulated and in print are derived from speculation, theory, investigations by archaeologists and anthropologists in cooperation with specialists in the physical sciences and by researchers in the origins of particular crop plants or food animals. A theory that agriculture developed by direct sequence from collecting, then hunting, then pastoralism, has been rejected by most researchers. One of the most widely discussed views on the center of food crop origin is that of Carl O. Sauer, a geographer, who set six presuppositions as a basis (here summarized):[2]

(1) Agriculture did not originate in groups or communities from a growing, chronic or desperate shortage of food. People living in the shadow of famine do

not have the necessary freedom from want to experiment with an alternate source of food.

(2) The hearths of domestication are to be sought in areas of marked animal and plant diversity, i.e., variety of climates and diversified physical terrain.

(3) Primitive agriculture did not originate in large river valleys subject to lengthy floods and requiring protective dams, drainage or irrigation.

(4) Agriculture began in hilly, wooded lands which have soils that are easy to dig or cultivate. Primitive agriculturalists did not have the implements to till sod or eradicate stoloniferous grasses.

(5) The inventors of agriculture had previously acquired special skills that predisposed them to experiment with new crops.

(6) Above all, the founders of agriculture were sedentary folk. Growing crops demand attention and care.

Sauer contended that the most likely people to begin agricultural practices were progressive fishing folk living in mild climates along fresh waters. He proposed Southeast Asia as the oldest center of crop agriculture. From Southeast Asia the agricultural revolution spread westward across India and the Near East, into Africa, and finally into Europe. He did not rule out the possibility that cultivation might have been transmitted from somewhere else to the New World.

In contrast to Sauer's hypothesis was the practical work of N. I. Vavilov, a Russian geneticist and agronomist. Vavilov was deeply concerned with the geography of crop origins. Based upon worldwide field work that he and his colleagues conducted between 1916 and 1934, Vavilov identified eight centers where the world's most important cultivated plants originated (here summarized):[3]

(1) China—the earliest and largest center of cultivated plant origin; an area of well diversified terrain and climatic parameters where indigenous peoples developed millets, buckwheat, soybeans, legumes, fruits—perhaps 136 endemic species.

(2A) India—India, Burma and Assam also are areas of climatic and physiogeographic diversity; rice, sugar cane, pulses, gourds, cucumbers, lettuce, radishes, citrus fruits, mango—a total of 117 significant species were developed here.

(2B) Indo-Malayan—the Indonesian and Philippine center contributed 55 cultivated plants.

(3) Central Asia—this center includes west India, Afghanistan, Tadzhikstan and Uzbekistan; a range of wheats, peas, lentils, beans and cotton were included in the 44 species that originated here.

(4) Near East—including segments of Asia Minor, Turkmenistan, Iran and Transcaucasia; among the 83 species listed are nine botanical species of wheat and rye, pear, grape, cherry, alfalfa, fig, walnut and almond.

(5) Mediterranean—an area noted for human activities in selecting and improving more promising varieties; 84 species were identified including the olive and many vegetables.

(6) Ethiopia—an independent center of origin, important for varieties of

wheat, barley, sorghum and millet. Vavilov listed 38 species endemic to this area.

(7) South Mexico and Central America—the primary center for maize (corn), sweet potato and upland cotton; 49 species were listed.

(8) South America—a center remarkable for its endemic plants, notably many species of potatoes; Vavilov listed 62 species.

Sauer differentiated centers on the basis of vegetative reproduction and seed reproduction; Vavilov delimited regions where agriculture had been practiced for extended periods of time. Sauer stated that plant growth initiated by seed rather than a cutting was initiated in northern China, western India and Ethiopia as a result of climatic limitations. Research since 1935 has revealed that Vavilov's patterns of food crop origin are extremely complex and many plants listed by Vavilov did not originate in his centers. Also, it should be noted that the agricultural region between the eastern Mediterranean and south-central Iran (Persia) was distinct for here was combined seed-grown food crops with animal herding (sheep, goats and cattle)—the beginning of modern mixed farming (Figure 4).

A synthesis of hypothesis and basic research on crop origins identifies four broad basic centers: (1) the Near Eastern; (2) African; (3) Southeast Asian and (4) American (Figure 5). The earliest archaeological evidence of cultivation of seed grains and evidence of the domestication of animals has been found in the Near Eastern center (southwest Asia and the eastern Mediterranean).[4] Hunters and gatherers here in the tenth millennium B.C. were reaping wild barley and

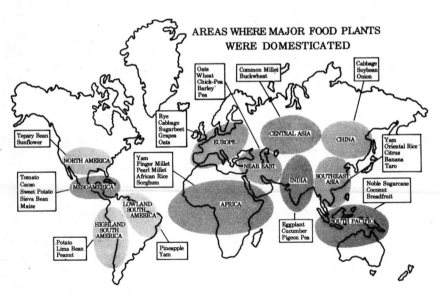

Fig. 4. The earliest archaeological evidence of cultivation of seed grains and evidence of the domestication of animals has been found in the Near Eastern center.

Fig. 5. Four basic centers of crop origins and animal domestication: (1) the Near Eastern; (2) African; (3) Southeast Asian; and (4) American.

wild wheat with knives, grinding grain and storing grain in pits. By the sixth millennium village communities were growing barley and wheat and keeping sheep and goats. Shortly thereafter, farmers began to move from communities in the foothills into newly established communities on the floodplains. Subsequently in the fourth millennium traditional Mediterranean crops were husbanded; the olive, grapes and fig.[5] High cultures that emerged within the Near Eastern center were supported and sustained by agricultural surpluses, for city dwellers were food consumers not food producers. In Mesopotamia and in Egypt emerged large cities and towns, stratification of professional classes, centralized government, concentrated economic and political power, metallurgy, standing armies, religious organizations and forms of writing. Much of the food used to maintain large concentrations of population came from four primary regional food sources: wheat, barley, sheep and goats. Although millet, emmer and einkorn wheat, lentils, chickpea, gardenpea, beets, turnips, carrots, radishes, rapeseed, mustard, safflower, flax, olives, melons, figs, date palm, pears, grapes, onions, garlic and various other cereals, pulses, root and tuber crops, fruits and nuts, oil crops, vegetables, spices and forage crops probably had their origins here—barley was the chief food crop.

There is little agreement among those who have studied and researched the origins of agriculture in Africa as to the geographic center and time early agricultural practices began. In the fifth millenium B.C. a vegetable-based system was practiced on the northwestern margins of the tropical rain forest. Two nodes of independent crop plant development have been identified, western Sudan and Ethiopia, but not verified. Agriculture was practiced in the savanna belt, between the desert and the tropical rain forest, by the third millennium B.C. The African center of crop origin did not provide the quantity and types of food surpluses that gave impetus to large cities. A system of large agricultural villages and towns evolved in the savanna belt at physically favored places. Although pastoral peoples from Arabia moved into the eastern margins by the second millennium with sheep, goats and cattle, a large segment of this belt was isolated from other centers.[6] High cultures supported by agricultural surpluses emerged in Mali, Ghana, Nok, Ife and Benin. Probable crop plants that originated here include finger millet, African rice, pearl millet, sorghum, Kersting's groundnut, cowpeas, yams, Kafir potatoes, oil palm, castor oil, watermelon, okra, coffee, cola and numerous local cereals, pulses, roots, tubers, fruits, nuts, vegetables, spices, fiber plants, forage crops and drugs. The African center of crop plant origin, extending from the Atlantic to the Indian Ocean and from the deserts to the north to the tropical rain forest of the south, is a complex center to study.[7] Perhaps here more than any other center of crop origin, each major food crop was a cultural unifier and a recognized cultural trait.

The Southeast Asian center of crop origin includes portions of present day China, Indochina, Thailand, Burma, India and Indonesia. Northern China and Burma-Indochina are the major nodes of independent crop plant development. Archaeological evidence suggests that the first farmers in northern China lived in the loess uplands of the Hwang Ho in the sixth and fifth millennia B.C. and grew foxtail millet and kept pigs. From the loess-covered hills, farmers moved eastward and settled on mounds found on the marshy Hwang Ho plains. Irrigation was not important in northern China until the first millennium B.C. and wet-rice cultivation did not originate here.[8] Chinese agriculture was basically garden agriculture (vegeculture), introverted and with little crop dispersal until modern historical times. Evidence of cultivated rice has been documented in Thailand c. 3500 B.C. Tropical vegetation agriculture was practiced in the upland areas of the Burma-Indochina node and wet-rice in lowland areas. Pigs and poultry were the dominant food animals. It is believed that in the Chinese node of the Southeast Asian center were first cultivated Japanese millet, buckwheat, rice, soybean, turnip, Chinese yam, Chinese radish, oil crop (tung, rapeseed and mustard seed), Chinese nuts (chestnuts, hickories, hazelnuts and walnuts), apricot, peach, water chestnut, cucumber, horseradish, bamboo, tea, plus other fruits and nuts, vegetables and spices, and drugs and narcotics. Crops first cultivated in the Burma-Indochina node of the Southeast Asian center include Job's tears, rice(?), pigeonpea, mat bean, taro, winged yam, arrowroot, coconut, sesame, breadfruit, lime, lemon, tangerine, grapefruit, orange, mango, banana, plantain, turmeric, clove, nutmeg, black pepper, eggplant, sugar palm, sago palm, sugar cane, numerous pulses, cereals, tubers, fruits, nuts, vegetables, spices and oils. It appears that agriculture in the Southeast Asian center of crop origin evolved from intensive gathering techniques focused upon roots and tubers, fruits and nuts and seed gathering.[9]

The American center of crop origin extends from the ecologically complex highland areas in central Mexico to central Chile, and along the northern coast of the South American continent from Peru to northeastern Brazil. An impressive listing of plants were first cultivated here and agricultural surpluses proved more than adequate to support the high cultures of the Maya, Aztec, Inca and others. American Indians were among the most talented and skilled of all food plant originators-developers. Crops indigenous to the American center were different from those first cultivated in other centers.[10] The major food plants were maize, potatoes, beans, manioc, squash and groundnuts; the only animals domesticated were the turkey, llama and alpaca. It appears that maize was cultivated in the sixth millennium B.C. in southern Mexico, and by the third millennium B.C. beans, squash, avocados, chillies and pumpkins as well as cotton. Along the coast in northern Brazil, evidence of plant cultivation in the fifth millennium B.C. has been recorded in fishing communities whose inhabitants grew beans, chilli peppers and squash. Here in the first millennium B.C. potatoes, manioc and groundnuts were cultivated.[11] Plant cultivation was far ranging and many food plants had their probable origin in the American center including Indian corn (maize), peanut, lima bean, common bean, yam, manioc, potato, pineapple, cashew, Brazil nut, papaya, tree tomato, avocado, pepper, squash, mate and many pseudocereals, pulses, root and tuber crops, oil crops, fruits, nuts, vegetables, spices, forage crops and drugs (Figure 6).

FOOD ANIMAL ORIGINS

Domestication of food animals occurred quite early in the Agricultural Revolution. Most of the important domesticated food animals originated in the Near Eastern food crop center. Domestication is a very complicated process in which humans interfere in the life cycle of certain animals. The purpose of domestication was to secure animal protein reserves and to have animals serve as living food conserves. Capturing animals, keeping them till they were needed for food and killing them is not domestication. Domestication is the breeding of animals under human control in artificial conditions. Although the distribution of potential animal domesticates is problematic, evidence indicates that plant cultivation and animal domestication began approximately at the same time in the Near East. Of the fifty or more animals that have been truly domesticated, only a dozen or so are of significance on a worldwide basis. Domesticated animals contributed to human survival and well being by providing a source of food, clothing, leather, bones for tools, work animals, transportation, amusement and religious offerings. Even-toed ungulates (hoofed animals) have been the prime domesticates, fifteen of the twenty-two most important. Of the even-toed ungulates, sheep, goats and cattle rank highest as food sources. Ruminants (cud-chewing animals), by the microflora in their stomachs, are able to convert second-rate protein sources into high quality, first-rate protein for human use. Ruminants were highly suitable for domestication for they did not compete with humans for the same food sources. Sheep, goats, cattle, etc., exist on a diet that

Fig. 6. Potatoes, the edible tubers of a cultivated plant (Photo by K. Kleven, Grand Forks Herald, N.D.).

has limited or no real nutritional value to humans. Domestication of most animals used as food sources was facilitated by the social rather than solitary habits of these animals.[12]

According to published archaeological records, sheep were the first animals to be domesticated. Remains dating back to the ninth millennium B.C. have been verified in the Near Eastern food crop center. The earliest determined date for the domestication of sheep antedates those known dates for any cultivated plants.[13] Sheep are unique among these animals domesticated for food. They are physically capable of surviving and adapting to harsh environments that are unfavorable for other food animal species. Early in history they became more widespread than goats for they possess a panting mechanism to dissipate heat which enables them to tolerate hot climates. Although dated remains of domesticated sheep are possibly two thousand years older than the dated remains of goats, there is a possibility that they were domesticated at the same time. The original domestication of goats most probably was in the Near Eastern food crop center. In contrast to other significant food producing animals, goats are browsers and grazers. Goats can survive in areas where the natural food supply is not adequate for other animals. Although not nearly as well appreciated as sheep, use of domesticated goats spread rapidly. Humans apparently preferred sheep and cattle meat more than goat meat, and sheep are superior fiber producers and cattle, superior milk producers.

Cattle were domesticated later than sheep and goats; the earliest archaeological finds date to the mid-seventh millennium B.C. Wild aurochs (wild cattle) were hunted, trapped and worshiped long before domestication. So far, domesticated cattle remains have only been found at archaeological sites where domesticated sheep or goats were maintained. It is probable that there was early domestication of cattle in India, but the earliest known remains have been discovered in Greece and then somewhat later in Anatolia. The original domesticated cattle were probably very large, strong and temperamental. Various breeds developed early as humans attempted to reduce the size and the ferociousness of early cattle. Cow's milk was utilized as a source of nourishment soon after domestication and milk remains as one of homo sapien's best foods. Cattle provided humans with milk, meat, hides for clothing, bones for tools, traction for field work and dung for fuel and plaster.[14] Of interest was the domestication of water buffalo in India after the third millennium B.C. The water buffalo is adapted to areas (hot, humid, tropical lowlands) and foods (aquatic and semi-aquatic grasses) that will not support traditional cattle. Its use as food is similar to that of cattle and it gives more milk than most breeds.

Pigs could have been domesticated in Europe or Asia for wild pigs are native to both. It seems that the earliest domestication of pigs may have been in the Near Eastern food crop center but there is no evidence of domestication here until about the seventh millennium B.C. No date or specific locality can be postulated for the origin of the Chinese pig. Delay in the domestication of pigs may have been related to the pig's inability to break down second-rate protein sources (grass, leaves, twigs, etc.) as ruminants do, and recognition that pigs compete directly with man for food. Pigs are scavengers and are primarily a household animal, not a herd animal. The pig is the most food productive, domesticated animal, per unit weight, of all the larger animals.[15]

The exact center of chicken domestication will probably never be known with certainty. However, most authorities on the subject are in agreement that the place of origin was in southwestern Asia, possibly derived from a jungle fowl of India. Chickens are the most important domesticated fowl and are one of a few domesticated food animals to come from the Southeast Asian food center. Date of domestication is not known, but chickens for some reason were not diffused to Iran (Persia) or Egypt before the second millennium B.C. Chickens, along with

Fig. 7. A turkey ranch in North Dakota. The wild turkey is native only to North and Central America. Domestic turkeys are descendents of the Mexican subspecies (Photo by T. A. Evanson, Grand Forks Herald, N.D.).

sheep, goats and cattle, were a dual-purpose domesticate; they provided eggs and meat. There are many other domesticated animals used for food in both the old and new world, including the camels, reindeer, rabbits, turkey, Muscovy duck, llama and alpaca. None of these animals figured prominently in early agriculture and none are as important a food source as those domesticates discussed (Figure 7).

FOOD CROPS AND FOOD ANIMAL DISPERSALS

The frequency of contact between people, communication networks, transportation accessibility, quality of information and the way people want to use a place and retain their distinctness play a part in the diffusion of food crops and animals. Every basic center of crop origin and animal domestication contained a great deal of information about the endemic plants and animals or foods developed there. People living in each center knew only a portion of the total information available and transmitted only what they appreciated, understood or wanted to transmit. The ability and willingness of people in other lands to receive and in turn send information depended upon their education, training and cultural characteristics. Distance was a significant factor, for the farther a group was away from a center, the less likely were chances of crop and animal dispersals. Food hearths, the four basic centers inhabited by groups of people whose inventiveness created new sources of food for human survival, generated diffusion waves. These diffusion waves moved outward from their sources carrying ideas about crops and animals like ripples expanding outward from a stone thrown into a pond. Also, individuals within food hearths transmitted ideas to their peers in other cultural areas without reference to geographic location or concern for space; in some cases leap-frogging cultural areas. Centrality and connectivity were significant in the hierarchies of food hearths and in the spread of innovations related to foods.

From the four basic food hearths, the Near Eastern, African, Southeast Asian and American, basic food crops and food animals were diffused throughout the world. Situated between two major food hearths, the Near Eastern center had the greatest impact prior to the Age of Great Discoveries. From the Near Eastern center a form of agriculture based upon wheat, barley, sheep and goats, spread westward into Europe and North Africa, and eastward to the Indian subcontinent and China. Wheat was introduced and successfully grown in the Nile delta of Egypt in the fifth millennium B.C. Slash-and-burn dry farming practices reached the Atlantic, North Sea and Baltic coasts and into the British Isles by the fourth millennium B.C. Wheat, barley, lentils and peas were all transported northward, and planted with good results, from the Near Eastern center. Oats and rye, initially weed seeds found in seed barley and wheat, were developed as food sources in Western Europe.[16] Due to moisture and temperature limitations, barley, rye and oats became the dominant food grains. Cultural preferences, combined with vegetal constraints, led cattle to becoming a more important meat and milk source rather than sheep or goats. Clearing of the woodlands in Europe enabled agriculturalists to increase the use of sheep for food (sheep could not feed well in forested areas with little grass). Also from the Near Eastern center, wheat, barley, cattle, sheep and goats diffused eastward into the Indian subcontinent and China by the end of the third millennium B.C. Seed crops and selected animals penetrated Africa south of the Sahara from the Near Eastern center, Egypt and Arabia in the third and second millennia B.C. Agriculture in the New World developed independently and distinctly from Old World food crop and food animal centers. Although early Mongoloid settlers had migrated from Asia across the Bering Strait into North then South America, they had completed their trek prior to plant cultivation and animal domestication in the Old World centers. By the middle of the first millennium B.C., there was some local unity but great regional diversity in food crops sown and food animals domesticated on the surface of the earth. Physical isolation and cultural preference led to marked differences among agricultural regions. With innovations in transportation and subsequent decline in isolation, food plants and food animals were slowly and selectively dispersed.

Literature reveals that at the beginning of the Christian era, there had been a considerable interchange of food plants and food animals between the Near Eastern, African and Southeast Asian food hearths. Although the Greeks were no great innovators, the superb transportation network of the Romans, combined with their need for food to supply their armies and citizens, led to a homogenization of food types in the Mediterranean area. The Romans developed the classical Mediterranean agricultural type; a combination of extensive farmed cereals with intensive tree crops (olives, grapes and figs). After the fall of the Roman Empire, the Arabs of North Africa and the Near East became the most important agents for food plant and food animal diffusion. The Islamic Empire, extending from Spain in Europe to Morocco in extreme northwest Africa to the Indian subcontinent and islands within the Indonesian group, introduced citrus fruits, rice, cotton and sugar cane, along with proven irrigation techniques, into north Africa and southern Europe. Arab traders also brought rice, citrus fruits, cucumbers and coconut palms (all indigenous to the Southeast Asian center) to the east coast of Africa. Contributions by the Romans and the Arabs to people's ability to survive and multiply as a direct result of better diets and fewer famines, were many. However, the Age of Great Discoveries led to the first world-wide exchange of food crops and food animals.

The discovery, exploration and colonization of the Americas led to the dispersal of indigenous Mesoamerican plants and animals, and the introduction of indigenous Near Eastern, African and Southeast Asian plants and animals to the New World. Wheat, rye, oats and barley were introduced quickly by the Spaniards, along with rice, yams, millet, cowpeas, grapes, figs, olives, citrus fruits, bananas, sugar cane and sugar beets. Cattle, sheep and goats were brought to the New World by Columbus, and pigs were brought from Europe a bit later. American food crops were diffused to Europe, Africa and Asia as rapidly as new food crops were brought to the New World. Manioc, sweet potatoes, cocoa and peanuts (groundnuts) were initially transported to Africa then dispersed. Corn, tomatoes, squash, potatoes and beans were brought to Europe first, then on to

Africa and Asia. Turkeys were taken to Europe and soon became a popular source of meat. Egon Larsen, in his interesting discourse on food, states:[17]

> The list of foods, and particularly of food plants which America gave the rest of the world is immense. There were many kinds of fruits and vegetables which contributed to the variety of European meals: pineapples, and tomatoes, 'french' beans and scarlet runners, red and green peppers, pumpkins and avocados, pears, peanuts and vanilla. The newcomers in America had to learn from the natives how to prepare and use these unfamiliar foodstuffs. Their seeds and plants were shipped eastward across the Atlantic, but it took a long time of experimenting until Europeans found out which of them would grow and where.

American plants had little influence upon agriculture or dietary habits in India or China. Peanuts and sweet potatoes are presently only important as supplementary foods. Two other new lands, Australia and New Zealand had no indigenous food plants or food animals of world value.

EARLY FOOD PATTERNS AND PREFERENCES

Each animal on earth is endowed with biological and psychological reactions which tend to harmonize their diets according to food availability, needs and functions. When given their choice of foods, animals will select the diet on which they survive best at a place. Older animals already accustomed to a particular diet will resist change even when change may be beneficial. Diets of animals vary from place to place and from region to region, concomitantly diets of human groups vary. Most of the food plants and animals humans use today were utilized from food-gathering and food-hunting times. There is an infinite variety of foods that will support the life process, and primitives appear to have used them all. Early homo sapiens served as the experimental animals in the testing of foods. They learned by trial and error to avoid and to use various plants and animals. When they erred they paid by illness and even death. Those who survived early experimentation developed a satisfactory pattern of food consumption for their place or area which enabled them to live and reproduce. Today, there are groups who are securing food by using methods similar to those devised by early homo sapiens. Conjectures about early human food habits are made by studying modern primitive groups. These conjectures may be misleading for the influence of highly developed groups must have touched these primitive peoples. More reliable insights can be secured for selected regions thousands of years ago by scientific archaeological excavations, examining the food ancient peoples placed in tombs for use of the dead in the afterlife, or food habits recorded in paintings, carvings or writings.

FOODS OF ANCIENT PEOPLES

The tombs of early Egyptians and the writings of early Jews provide a wealth of information about foods used in the Near Eastern food hearth. Neolithic inhabitants of settlements on the banks of the Nile River and near the Nile Valley cultivated wheat and barley, raised a few domestic animals for meat, fished and hunted. Poultry and fish were plentiful, and beans, radishes, onions, leeks, garlic and parsley were grown. Eggs were a favorite food; hen eggs, turtle eggs, ostrich eggs and crocodile eggs. Later Egyptians prized cabbage, beer made from barley, mushrooms and locusts. Egyptians are best known for developing the art of bread making. Bread was a preferred food and the ancient Egyptian revered wheat bread. It was a grave offense to refuse bread to anyone. Bread was used as wages and grain collected as taxes. Bakers in ancient Egyptian society were as well regarded as priests.[18] Egyptian wheat was considered to be a superior food raw material and was widely exchanged for dried fish and fruits and for the various cheeses of Asia Minor.

Although the basic foods of the early Jewish people were similar to the foods of the Egyptians, certain foods were forbidden and foods were prepared in a different manner. Bread and fish were the basic foods of the common people. Meat was consumed only at special times and festivals. Chicken was scarce, pigeons inexpensive and nuts were prized. Wheat and barley were cooked into a special stew with lamb or mutton, and beans, lentils, cucumbers and onions played a significant role in the diet. Wine was the most important food beverage. Graubard stated:[19]

> Because the Bible relates the life and customs of the Hebrew tribes, it also records their dietary practices and beliefs. All animals with uncleft hoofs and not ruminating were declared impure. So were fish without fins and scales, all worms, shellfish (Crustacea), snails, squid (Molluscs) and most birds. The reason for the prohibition is not that these items are detrimental to health. They were not then, nor are they today. The Bible merely reiterates that they are "an abomination" and "unclean." "All fowls that creep going upon all four shall be an abomination unto you. Yet these may ye eat of every flying creeping thing that goeth upon all fours which have legs above their feet to leap withal upon the earth . . . the locust after his kind, and the bald locust, and the beetle after his kind and the grasshopper after his kind." The warning "Thou shalt not seethe a kid in its mothers milk" is given three times.

Foods and food preferences of the peoples who dwelled in the East Asian food hearth have a long documented history. Chinese diets were characterized by the assemblage of plants and animals that were found in the places people lived for a long time. A distinctive aspect of Chinese food is the division between grains and other starch foods, and vegetables and meat dishes. Traditional balanced meals had the appropriate amount of both groups. Starch staples included millet and rice; vegetables included soybeans, mung beans and Chinese cabbage; meats included pork, dog, pheasant, chicken and fish. Foreign foodstuffs were readily adopted since the dawn of Chinese history and the Chinese way of eating has always been characterized by flexibility and adaptability. Wheat and sheep were introduced from the west, many fruits and vegetables from the south and southwest and peanuts and sweet potatoes from the southeast. Despite continuous introduction of dairy products, milk and most dairy products never played an important role in the diet. Soybeans eventually became the equivalent of the Near Eastern food hearth's protein-rich milk and cheese. It is believed that the early Chinese preserved their foods in many more ways and in larger amounts than most other cultural groups. They preserved food by pickling, smoking, salting, drying, sugaring and soaking in sauces. Thorough understanding of wild plant food sources, methods of food preservation and dietary flexibility has helped the Chinese peoples through many periods of food scarcity. Knowledge of "famine foods" was transmitted from generation to generation.[20]

Of great interest are food preferences of the early inhabitants of the Indian subcontinent and the complex dietary rules which evolved. The earliest inhabitants of postglacial India cultivated wheat, barley, rice and sugar cane. Grapes, pears, plums, peaches, mulberries and oranges were consumed fresh and preserved with sugar. Cattle were raised for domestic consumption as well as pigs, dogs, buffalos, sheep and poultry. Dietary constraints for religious and social reasons more complex than those of the Jews, evolved slowly. By approximately 1000 B.C. the cow became sacred and by 500 B.C. vegetarianism became a Hindu requirement. Graubard observed:[21]

> Here, too, prohibited food is considered "unclean" and an "abomination." In addition, all dietary restrictions center about the institution of caste as does most of Hindu life. Thus, Brahmans, the highest and the divine caste, regard as polluted all water and food touched by any other castemen. Food upon which the shadow or even the gaze of a lower castemen, or a Christian or foreigner, happened to fall is polluted, uneatable and must be destroyed lest others eat it and suffer unconscious pollution. "Clean castes do not pollute water; but below them are caste which pollute an earthen vessel, then castes which pollute a brass vessel." From some castes a traveling Brahman may only accept dry food; from others, only food cooked in water; from still others, food cooked in oil. Partaking of certain foods leads to loss of cast which means becoming an outcast. That state is held in contempt even by the lowest groups and incurs endless misery and abuse. Brahmans and other high castemen normally eat no meat or fish which are considered polluting. Members of different castes may not dine together, just as they may not intermarry. Interdining is a serious social and religious offense and leads to grave consequences.

Unlike the Near Eastern food hearth, early foods in the African food hearth were regional rather than universal, many having very limited distribution. Foods in the African food hearth initially were totally derived from a savanna ecosystem by hunting and grain gathering. Sorghum, the prime food base, was a savanna plant that was not suited to high rainfall regimes, and pearl millet was one of the most drought-resistant of all food crops. African rice was initially a plant of water holes in the savanna zone. Even the yams, which were the staff of life for most forest belt tribes, and watermellons were basically savanna plants.[22] Oil palms originally were trees of the savanna-forest margin. Finger millet was a plant of the cool East African highlands. Cola and coffee were true forest plants. Diets within this wide but narrow food hearth consisted basically of sorghum and millet, tubers, legumes, green leaves, berries, roots, bark, fish, milk, flesh from domesticated and wild animals and selected game birds. There developed early a sharp demarcation between cultural groups who preferred to build their diets around one basic food source; most pronounced were the spatial differences between rice-eating and yam-eating groups. Sheep and goats were kept by indigenous groups in the savanna belt and in the Sahara. Dating these pastoral activities is difficult, but they began in the fifth millennium B.C. when both the savanna and the Sahara regions received more rainfall than today. Milk from cows, goats and sheep was consumed but meat from domesticated livestock was rarely eaten.

Early food patterns and preferences in the American food hearth were developed in isolation. Asian and African food plants and food animals were not available. New World early food production focused upon plant cultivation rather than animal rearing. Archaeological evidence for agricultural evolution and foods in the Americas is sketchy. Still the American Indians were manipulating for food purposes many plants and a few animals by the seventh millennium B.C. The diet of early hunter-gatherers consisted largely of harvested wild plants, i.e., white and sweet potatoes, corn, squash, pumpkins, chili peppers and beans, plus Muscovy ducks, turkeys, deer, bison, rabbits and various fish that were hunted or trapped.[23] Later, within the American food hearth three distinct nodes of basic food preferences developed. The inhabitants of the Mesoamerican node favored a corn, bean, squash, avocado and cacao diet with domesticated dog, turkey and small game meat. Corn became the major staple by the first millennium B.C. The inhabitants of the Andean Highland node, with its enormous topographic and climatic diversity, consumed a diet based upon potatoes at one elevation; peanuts, cacao, lupines and beans at mid-elevations; and manioc, pineapples, cashews, papayas, avocados, Brazil nuts and peppers in the lowlands.[24] Llamas, alpacas and guinea pigs were the prime source of domesticated meats in the Andean Highlands. Food was easy to secure, there was much leisure time and civilizations were able to develop to a high degree. The white and sweet potato were of supreme importance to the native population of highland South America, manioc to the inhabitants of northeastern South America, and corn to the Mesoamericans. Hundreds of cultivated varieties of potatoes were grown in the Andes and they were preserved in many ways including freezing and dehydration. Maize was not only consumed unripe, boiled, baked and ground into meal for soups, cakes and mixed with the blood of animals, it was made into a variety of alcoholic drinks. Flour was prepared from the manioc root by shredding and soaking it to remove toxic qualities. Cassava bread was made from this flour.

FACTORS WHICH RETARD CHANGES IN EARLY FOOD HABITS

Relative isolation for a great number of years at places and regions led groups to standardize the behavior of individuals towards foods and develop unifying common patterns of eating. Standardization of group dietary habits have both positive and negative effects especially in times of acute food shortages. Food habits are a product of the group's past history and present physical and social environments. Meaningful food habits and customs are carefully observed and change slowly. Cultural pressures determine what foods are eaten, number of meals per day, meal pattern, methods of consuming food and utensils used. However, food sources, food choices and cultural food biases are carefully made only when there is plentiful food to permit choices. Food restrictions and food taboos must be relaxed during famines or the faithful will starve. Identifiable, strong cultural food habits are most likely to be perpetuated in societies where communication and cultural exchange are not highly developed. Food habits and preferences are carefully transmitted to succeeding generations through the training of children. A mother, in particular, exerts a strong influence on the eating habits of her children. Differences do exist within subgroups of major cultural groups, but the profound effects of cultural pressures on food habits cannot be underestimated.

NOTES

[1] For insights into various views of agricultural origins see E. Hahn, *Die Haustiere und ihre Beziehungen zur Wirtschaft de Menschens* (Leipzig: Dunker und Humbolt, 1896) and his *Die Entstehung de Pflugkultur* (Heidelberg: C. Winter, 1909); Hahn proposed a theory of animal domestication for religious reasons. C. Darwin, *The Variations of Animals and Plants Under Domestication*, 2nd ed. (New York: D. Appleton, 1896) and his *The Descent of Man and Selection in Relation to Sex*, 2nd ed. (New York: D. Appleton, 1909); Darwin developed a model that led him to believe cultivation of plants was an invention or a discovery, i.e., a happy accident. C. Sauer, *Agricultural Origins and Dispersals* (New York: American Geographical Society, 1952); Sauer deduced that it was the idea of cultivation that diffused and he attempted to locate the cradle of agricultural origins theoretically. R. Binford and L. Binford, eds., *New Perspectives in Archaeology* (Chicago: Aldine, 1968); the Binford model concludes that plant domestication likely occurred simultaneously and independently in many places on earth. N. Vavilov, *Teoreticheski osnovi selektsi rastene* (Moscow: 1935). Vavilov proposed eight centers of cultivated plant origin based upon his theory that the greatest genetic diversity was the center of origin. And, J. Harlan, "Agricultural Origins: Centers and Noncenters," *Science*, Vol. 174 (1971), pp. 468–474, and his *Crops and Man* (Madison: American Society of Agronomy and Crop Science, 1975). Harlan has identified centers and noncenters of agricultural origins but supports a no-model model which takes into account the possibility that domestication began in different regions for a variety of reasons.

[2] Sauer, op. cit., note 1, p. 21.

[3] Vavilov, op. cit., note 1.

[4] J. Harlan and D. Zohary, "Distribution of Wild Wheats and Barley," *Science*, Vol. 173 (1966), pp. 1074–1080.

[5] H. Helbaek, "Domestication of Food Plants in the Old World," *Science*, Vol. 130 (1959), pp. 365–372.

[6] H. Hugot, "The Origins of Agriculture in Africa: The Sahara," *Current Anthropology*, Vol. 9 (1968), pp. 483–488.

[7] O. Davies, "The Origins of Agriculture in West Africa," *Current Anthropology*, Vol. 9 (1968), pp. 479–480.

[8] K. Chang, "The Beginnings of Agriculture in the Far East," *Antiquity*, Vol. 44 (1970), pp. 175–189.

[9] P. Ho, "The Loess and the Origin of Chinese Agriculture," *American Historical Review*, Vol. 75 (1969), pp. 1–36.

[10] G. Willey, "New World Prehistory," *Science*, Vol. 131 (1960), pp. 73–86.

[11] R. MacNeish, "The Origins of American Agriculture," *Antiquity*, Vol. 39 (1965), pp. 87–94.

[12] C. Curtain, "On the Origin of Domesticated Sheep," *Antiquity*, Vol. 45 (1971), p. 303.

[13] For insights into the early domestication and exploitation of animals for food, see: S. Bökönyi, "Archaeological Problems and Methods of Recognizing Animal Domestication," pp. 219–229, and B. Cranstone, "Animal Husbandry: The Evidence from Ethnography," pp. 248- 263, in P. Ucko and G. Dimbleby, eds., *The Domestication and Exploitation of Plants and Animals* (Chicago: Aldine, 1969).

[14] C. Reed, "Animal Domestication in the Prehistoric Near East," *Science*, Vol. 130 (1969), pp. 1629–1639.

[15] B. Bender, *Farming in Prehistory: From Hunter and Gatherer to Food-Producer*, (New York: St. Martin's Press, 1975), pp. 102–106.

[16] D. Grigg, *The Agricultural Systems of the World: An Evolutionary Approach*, (Cambridge: Cambridge University Press, 1974), p. 16.

[17] E. Larsen, *Food: Past, Present and Future*, (London: Frederick Muller Ltd., 1977). p. 37.

[18] J. Leonard, *The Emergence of Man: The First Farmers*, (New York: Time-Life Books, 1973), pp. 115–125.

[19] M. Graubard, *Man's Food: Its Rhyme or Reason*, (New York: Macmillian, 1943), p. 11.

[20] K. Chang, ed., *Foods in Chinese Culture*, (New Haven: Yale University Press, 1977), pp. 6–21.

[21] Graubard, op. cit., note 19, pp. 11–12.

[22] D. Coursey, "The Origins and Domestication of Yams in Africa," in M. Arnott, ed., *The Anthropology of Food and Food Habits*, (The Hague: Mouton Publishers, 1975), pp. 187–212.

[23] C. Levi-Strauss, "The Use of Wild Plants in Tropical South America," in the *Handbook of South American Indians* (Washington, D.C.: Smithsonian Institution, Bur-Amer. Ethnol. Bul. 143, Vol. 6, 1950), pp. 465–486.

[24] D. and P. Brothwell, *Foods in Antiquity: A Survey of the Diet of Early Peoples* (New York: Praeger, 1969), pp. 103–104, 112–115.

Chapter 3

Nutrition and staple foods

People must eat to live; if they do not they starve to death. Food is necessary for physical, mental and emotional health. Humans have devoted much thought, time and effort into producing, processing, distributing, preparing and serving food. Both the quantity and quality of food are important for children to grow normally, and adults to maintain their health and their capacity to do work. People of all ages and all occupations require food in sufficient kinds and amounts that enable their bodies to maintain the optimum possible internal environment for cells, tissues and organs. Observations of the comparative well-being of cultural groups that have subsisted for many generations on diets that differ widely, along with experiments with human subjects and animals, leave little doubt that proper nutrition makes an important contribution to maintaining an individual's health throughout the individual's life. The human body must secure approximately fifty different substances from the food ingested. These substances are collectively called nutrients. Each nutrient has a specific function, individually or synergestically with other nutrients, and is needed to perform services for the body. Some furnish the body fuel, others provide materials for the building and maintenance of body tissue and a third group acts to regulate body processes. Nutrients, in proper amounts and proportions, enable the body to function normally and make the internal changes necessary as a person passes through the various phases of the life cycle. People who do not consume enough food or do not eat the right kinds of food to maintain body functions die.

NUTRIENTS AND ENERGY

Foods vary in their ability to satisfy hunger, and nutritive values of foods depend upon their chemical composition.[1] The six general classes or kinds of nutrients are: (1) carbohydrates; (2) fats and other lipids; (3) proteins; (4) vitamins; (5) minerals and (6) water. Carbohydrates, fats and other lipids and proteins are organic combustible energy nutrients and the only substances the body can use to supply energy for work and heat. Mineral elements and water, inorganic nutrients, are non-combustible for they do not contain carbon. The desire to eat is related to the body's need for energy rather than its need for other nutrients. A person could die for lack of a particular food nutrient with no feeling of hunger. Body tissue is built and repaired mainly by proteins, with the assistance of vitamins, minerals and water. Body processes are regulated by vitamins and mineral salts which occur in minute quantities in foods. Body temperature is regulated by water, and water aids body processes by holding substances in solution, facilitating circulation and aiding in elimination of waste. Intestinal elimination is assisted by vegetable fiber and water. The three main energy nutrients, carbohydrates, fats and proteins, can be used more or less interchangeably to supply energy. Chemical energy which may be released upon combustion is measured in heat units, calories. Georgian Adams has succinctly defined the calorie as:[2]

...a unit measure of heat. The word itself is derived from the Latin "calor," meaning heat. Heat quantity is measured by the change of temperature produced. The calorie, therefore, is the quantity of heat necessary to raise the temperature of 1 gram of water, 1 degree centigrade. The unit quantity of heat varies slightly at different points on the thermometric scale. If the degree interval chosen is from 14.5° to 15.5°C, the value of the unit is almost exactly that of the "mean" calorie, which is 1/100 of the quantity of heat necessary to raise the temperature of 1 gram of water from 0° to 100°C, that is, from the melting point of ice to the boiling point of water. The calorie, thus defined as the amount of heat required to raise the temperature of 1 gram of water from 14.5° to 15.5°C, is a very small unit, and is referred to as the small calorie (spelled with a small c). A larger unit, often convenient to use, is the kilogram calorie. This is the Calorie (spelled with a capital C). It represents the amount of heat necessary to raise the temperature of 1 kilogram (2.2 pounds) of water 1°C. The Calorie, equal to 1,000 small calories, is also called the "large" or "great" calorie. It is the unit generally used in expressing the heat-producing or energy-producing value of food. A teaspoonful of sugar (4 grams), for example, provides about 16 Calories (16,000 calories). The body requires a source of energy, which is normally supplied by food. In the process, food is fragmented by digestion into simple components, which are absorbed through the intestinal wall and transported to the body tissues. When these food components are oxidized within the tissues, energy is released, to be utilized in maintaining body temperature and muscle tone or to be expended in muscular work and other body activities. If the food intake is more than enough to meet the body's energy needs, there is storage of the excess, chiefly as body fat, and a gain in weight results. If the food intake is insufficient, the body draws on its own reserves, oxidizing them to furnish needed energy, with resultant loss in body weight. Whether we gain, lose, or maintain weight depends on food energy intake in relation to body energy requirements.

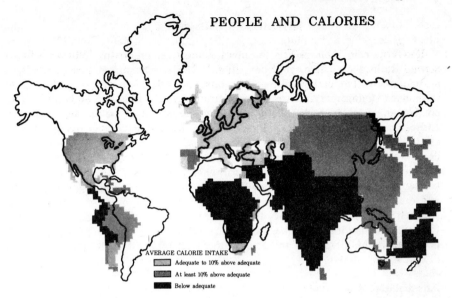

PEOPLE AND CALORIES

AVERAGE CALORIE INTAKE
- Adequate to 10% above adequate
- At least 10% above adequate
- Below adequate

Fig. 8. Both the quantity and quality of food are important for children to grow normally, and adults to maintain their health and their capacity to do work.

A certain amount of energy is required by the body for maintenance of vital processes and tissue, i.e., a base energy requirement. The amount of energy required to maintain life at rest is defined as the "basal metabolic" rate of a body. Extra energy needed as a result of muscular work, adjustments to new climatic environments and for the formulation of new tissues is superimposed upon this base metabolism rate. No one could live for very long on the base level of energy requirement. Everyone must eat to supply the energy necessary to maintain life (Figure 8).

Carbohydrates

Carbohydrates are a major source of most of the human body's energy. They are composed entirely of carbon, hydrogen and oxygen. All green plants form carbohydrates.[3] Cereals, high in carbohydrates, are a universal staple food for they provide the human body with the greatest amount of energy per unit area of land cultivated, are easy to store and transport and are inexpensive. Carbohydrates are subdivided into three groups according to complexity and molecular weight. They are the monosaccharides (glucose, fructose and galactose), disaccharides (sucrose, maltose and lactose) and polysaccharides (starch, dextrins and glycogen). All carbohydrates must be broken down by digestion into simple sugars before they can be absorbed by the body. Nutritionally, starch is the most important carbohydrate. Starch is found in seeds, tubers and roots, and functions as an energy store for future use of the plant. Rice, wheat, sorghum, corn, millet and rye contain about 70 percent starch. Potatoes, other tubers, beans and legumes are more than 40 percent starch. Refined cane sugar and beet sugar are relatively pure carbohydrates. The only carbohydrate of animal origin significant to human nutrition is lactose or milk sugar. Carbohydrates, when converted to sugar within the body, are highly soluble and can be used directly by the tissue or stored as an energy reserve. Inadequate carbohydrate intake reduces the body's ability to oxidize fat or reduce protein wastage. During periods of starvation, the body uses stored fat for energy and oxidizes amino acids from proteins in order to obtain the required energy. Utilization of amino acids for energy can produce an acute protein deficiency. This deficiency can lower the rate of body growth and maintenance and even increase the osmotic pressure in the stomach causing distention of the stomach and reduction of the desire to eat, accompanied by edema.[4] Another form of carbohydrates is fiber, and although not digested by humans, fiber is needed as a bulk material to regulate the mechanism of excretion and prevent constipation.

Fats and Lipids

Fats are the most concentrated source of energy for body needs. They are a source of needed essential fatty acids, carry fat-soluble vitamins A, D, E and K, promote efficient body use of carbohydrates and proteins and make food appetizing and satisfying. Fats are chemically formed by combining three fatty acids with glycerol (organic alcohol). Their fuel value relates to their composition, i.e., large amounts of carbon, hydrogen and oxygen. Fats are the chief form by which animals store extra energy for future use. Many food fats are of animal origin: butter, lard, fatty fish and meats, egg yolk, cream and cheese. Some plants such as olive, coconut, peanut, soybean, etc., store fats in fruits, seeds or nuts. Fats in liquid form, at room temperature, are commonly called oils. The physical properties of fats sometimes affect their nutritive value. Emulsified fats, as in egg yolk and in milk, can be digested quickly because the tiny droplets can be easily worked upon by digestive enzymes. Some fats are considered saturated when they cannot take up any more hydrogen, unsaturated when they can absorb some hydrogen, and polyunsaturated when they have the ability to incorporate much more hydrogen. Polyunsaturated fats have great nutritional importance, especially linoleic acid.[5] Linoleic acid is necessary for growth, reproduction and reduction of damage from radiation. It also lowers blood cholesterol and protects against excessive loss of water. A "lipid" is any substance with physical properties similar to fats and is characterized by the presence of one or more fatty acids. Cholesterol, a common lipid, is an essential constituent of the blood and it assists the body to form vitamin D from ultraviolet light. High plasma cholesterol is indicative of disturbed metabolism and can cause serious damage to arterial walls. Amounts of fats and lipids in a diet vary widely according to the availability of fat-rich foods, money available for food, tradition and personal tastes.

Proteins

Proteins, a group of complex organic compounds containing nitrogen, carbon, hydrogen and oxygen, are essential for life and growth. Molecules of proteins are made up of nitrogen-containing compounds called amino acids. Protein, named from a Greek word meaning first place, is used by the human body to: (1) build new tissue; (2) maintain tissue and for replacement of regular tissue loss; (3) serve as regulatory substances and influence water balance; (4) make enzymes essential for digestion and metabolic processes; (5) form milk; (6) supply energy; and (7) make hormones and antibodies. Unlike nitrogen and oxygen, proteins do not exist in the air humans breathe. Proteins must be made by living cells. Humans must secure necessary proteins from plants and animals.[6] Plants, utilizing radiant energy from the sun along with nitrogen from the soil and carbon dioxide from the air, make their own protein. Animals secure their proteins from plants and other animals.[7] Ruminant animals such as sheep, goats and cattle, are unique in that micro-organisms in their paunches can utilize nitrogen-containing pasture grasses as a base for making digestible proteins. Amino acids in proteins determine their chemical characteristics, nutritive value and usefulness in body metabolism. Although many amino acids are found in standard proven diets, eight are nutritionally essential and indispensable. The human body must have their eight amino acids but it cannot synthesize them. These eight must be ingested completely formed and ready for the body to use.

The usefulness of a protein depends upon its mixture of amino acids after digestion and absorption into the blood. A complete protein supplies the body with all essential amino acids in proper amounts and proportions. Meat, milk, fish, poultry and eggs, and cheese, nuts, peanuts, peas or beans are protein-rich foods. Proteins of animal origin are well balanced in their ratio of essential and non-essential amino acids and have higher biological value than other proteins. Vegetable proteins supply important amounts of amino acids but not all. Proteins from cereals alone are not of high quality for normal human growth and sufficient human body maintenance.

If a diet does not furnish enough protein for the body's daily needs, the body draws on its own tissue protein. Protein deficiencies for extended periods of time can lead to stunted growth, lack of muscle development and lowered resistance to disease. Young children immediately after weaning are most apt to show marked symptoms of protein deficiency. This is especially true in developing nations where protein-rich foods, particularly those of animal origin, are unavailable to the poorest segments of the population. Infants and adults may show marked swelling of the legs and abdomen (edema), contract infectious diseases and be weakened by intestinal parasitism. Kwashiorkor (a West African word meaning "the disease the child gets when another body is born") and Marasmus (from the Greek word meaning "to waste away") are two different types of protein-calorie deficiencies.[8] Kwashiorkor is common to infants who are fed a diet adequate in calories, but low in protein. The child's body becomes bloated for the tissues contain excessive water, hair color changes to reddish-orange and a skin rash covers the body. Marasmus is common in infants who are weaned early in life from a diet of nutritious mother's milk and are fed a low-calorie, low-protein substitute.[9] Infants develop atrophied muscles, physical stunting, brain damage and are very susceptible to infectious diseases. Their mortality rate is high. Any severe lack of protein impairs a child's mental abilities whether this void occurs during pregnancy or during the first years of life. Supplies of protein foods are a critical problem for many populous, developing nations. Hundreds of millions of children are now growing up with inadequate physical and mental characteristics to meet the challenges of adult life, to make and carry out the decisions necessary to insure survival in a famine or to compete in a complex space-age world.

Vitamins

At the turn of this century, only carbohydrates, fats, protein, mineral elements and water were believed needed for normal human nutrition. A number of chemists and physiologists, working independently, determined that the body needed selected organic compounds in small amounts that had to be supplied from a source outside the body. Dr. Casimir Funk, a Polish chemist, coined the word "vitamine" (an amine compound) in 1912 and wrote the first book on "vitamines" in 1914. Vitamins promote growth and the ability to produce healthy children, maintain health, long life and mental alertness, utilization of amino acids and energy source metabolism and assist in developing resistance to bacterial infections. They act as organic catalysts which speed up chemical reactions. Any ordinary mixed diet contains a good supply of vitamins. When food choice is limited, a diet low in certain vitamins causes specific vitamin deficiency diseases.[10] Vitamins are classified on the basis of their solubility. Vitamin C and vitamins of the B complex are water soluble; vitamins A, D, E and K are fat-soluble vitamins. A deficiency of vitamin A lowers resistance to respiratory infections and vision impairment; vitamin A is found in yellow and dark green leafy vegetables, egg yolk and cod-liver oil. Diets low in the B complex vitamins result in beriberi (a Chinese word meaning "I cannot") and pellagra (from the Italian "pelle agra" meaning painful or rough skin). Beriberi is a disease characterized by heart disease, muscle atrophy, paralysis and death. Pellagra is a disease characterized by a reddish skin rash, skin lesions, diarrhea and mental apathy. The B complex vitamins are abundant in lean meats, wheat germ, dry beans, peas and yeast.

Vitamin C is needed for the formulation of collagen (wound healing) and is important for scurvy prevention. It is found in nature within citrus fruits, apples and potatoes. Scurvy, one of the oldest recorded diseases and one prevalent in times of famine when fresh foods are not available, results in the loss of teeth, pains in the joints, rough skin, fatigue and degeneration of body tissue. Vitamin D is sometimes called "the sunshine vitamin" because sunlight striking the skin converts provitamins into a form of vitamin D. Lack of vitamin D is most serious in children, and is reflected in bowlegs, knock-knees, enlarged joints and shrunken chests (pigeon chest). Vitamin D may be secured from an oil concentrate (eggs, liver or fatty fish) or generated in the body by exposure to ultraviolet rays from sunlight. Vitamin E is necessary for the prevention of blood disorders, reproduction and the normal excretion processes. Palm oil, safflower oil, wheat germ oil, shortening and margarines are common sources of vitamin E. Vitamin K, the "koagulation" vitamin, is used primarily by the body for blood clotting. An average individual eating a varied diet of traditional foods receives adequate supplies of vitamin K. Additional organic compounds, some yet unidentified, do exist and do play a significant role in human life support.

Minerals

The human body is composed of chemical and mineral elements in numerous combinations. Calcium, phosphorus, sodium, potassium, sulfur and magnesium are important macro inorganic minerals and are present in the body in relatively large amounts. Iron, manganese, copper, zinc, cobalt, iodine and others are vitally important but present in minute quantities. Approximately 99 percent of the calcium and up to 90 percent of the body's phosphorus are in the bones and teeth. Calcium is essential for blood clotting, heart muscle contraction and relaxation and enzyme activation for metabolism. Phosphorus participates in chemical reactions with proteins, fats and carbohydrates to provide the body with energy and to assist in body growth and repair. Phosphorus, when combined with calcium, is very important in providing rigidity and hardness to the bones and teeth. Dietary deficiencies of calcium and phosphorus, particularly in children who need large amounts, lead to growth stunting, poor quality teeth and bone malformation.[11] In parts of the world where a large proportion of the normal diet comes from vegetable sources, calcium and phosphorus deficiencies are endemic. Cereal grains, unlike milk and meats, are low in calcium. Children with inadequate intake of calcium and phosphorus may never develop the full height of which they are genetically capable. Milk is a superb source of calcium and in parts of the world where milk is not available, calcium must come from other sources such as bones, bony meats, grains and vegetables consumed in large amounts, drinking water, dark leafy vegetables, etc. Diets that supply adequate amounts of protein usually are adequate in phosphorus.

The function of magnesium in the body is related to both calcium and phosphorus. Approximately three-quarters of the magnesium in the body is found in the bones. Magnesium is necessary in the body to synthesize protein, regulate temperature and assist in nerve contraction processes. A deficiency of magnesium in the body is uncommon, for diets adequate in other essential elements generally supply adequate magnesium. Trace or micro-minerals are necessary in the human body in small amounts. They include iron, iodine, copper, manganese, zinc, etc.; and vary in function, distribution, body requirements and chemical properties. People who eat a mixed plant and animal diet seldom experience deficiencies or toxicities from lack of trace mineral elements.

Water

Water is second only to oxygen in importance for the survival of humans. A person can survive without food for weeks, but only a few days without water.

Approximately 60 to 65 percent of an adult's body weight is water and a body water loss of 10 percent is fatal. A body loses 2 to 2½ liters of water per day through excretion, expired air and by perspiration. Water replacement is by fluid in-take, water in solid foods and water produced by metabolic processes.[12] Acute water deficiency or dehydration produces weakness, lassitude, thirst, loss of weight and mental confusion. In warm, dry climates a dehydrated person needing water may develop heat cramps, heat exhaustion or heat stroke before he dies. Water losses may result from persistent diarrhea. The body's water content must be maintained for water is the medium for transporting dissolved nutrients and wastes, and for regulating body temperature.

Neither muscles nor nerves function properly unless bathed in a tissue fluid that contains mineral salts. Excessive sweating at high temperatures causes both water and sodium chloride (salt) losses from the body. Sodium is a key element in regulation of body water and acid-base balance. Depletion of sodium leads to muscle cramping, mental apathy, convulsions, comas and even death. Calcium ion imbalances in tissue fluids can result in convulsions and paralysis. Lack of necessary potassium produces muscular weakness, abdominal distention (by gas), and heart muscle stoppage. Need for potassium increases in times of acute hunger or famine when the human body begins to utilize its own muscle as a body energy source.

UNDERNUTRITION AND MALNUTRITION

Undernutrition, malnutrition and hunger are terms utilized to describe diets and alimentary desires in food deficient places and regions of the world. They are social diseases, not medical problems, which have been a part of human experience since humans became social beings. Causes are built into the regional, national and international socioeconomic and political structures. Scarcity of food is rarely the main factor responsible for undernutrition. malnutrition and hunger. Internal, external, regional, national and international maldistribution of food is the main factor responsible.[13] Historically, many places have suffered severely from malnutrition and undernutrition and people went hungry and died, yet there were surpluses of food and foodstuffs were even a major trade or export item. Undernutrition or undernourishment refers to an inadequacy in the quantity of a diet, specifically lack of calories (not enough to eat). Malnutrition refers to an inadequacy in the quality of a diet, specifically the lack of essential nutrients in a diet (not the right types of foods). Hunger is acute and persistent undernourishment that causes physical discomfort and pain. A rational diet must be both sufficient to temper hunger and complete for full body realization. It should supply the body with all the energy needs and all the essential substances to maintain body health and vigor. If a body does not take in as much energy as it expends, it suffers from energy hunger and then semistarvation; if the energy deficiency is acute life may be terminated. A body adequately supplied with energy foods but lacking in one or more essential chemical nutrients suffers from partial or hidden hunger. Many qualitative nutritional deficiencies have no external symptoms, while others result in open and visible deficiency diseases. Common malnutrition and/or hidden diseases are a ramification of diets inadequately supplied with proteins, vitamins, certain fats and/or lipids or mineral salts. William Shurtleff wrote in September 1978:[14]

> During the 1970s, 15 million died each year of starvation and malnutrition-caused diseases. Seventy-five percent of those who died were children. This is 41,000 deaths each day and over 1,700 each hour. In the 15 minutes it will take you to read this article, 428 people will die of starvation. Malnutrition causes millions of premature deaths each year and in some societies 40% of the children die before the age of 5, mostly from nutrition-related causes. The survivors often suffer such severe and chronic malnutrition that their physical and mental growth is permanently retarded. Malnutrition and infectious diseases commonly occur in the same child and each magnifies the other. Infection can precipitate malnutrition and malnutrition increases susceptibility to infection. The vicious circle soon becomes a downward spiral as malnutrition leads to poor work, education and health, which in turn generate more poverty and malnutrition. This is the cycle of suffering which is quickly becoming the dominant reality of daily life for poor people throughout the world.

It is very difficult to determine the total number of persons who lack adequate quantity and quality of food, so estimates of these numbers are only academic exercises. Nevertheless, reliable data shows that in the last quarter of the twentieth century, most of those who suffer from undernutrition and malnutrition live in the developing countries of Latin America, Asia and Africa, characterized by high rates of population growth. Pockets of rural and urban human malnutrition and undernutrition exist also in the most technologically advanced countries.[15]

There is a close connection between a person's diet, outlook on life and general health. Diets influence health and balanced physiological development prior to birth. After birth, nutrition affects growth, mental development, efficacy and longevity. An ill-nourished and weak human body is susceptible to various pathogenic agents which it may not have the ability to fight. People who are suffering from undernourishment or caloric deficiency are characterized by withered bodies, open skin wounds and changed social behavior. The first stage of undernutrition or hunger is exemplified by nervous excitement, extreme irritability, loosening of social bonds and lessening of morale. Food riots, violent protests, social strife and individual overt anti-social activities generally occur at this stage, if they occur at all. The second stage of undernutrition or severe hunger may be described as a time of individual apathy, mental depression, nausea and inability to concentrate. There is lack of ambition, melancholy, submissiveness and little interest in sex. Males and females begin to lose aspects of their outward physical sexual differences, and males begin to resemble females by loss of beards, enlargement of breasts and development of smooth, soft skin. The third and final stage of acute undernourishment or starvation leads to the disintegration of the human personality and internal disintegration of the body. Self-preservation and mental control are lost, scruples and inhibitions disappear, then madness, stupor and finally death. Undernourishment can be "chronic", leading to marasmus but not to death specifically by starvation, or "infrequent" but leading to death by acute calorie deficiency starvation. Chronically undernourished populations may become insensible to their lack of food and experience only facets of the first stage of undernutrition and selected aspects of the second stage. Infrequent acutely undernourished populations suffer the gamut of human physical and mental pain, including the total ramifications of the third stage and death.

For millenniums an important factor in morbidity and mortality of great numbers of humans, who believed they were eating well, was the deficiency of proteins. Protein is probably the single most common nutrient deficiency in any diet.[16] Protein deficiency exerts its most devastating effects on the young, causing a high rate of premature births, stillbirths and a high mortality rate during the first years of life. Children, who at an early age experience a period of inadequate protein intake, eventually reflect this paucity in their subnormal physical condition. Incidence and virulence of diseases such as tuberculosis, pneumonia, dysentery and typhoid fever are related to a reduction in organic resistance as a result of an absence of protein. Kwashiorkor or severe protein deficiency produces bloated bellies, deformed faces, apathy, irritability, "flaky-paint" skin and dispigmented hair. Children are very susceptible to kwashiorkor and can be identified by their swollen bellies, enlarged for the muscles are weak and tissues contain too much water, on an otherwise shrunken body and supported by little legs resembling withered twigs.[17] Protein malnutrition in children reduces the possibility of them achieving the mental and physical potential with which they were born.

There are five principal deficiency diseases in the world today: anemia, endemic goiter, kwashiorkor, marasmus and xerophthalmia. Marasmus, a severe caloric deficiency, and kwashiorkor, a severe protein deficiency, have been discussed. Xerophthalmia is a vitamin A deficiency disease which in its most severe form, involves drying of the eyes, night-blindness, corneal ulcerations and other changes that cause destruction of the eyes and lead to blindness. Young children are most frequently affected and by far the greatest incidence in recent years occurs in Southeast Asia. Diets composed primarily of starchy foods with only occasional fruit and green vegetables can produce xerophthalmia. The mortality rate of malnourished children with this vitamin deficiency disease is high. Other vitamin deficiency diseases include beriberi, scurvy, pellagra and types of vitamin B and C anemia. Fat and lipid malnutrition results in poor growth and scaliness of the skin. Humans need many different fatty acids to manufacture certain cellular structures, but lack the ability to synthesize a number of them. Dietary fats also help in the body's absorption of certain vitamins. Mineral malnutrition is of importance for mineral salts are as significant to the human body as calories or proteins. Minerals have a myriad of functions in the body and they cannot be substituted for each other in these functions. The minerals which cause special concern are calcium, phosphate, iron and iodine. Two of the five principal deficiency diseases are mineral deficiency diseases, anemia and endemic goiter. Anemia, a recurring global problem among malnourished individuals, is mainly an iron deficiency disease whose symptoms include pallor of the skin and mucous membranes, general fatigue, breathlessness

MARASMUS
Calorie Deficiency Disease

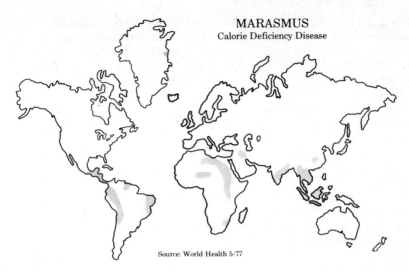

Source: World Health 5/77

Fig. 9

after exertion, loss of appetite and indigestion. In pregnant and lactating women and growing children, the demands for hemoglobin are greatest. Hemoglobin, the iron-containing component of the blood, assists the blood in performing its oxygen carrying function. Endemic goiter, a disease known for thousands of years, is the enlargement of the thyroid gland resulting from iodine deficiency.

KWASHIORKOR
Protein Deficiency Disease

Source: World Health 5/77

Fig. 10

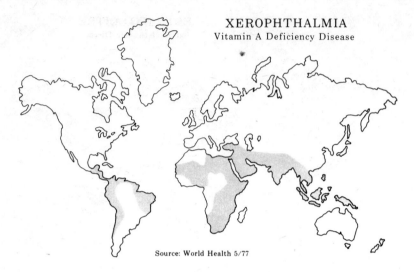

Source: World Health 5/77

Fig. 11

Its main symptoms include deformity of the lower part of the neck, mental retardation and deaf-mutism. Goiter has occurred in some part of almost every region and nation of the world. Deficiency diseases are especially prevalent where the basic diet is composed of five calorie-producing world food staples: rice, wheat, millet, corn or cassava (Figures 9, 10, 11, 12 and 13).

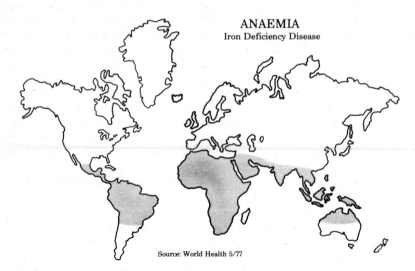

Source: World Health 5/77

Fig. 12

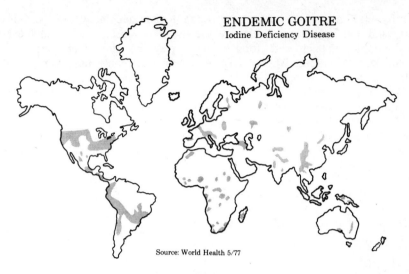

ENDEMIC GOITRE
Iodine Deficiency Disease

Source: World Health 5/77

Fig. 13

Most places, regions, or nations where undernutrition and malnutrition are prevalent have not suffered from a famine. Only a small segment of any population in non-famine years suffers from acute malnutrition, mainly infants and small children. People in most societies know what they should eat to provide them with a balanced diet, but many lack financial resources and facilities to prepare or store food. Transculturation has historically created food-hunger problems when parents find their traditional way of life and traditional foods socially unacceptable or applicable. Mothers, at times, are caught in a cultural dilemma and may feed their children improperly because they have adopted practices and new foods they do not understand. Inadequate knowledge of new foods and lack of appreciation at times for old foods are important factors in inducing malnutrition. Another significant factor in undernutrition and malnutrition is the range of common infectious diseases resulting from unsanitary environments which interfere with the human body's ability to properly utilize the food consumed or which may have drastically reduced the individual's appetite. An insufficient diet with a severe calorie deficit frequently is the cause of malnutrition. Providing individuals and cultural groups with the necessary quantity of high quality foods is the only permanent solution to undernutrition and malnutrition.

STAPLE PLANT AND ANIMAL FOODS: A SPATIAL PERSPECTIVE

Staple food consumption patterns vary greatly on the surface of the earth. Food supply is the most significant factor affecting consumption, and food quantity and quality vary from one region to another. Many taboos, cultural biases and much ignorance influence the use of nourishing plants and animal foods. Food supplies and food sources play an important part in the development of nations. Where staple food is scarce, people must spend most of their time securing enough food to eat and little time to the arts, sciences or activities that ultimately lead to socioeconomic progress. Where staple food is plentiful, people have more time to invest in activities that lead to making this world a better place to live, economic progress and the enjoyment of leisure. Much human suffering and many wars have occurred when people found it necessary to fight for known food reserves or perceived food-rich lands. People associate specific food or foods to places, and traditional regional foods are reflective of what plant grows best or what animal thrives in a particular climate-soil-landform region. Most of the staple foods for human consumption comes from a small number of plants and animals.

The most important food crops in the world are:

(1) Wheat	(6) Manioc
(2) Rice	(7) Sorghums and millets
(3) Corn	(8) Soybeans
(4) Potatoes (white and sweet)	(9) Beans, peas and chickpeas
(5) Barley	(10) Peanuts

Wheat and rice are by far the most important staples (average annual world production of each ranges between 300 and 350 million metric tons, and currently about one-third of all cultivated land is used to grow these two food crops). Wheat and rice, along with corn, barley, sorghum, millet and rye, are cereals. All have starchy edible seeds and have been grown throughout historic time. The principal basic food source for every major civilization was a cereal. Cereals can be easily produced, stored and transported. They yield more food, both quantitatively and qualitatively, per unit of land and labor than any other major crop and serve as feed for animals that produce meat, milk, fats and eggs. Cereals are consumed in grain form, processed or milled, brewed into beer, or distilled into potable spirits. Per capita consumption of cereals initially increases with elevation of living standards, but after a level has been reached more diverse foods are sought and consumption slowly declines. Highly developed societies have the lowest per capita consumption of cereals. In the past century or so, world production of cereals has kept pace with world population growth and also with the elevation of levels of living.

Wheat, the leading bread grain, is the dominant staple in North America, Europe, North Africa and the Near East. There are two basic types of wheat, winter wheat and spring wheat. Winter wheat is autumn sown and accounts for three-quarters of all wheat produced. Hard spring wheats, sown where winters are too severe for growing winter wheat, are the best bread-making varieties. Wheat can be grown in most temperate climates and its moisture requirements range from 250 to 900 mm. Duration of daylight and total heat-degree days determine the growing period, which ranges from about 90 to almost 240 days. Rice is the dominant staple of most of south and east Asia. Asia historically has produced and inhabitants consumed nine-tenths of the world's average annual rice crop. Unlike wheat, rice can tolerate high temperatures and high relative humidities. Rice requires high light intensities and is normally grown in standing water. Minimum temperatures for its germination are 18° to 20°C and 22° to 24°C for vegetal growth. Rich alluvium soils with impervious subsoils that retain irrigation or flood waters are ideal for rice. It has proven to be an excellent staple because of its high productivity per unit area cultivated and its ability to yield well under continuous cultivation. Although world corn production approaches that of wheat and rice, corn directly supplies much less of humanity's food calories. Corn is used primarily as animal food in developed nations, but as a food staple in some developing nations. It can be grown in most tropical and mid-latitude warm climates if the growing season's temperatures average 24°C by day, receives 650–1000 mm of precipitation and has a long frost-free period. Corn is processed to make oil, starch and syrup, or dry milled for the production of cornmeal, hominy, grits and breakfast foods. It is eaten in Central America and Mexico in the form of baked cakes or bread called tortillas, and in southeast Africa as doughy balls, gruel or paste.

Potatoes rival wheat and rice as a source of human food, and white potatoes provide more nutrients per hectare than wheat or rice. White potatoes require a long growing season, a stable moisture supply and sandy-loam soils. They are a staple food in the highlands of South America, and in Eastern and Central Europe. Sweet potatoes, manioc and yams are tropical starch-producing root crops. These starchy foods are staples in portions of lowland South America, along the west coast of Africa and in the Far East. Generally, the highest consumption areas are in equatorial regions where the use of starchy foods is abundant. Barley has the shortest growing season of all cereals and can be grown in a wide range of climates and soils. Climatic requirements for food barley and malting barley differ, for malting barley needs cooler temperatures in the final phase of the ripening cycle. Most barley is used for animal feed, but it is consumed by humans in bread form within selected African, Asian and South American countries with extreme climates. Sorghums and millets are staple subsistence foods in the savanna regions of Africa and India. Their importance in Africa is revealed by statistics which rank these as the most important grain crops in more than fifteen countries. Sorghums and millets are consumed as bread and gruel and fed to food producing animals as a grain meal and as forage. Soybeans, beans, peas, chickpeas and peanuts are a few of many edible leguminous seeds. Normally, they have a protein content that ranges from eight to fifteen percent of dry weight. They are a very important source of protein for a large segment of the world's population. Unfortunately, plant proteins are usually low in certain essential amino acids. Human consumption is highest in parts of tropical Africa, Southeast Asia and Central and South America. Soybeans are an exceptional source of high quality protein and are used for human nourishment as flour, paste, curds and sauce. Peanuts are a good source of niacin, their skin is rich in thiamine and they contain large amounts of fats. Peanuts are an important subsistence staple in southeastern and west-central Africa, and in southern and eastern Asia.[18]

Fig. 14. Animals have been used for food from the time humans learned to scavenge and hunt. Here, in 1974, a desperate individual tried to satisfy hunger by searching for small scraps of meat on the bones of a dead animal in the Sahel (Photo by UNICEF/Leon Davico, ICEF 6918).

People who live in areas of the world where plant foods are the principal source of proteins are those who suffer most from undernutrition, malnutrition, hunger and famine. There is a lower protein-to-energy ratio of staple plant foods to animal food products. Reliance on a single staple plant food often provides an inadequate supply of essential amino acids. Supplementing vegetarian diet with plant protein from different sources or including small amounts of animal protein can correct critical deficiencies. If high quality protein sources are unavailable to a population whose diet is composed of vegetables or seed staples, protein malnutrition can become endemic.

Animals have been used for food from the time humans learned to scavenge, hunt and fish (Figure 14). Of the many animals originally hunted or fished and found suitable for food, only a few were domesticated. Fewer still of these early domesticated animals are considered staple food sources. These include:

(1)	Cattle	(6)	Water buffaloes
(2)	Sheep	(7)	Camels
(3)	Goats	(8)	Yaks
(4)	Pigs	(9)	Llamas
(5)	Chickens	(10)	Rabbits

Fish and other aquatic creatures are excellent food sources but few have been domesticated. Domesticated food animals are in essence stored "food on the hoof". A live animal is its own storage facility and can be slaughtered when needed. Animals can produce food, such as milk or eggs, for extended periods of time and during the long period between plant harvest. Animal food and animal products are very significant during the preharvest hunger period.[19] Foods of animal origin are more expensive to produce than foods of plant origin, but animals are able to thrive on plant materials unsuitable for human consumption.

Cattle, as producers of meat and milk, are the most important staple animal food source. As ruminants, they utilize cellulose from plants as their main source of energy. Plant-based cattle feed includes actively growing plants, dormant plants and preserved plant materials (hay or silage). Dairy cattle must consume large quantities of feed for efficient milk production. Two distinct types of cattle exist that provide foods for humans, European or temperate and humped or tropical cattle. European cattle were bred for milk and meat, and thrive best in areas where the mean monthly temperatures are less than 18°C. Tropical cattle thrive best where temperatures exceed 21°C, and are used primarily as field animals. Dairy farming is very important in northeastern United States and northwestern Europe. Ranching or commercial beef cattle operations are a major industry in the grassland areas of the North American Great Plains, northern Argentina, Uruguay, and eastern Australia. Zebu, water buffaloes and other humped cattle are of great importance in the food production tasks of those who dwell in tropical Africa and Asia.

Sheep and goats are closely related ruminant animals used by humans as a food source of meat and milk. For thousands of years, fat lambs have been prized for their meat. Mutton, or meat from mature sheep, and goat meat have a stronger flavor than fat lambs. Sheep and goats can forage on sparse vegetation and thus make extremely marginal range land a producer of high quality food. Australia, Soviet Union, Peoples Republic of China, Turkey, India and New Zealand are noted food sheep and goat producing nations. Sheep and goat meat are of great importance in the diets of those who live in the Middle East, Eastern Europe, Australia and selected west European nations. Unlike cattle, sheep or goats, pigs are omnivorous animals that cannot digest cellulose. Food requirements of a pig are similar to those of a human. However, pigs do eat items people cannot such as garbage, fish by-products, low-quality grains, dry corn, etc. Pigs can adjust to most climates but must be protected from extreme hot or cold temperatures. The main food products secured from pigs are pork, bacon and lard. Pigs are bred and reared for food on a large scale in the Peoples Republic of China, the United States, Brazil, Soviet Union and in Europe. Chickens are the most important domesticated fowl used as a human food source. Other domesticated birds used for human food include turkeys, ducks, geese and guineas. Chickens are very efficient producers of meat and eggs. Egg protein has the highest nutritive value of any common food. Like pigs, chickens consume foodstuffs humans cannot eat or could eat only with difficulty. Chickens have extraordinary biological adaptability and are an important food source for most of the inhabitants of the world.[20] Water buffaloes, camels, yaks, llamas and rabbits are staple food sources in regions where traditionally there is low consumption of meat for cultural or religious reasons.

NOTES

[1] N. Scrimshaw and V. Young, "The Requirements of Human Nutrition," *Scientific American*, Vol. 235 (1976), pp. 51–64.

[2] G. Adams, "Calorie," and information footnote in *Food: The Yearbook of Agriculture 1959* (Washington, D.C.: Government Printing Office, 1959), p. 56.

[3] J. Janick, C. Noller and C. Rhykerd, "The Cycles of Plant and Animal Nutrition," *Scientific American*, Vol. 235 (1976), pp. 75–86.

[4] A. Berg, *The Nutrition Factor* (Washington, D.C.: The Brookings Institution, 1973), pp. 9–30.

[5] H. Wiese, A. Hansen and D. Adams, "Essential Fatty Acids in Human Nutrition," *Journal of Nutrition*, Vol. 66 (1955), p. 345.

[6] J. Overbeek, "Plant Physiology and the Human Ecosystem," *Ann. Rev. Plant Physiology*, Vol. 27 (1976), pp. 10–11.

[7] B. Ortiz de Montellano, "Aztec Cannibalism: An Ecological Necessity?", *Science*, Vol. 200 (1978), No. 4342, pp. 611–617.

[8] L. Brown, "Death at an Early Age," *UNICEF News*, Vol. 85 (1975), No. 3, pp. 3–9; and D. Jelliffe and E. Jelliffe, *Human Milk in the Modern World* (Oxford: Oxford University Press, 1978).

[9] J. Dwyer, "The Decline of Breast-Feeding: Sales, Sloth or Society?", *UNICEF News*, Vol. 86 (1975), No. 4, pp. 14–18.

[10] "The Five Principal Deficiency Diseases in the World Today," *World Health*, (May 1977), pp. 16–17.

[11] D. Jelliffe and E. Jelliffe, "Human Milk, Nutrition, and the World Resource Crisis," *Science*, Vol. 188 (1975), No. 4188, pp. 557–561.

[12] K. Schmidt-Nielsen, *Animal Physiology* (Englewood Cliffs, N.J.: Prentice-Hall, 1964), pp. 47–67.

[13] W. Cochrane, *The World Food Problem* (New York: Thomas Y. Crowell, 1969), pp. 38–39.

[14] W. Shurtleff, "New Foods from Old Ways," *Contents*, Vol. 1, No. 8 (1978), p. 18.

[15] *Hunger, U.S.A.* (Washington, D.C.: New Community Press, 1968), pp. 16–38.

[16] M. Benarde, *Race Against Famine* (Philadelphia: Macrae Smith Co., 1968), pp. 13–24.

[17] J. de Castro, *The Geography of Hunger* (Boston: Little, Brown & Co., 1952), p. 40.

[18] D. Jones (adv. ed.), *Oxford Economic Atlas of the World* (Oxford: Oxford University Press, 1972), pp. 9–20; and N. Vietmeyer, "Poor People's Crops," *Agenda*, Vol. 1, No. 8 (Sept., 1978), pp. 12–17.

[19] J. Hunter, "Seasonal Hunger in Part of the West African Savanna: A Survey of Bodyweights in Nangodi, North East Ghana," *Transactions and Papers, The Institute of British Geographers*, 41 (1967), p. 171.

[20] Jones, op. cit., note 18, pp. 21–23.

Part II

**Famines of the past:
4000 B.C. to A.D. 1978**

Chapter 4

Famine: Problems in definition

According to ancient chroniclers and modern records, every society has people who suffer from hunger. Demands for food by humans are daily, while the biological inputs and outputs of food production have definite seasonal patterns. The seasonality of food production patterns places a premium on efficient storage facilities or food preservation techniques. In traditional cultures, the most serious problems arise in the pre-harvest season when substantial labor input coincides with a period when stored food runs low. At this time, there is little food available and that which is bartered or sold commands a high price. Hunger, in an extreme form, occurs more frequently among the poor. There is no measure of the extent of hunger and no scientific studies to determine if hunger in the most affluent nations of a time has been sufficiently severe and prolonged to produce national psychological effects, although national psychological health has undoubtedly been impaired. The existence of hunger in societies that can afford to eliminate hunger is morally and economically indefensible. A society, in any time frame, cannot excuse itself from not providing adequate food for all its people on the grounds that those who suffer from hunger are ignorant of proper nutritional practices. Hunger in any form damages the moral and economic base of society, regardless of the reason for hunger's existence. Hungry members of a society are frequently resentful people. As long as those who suffer from hunger do not chronically feel the pains of hunger, have loved ones die from hunger or see their friends starve to death in mass, their resentment is seldom translated into action. Acute or chronic hunger produces resentful people who begin to hope for better things. If hope is combined with a social program to change the status of those who are hungry, a stage is set for social unrest and revolution.

Malnutrition has been a greater cause of affliction throughout recorded history than chronic hunger. Primary malnutrition is inadequate intake of nutrients for normal body requirements caused by food shortages, faulty selection of food or lack of the ability to purchase adequate quality food. Secondary malnutrition results from factors which interfere with proper utilization of ingested essential nutrients. Not all forms of malnutrition are caused by dietary inadequacies. The most commonly used criterion to estimate a nation's dietary level is measuring food energy supplies in terms of calories. Ned Greenwood and J. M. B. Edwards noted:[1]

> The F.A.O. has established what it calls the Standard Nutritional Unit (SNU), which consists of 2,350 calories per person per day or 857,750 calories per year. The SNU is based on average caloric need, but it can also be used to imply a particular balance of nutritional elements. Below this average level work capacity falls rapidly. At 1,600 or 1,700 calories per day the body generally reaches the level of basal metabolism, that is, it is barely capable of maintaining the respiratory, digestive, and other basic systems in working order. Most prisoners assigned to hard labor in the Auschwitz concentration camp received between 1,000 and 1,300 calories a day; those who were unable to obtain special privileges died in about three months. Individual nutritional needs vary with age, sex, body build, activity, and climate. A manual worker in a cold climate may require as many as 5,000 calories. Other things being equal, higher average caloric intake is required in temperate and cold countries than in tropical countries, though the same is not necessarily true of protein requirements. It may seem as if Europeans and those of European origin need more calories, but this is only because a high-protein diet has enabled them to develop to full body size. The F.A.O. now assumes that if this were true of all the world's peoples, nutritional requirements would be about the same everywhere.

There is a great difference between hunger or malnutrition and famine, but to many the dividing line between hunger and famine is uncertain. Most people would agree that there are degrees of hunger or even food shortages which do not justify the use of the term *famine*. Yet famine is a term applied to many occurrences and conveys thoughts and impressions not related to mass deaths by starvation. The question of a standard definition for famine is important if scholarly study of the topic is to make contributions to the literature. Lack of a standard definition may be partly responsible for the paucity of published scientific famine research. Famine, as a descriptive term for a devastating social hazard, carries emotional overtones. It is constantly being improperly raised to attract aid for brief food shortages, drawing attention from a more desperate need elsewhere or negating potential future relief for a real famine. Predictions of world famine were heard so frequently that most people ceased to question "what is a famine?" and accepted famine as something common such as a storm, a flood or an earthquake. Thomas Malthus, a British political economist, concluded in 1798 that famine was a natural means by which population was held in balance with food supply. He postulated:[2]

I think I may fairly make two postulata. First, that food is necessary to the existence of man. Secondly, that the passion between the sexes is necessary, and will remain nearly in its present state.... Assuming then, my postulata as granted, I say, that the power of population is indefinitely greater than the power in the earth to produce subsistence for man. Population, when unchecked, increases in a geometrical ratio. Subsistence increases only in an arithmetical ratio. A slight acquaintance with numbers will show the immensity of the first power as compared with the second. By that law of our nature which makes food necessary to the life of man, the effects of these two unequal powers must be kept equal. This implies a strong and constantly operating check on population from the difficulty of subsistence.... The race of plants, and the race of animals shrink under this great restrictive law. And the race of man cannot, by any efforts of reason, escape from it. Among plants and animals its effects are waste of seed, sickness, and premature death. Among mankind, misery and vice. The former, misery, is an absolutely necessary consequence of it. Vice is a highly probable consequence.... I see no way by which man can escape from the weight of this law which pervades all animated nature....

Acceptance of famine as a necessary state and inevitable fate of the weak and the poor has led to actions which create famines and perpetuate famines. Many famines which have occurred might have been prevented or reduced in intensity by human efforts had decision-makers understood the meaning of the word famine and the causes of famines.

William and Paul Paddock, an agronomist and a Foreign Service Officer of the State Department, mused over this definitial problem and in their unique book concluded:[3]

Perhaps when a man keels over and collapses from lack of food, then that can be accepted as the dividing line between malnutrition and starvation. Perhaps when whole families and communities keel over, then it can be called a famine. All this, unfortunately is bad scientific terminology.

A nutritional advisor and Chief, Research and Institutional Grants Division, AID, Miloslav Rechcigl, accepted the conclusion that the 124 famines listed in a number of early British records from 500 to 15000 A.D. were caused by crop failures induced by adverse climatic conditions.[4] Many researchers and writers believe famines are synonymous to crop failures produced by abnormal climatic conditions. Meteorological factors such as persistent rains, frost, droughts, etc., are more readily understood than social causes of famine. Others feel that famines are simply periods of extreme want. Father Noel Drogat, S.J., wrote:[5]

Around the year 1000 A.D., at the time of the Great Famine, countries in the West went through periods of extreme want which were marked, in some places, by the re-emergence of untamed instincts. People gathered what they could for food: acorns, roots, grass, leaves. Crushed reeds and rushes were used for making porridge. Some people were reduced to eating the bark of trees and thatch from the roofs. The tale of Tom Thumb and the giant who ate children was not altogether fictional. Chroniclers of the time furnish us with convincing details. Folk did not always content themselves with robbing the traveller:

sometimes there were other explanations for his disappearance, reasons into which it would be repugnant for us today to look more closely.

A Soviet Marxist writer, K. Malin, stated famines are "engendered by the capitalist system, by its mode of production, which aims not at satisfying the people's needs but at securing the highest possible profits for the entrepreneurs."[6] Malin defines famine as an inherent by-product of capitalism. The Paddocks, Rechcigl, Drogat and Malin exemplify those authors who employ *famine* as a term so well understood that it needs no definition or those authors who attribute famine to pure physical or pure cultural factors.

Cecil Woodham-Smith, an award-winning biographer, reasoned famine is nothing more than a great hunger.[7] Josue de Castro, Chairman, Executive Council, Food and Agricultural Organization (FAO), United Nations, observed that hunger ". . . has unquestionably been the most potent source of social misfortunes." He defined famine as epidemic hunger affecting great human masses.[8] A specialist in economic development, Donald Hughes supports de Castro, but he adds a new dimension. He implies famine is mass hunger and abject poverty, and describes famine as a ". . . vicious cycle of hunger and disease" created by poverty.[9] Both de Castro and Hughes are correct, hunger is a potential source of social misfortune and can embrace everything from latent deficiencies to absolute starvation. It is an extremely variable phenomenon that can turn a victim into a veritable walking skeleton or produce subtle chronic deficiencies with limited outward signs. Hunger can be a craving, an urgent need for food, or a strong desire; but *hunger is not famine*. Two biologists, Maarten J. Chrispeels and David Sadava, wrote famines ". . . are periodic hungers caused by natural disasters . . . ."[10] An anthropologist, K. Chang, in his superb book on food in Chinese culture, suggests famine is undernourishment and drought.[11] Undernourishment can and has produced weakened individuals and drought has caused crop failures, but neither undernourishment nor drought is a famine. B. H. Farmer, President of St. John's College and Director of the Center of South Asian Studies, University of Cambridge, England, wrote in a paper on available food supplies, ". . . whereas famine in the nineteenth century meant no food, it now means less than one, or perhaps two square meals a day: so that famine is a political problem too."[12] These seven authors expanded a simple famine definition from a "crop failure" and a "want" to a definition with food scarcity being a critical component (Figure 15).

Don Brothwell, an archaeologist, and Patricia Brothwell, a linguist, explained famine as "severe malnutrition" and wrote:[13]

The records show that from the beginning severe malnutrition occurred in widely separated parts of the world. It resulted from one, or a combination, of the following; detrimental climatic conditions, disease, political strife resulting in agricultural neglect, food destruction, or the breakdown of food-distribution. Populations close to, or possibly exceeding, the optimum for the territory farmed were the most susceptible to these factors, though none was immune from major catastrophies.

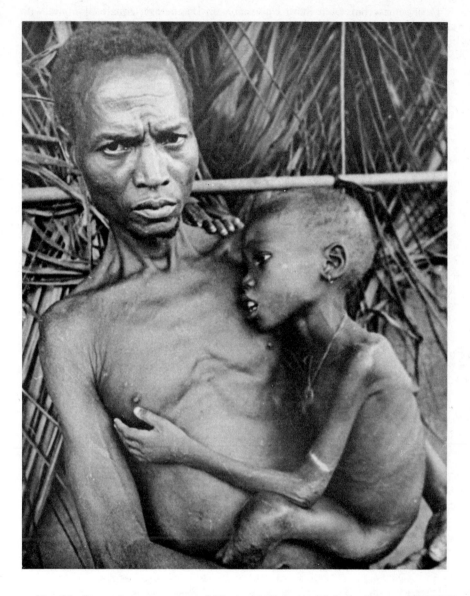

Fig. 15. Starvation was a way of life in 1968 during Biafra's civil war (UNICEF Photo by Gamma, ICEF 5636/37).

A biochemist from Ohio State University, F. Deatherage, equated famines with chronic food shortages. He concluded that food shortages in traditionally well-fed nations are different than food shortages in regions of the world where they are chronic. Deatherage observed ". . . insufficient food and malnutrition are a way of life for large numbers of people."[14] B. M. Nicol, Deputy Director, Nutrition Division, FAO, Rome, professed ". . . I believe that famine and starvation . . . are synonymous," and chronic hunger and starvation result from inequities of available food within countries.[15] In the same symposium dealing with nutrition and relief operations in times of disaster, William H. Foege, Director, Smallpox Eradication Program, U.S. Department of Health, Education, and Welfare, began his paper by declaring "first, it must be understood that famine is itself an epidemic; an epidemic of malnutrition."[16] A member of the Department of Agriculture, University of Oxford, England, G. Masefield implied famine was a prolonged shortage of food resulting in increased human death rates, but noted that difficulties in definition are real and significant. He quoted the FAO action definition as ". . . a food situation in which there are clear indications, based on careful and impartial study, that serious catastrophe and extensive suffering will occur if international assistance is not rendered."[17] Standard dictionaries generally define famine as "scarcity of food producing hunger and starvation."[18] It is not uncommon for published definitions of the word famine to range from severe malnutrition, or chronic food shortages, to starvation. These published statements, positions and definitions are interesting and reflect concern but are incomplete.

Masefield, although citing the FAO famine definition, developed a minimum acceptable definition of:[19]

> a wide and prolonged shortage of food resulting in an increased human death-rate. This is not the place to pursue definitions further. But it may be noted that none of these definitions are much use to authorities faced with an imminent emergency, when no one can tell how widespread or how long-lasting the effect will be, or how many people will die. In other words, an incipient famine never does become a famine if it is relieved in time, and it is for this situation that the lack of a suitable term most makes itself felt.

John D. Post, a political scientist-economist, in his fascinating book on what he considered to be the last great subsistence crisis in the western world, contended famines were ". . . deaths from starvation."[20] Food and nutrition specialist Mirian E. Lowenberg and her colleagues contended:[21]

> A famine differs from a period of scarcity of food in several ways. A famine is usually agreed to be a general, acute, and extreme shortage of food within a region, which is not relieved by supplies of food being sent in because of inadequate distribution. Famines cause deaths from starvation and disease, which follow the extreme shortage of food, calories and nutrients. Infections readily take their toll under these circumstances.

Death becomes part of a famine definition by Jack R. Harland, a plant geneticist, in his excellent study of crops and man. Harland associates famine with agricultural systems where "... crop failure means starvation and death. The threat of famine has become a characteristic of agricultural systems; we have no evidence that this was a part of preagricultural system."[22] Joseph D. Tydings, a United States senator from the state of Maryland, linked famine with population and believed Nature uses famine as a culling tool. He wrote:[23]

> Man's day of reckoning with this problem cannot be put off six hundred years, or even fifty years. Whether we wish it or not, the present imbalance between births and deaths will be redressed within our lifetimes. Either the nations of the world will act in time to defuse the population bomb with humane programs to sharply reduce birth rates, or Nature will ruthlessly restore the balance with her traditional culling tools of war, famine, and disease—the feared Horsemen of the Apocalypse. Either a birth rate solution or a death rate solution: the choice is still ours, though not for very long.

Both a biologist, Paul E. Ehrlich, and a physicist, Harrison Brown, skirt the painful process of famine definition but lead their readers to conclude that overpopulation and famine have the same or very nearly the same meaning.[24] Ehrlich implied and Brown stated "... recurrent famines ... play an important part in determining the average population level." A famine could not occur without a very serious food-population imbalance, but overpopulation in underdeveloped parts of the world has been only a contributing factor in selected famines. Masefield, Post, Lowenberg and her colleagues, Harlan, Tydings, Ehrlich and Brown have added another thought and dimension to famine—death by starvation.

Jean Mayer, a nutritionist, expanded his definition of famine to include place and time. He wrote "a famine occurs in a definable area and has a finite duration; as long as food is available somewhere, relief agencies can undertake to deal with the crisis."[25] A more specific definition was penned by Brian Ferris and Peter Toyne:[26]

> A temporary, but severe, local shortage of food is called a famine. It is generally the result of an almost complete crop failure in an area of subsistence or near subsistence farming. This failure can be caused by one or more factors which, in the past, have included prolonged drought, e.g., failure of the annual rains, untimely frost or a severe attack by insects.

They not only include time, intensity, food shortage in their definition, but also place as Mayer had in his definition. Famines, to Ferris and Toyne, have a definite spatial and temporal aspect. Richard G. Robbins, Jr., a historian, not only believed that famines were place-time-social phenomena, he made some very important distinctions (Figure 16):[27]

> So far we have spoken of crop failure, but not of famine; and we should be aware of the distinction between these two words. A nation can suffer one or even a series of bad harvests, and not experience famine. On the other hand, famine may occur in a time of relatively good harvest when, for one reason or another, human decisions deprive areas of a country of needed food supplies.

Fig. 16. Peasants being fed in Niji Province during the Russian famine of 1892, (Photo from the Prints and Photograph Section of the Library of Congress).

The harvest of 1891 in Russia was extremely small, but there was enough food available to feed the population. Moreover, the harvest was not appreciably poorer than those of 1880 and 1885; yet in those years the nation survived without resort to the extraordinary relief measures which were necessary in 1891. To understand why famine occurred in the winter of 1891-92, we must look at the situation of the peasantry and investigate some of the economic and financial policies of the tsarist regime. Famine rarely strikes a prosperous nation. It happens only when a country's agricultural population has been reduced to a condition of chronic poverty and misery.

Robbins discovered, as most researchers do when they study a famine, there are many factors that can cause a crop failure, but humans, by failing to help those who desperately need food, create a famine. In a classic article on famine published in the *International Encyclopedia of the Social Sciences*, M. K. Bennett, a respected expert on world food problems, defined a famine as a:[28]

shortage of total food so extreme and protracted as to result in widespread persisting hunger, notable emaciation in many of the affected population, and a considerable elevation of community death rate attributable at least in part to deaths from starvation. Criteria do not exist to measure the degree of hunger, emaciation, or elevation of death rate serving to differentiate famine from shortage. The archetypical famine extends over a wide area and affects a large population.

Bennett included extreme food shortage, time, persisting hunger, starvation and death in his definition. William A. Dando, a geographer, synthesizing the writings of chroniclers and learned men and women who wrote on famine in a time span in excess of 6,000 years, defined famine as "...*a protracted total shortage of food in a restricted geographical area, causing widespread disease and death from starvation.*"[29] Famines- have existed throughout human history and have generally been short term events, confined to restricted geographical areas and to relatively small local populations. Contemporary reporters and most generalists when writing on famine occurrence have consistently labeled natural disasters, particularly drought, as the cause of famines; albeit, chroniclers who recorded famine occurrence and those who lived through a famine cite numerous factors which led to a famine situation, least of all a drought. In the past decade or so, a number of respected population specialists and researchers in human ecology have postulated that the famines of tomorrow will be long term events, covering broad geographic areas, and involving tens to hundreds of millions of people. They predict the population-food collision is inevitable, imminent famines in Latin America, Africa and Asia and some are actively striving for a worldwide contingency plan to alleviate these impending famines or to shorten their length. Yet a geographic analysis of the famine literature reveals that: rarely did one factor directly cause a famine (particularly a drought); famine duration has varied greatly in the past; famine regions differ significantly in time, size and intensity; famine deaths or deaths related to famine ranged from the thousands to the millions; famines were not restricted to certain cultural areas and famines did not occur more frequently in selected racial groups. Famines are a social problem, a man-made unnatural phenomenon and should be defined as such.

NOTES

[1] N. Greenwood and J. Edwards, *Human Environments and Natural Systems: A Conflict of Dominion* (North Scituate, Mass.: Duxbury Press, 1973), p. 103.

[2] These statements, taken from *An Essay on the Principle of Population as it Affects the Future Improvement of Society* (reprinted by Macmillan & Company, London, 1926, and reissued in 1966 under the title, *First Essay on Population 1798*), represent the core of the Malthusian argument. See Chapter 1, pp. 11–17.

[3] W. Paddock and P. Paddock, *Famine–1975! America's Decision: Who Will Survive* (Boston: Little, Brown & Co., 1967), p. 50.

[4] M. Rechcigl, Jr., *Man, Food and Nutrition* (Cleveland: CRC Press, 1973), p. 164.

[5] N. Drogat, *The Challenge of Hunger* (Westminster, Md.: Newman Press, 1962). p. 4.

[6] K. Malin, *How Many Will the Earth Feed?* (Moscow: Progress Publishers), p. 5.

[7] C. Woodham-Smith, *The Great Hunger* (New York: Signet Books, 1962).

[8] J. de Castro, *The Geography of Hunger* (Boston: Little, Brown & Co., 1952), pp. 5, 23.

[9] D. Hughes, *Science and Starvation* (New York: Pergamon Press, 1968), p. xi.

[10] M. Chrispeels and D. Sadava, *Plants, Food, and People* (San Francisco: W. H. Freeman, 1977), p. 1.

[11] K. Chang, *Food in Chinese Culture: Anthropological and Historical Perspectives* (New Haven: Yale University Press, 1977), p. 13.

[12] B. Farmer, "Available Food Supplies," in Sir Joseph Hutchinson, ed., *Population and Food Supply* (Cambridge: The University Press, 1969), p. 89.

[13] D. and P. Brothwell, *Food in Antiquity: A Survey of the Diets of Early Peoples* (New York: Praeger, 1969), p. 176.

[14] F. Deatherage, *Food for Life* (New York: Plenum Press, 1975), p. 304.

[15] B. Nicol, "Causes of Famines in the Past and in the Future," in G. Blix, Y. Hofvander, and B. Vahlquist, *Famine: Nutrition and Relief Operations in Times of Disaster* (Uppsala: Almquist & Wiksells, 1971), p. 10.

[16] W. Foege, "Famine, Infections and Epidemics," in G. Blix, Y. Hofvander, and B. Vahlquist, *Famine: Nutrition and Relief Operations in Times of Disaster* (Uppsala: Almquist & Wiksells, 1971). p. 32.

[17] G. Masefield, *Famine: Its Prevention and Relief* (London: Oxford University Press, 1963), p. 5.

[18] R. Durrenberger, *Dictionary of the Environmental Sciences* (Palo Alto: National Press Books, 1973), p. 85; *Webster's New International Dictionary of the English Language* (Springfield, Mass.: G. & C. Merriam, 1950), p. 916; C. Bernhart and J. Stein, eds., *The American College Dictionary* (New York: Random House, 1962), p. 437; and *The New Merriam-Webster Pocket Dictionary* (New York: Pocket Books, 1973), p. 178.

[19] Masefield, op. cit., note 17, p. 4.

[20] J. Post, *The Last Great Subsistence Crisis in the Western World* (Baltimore: The Johns Hopkins University Press, 1975), p. xiii.

[21] M. Lowenberg et al., *Food & Man* (New York: John Wiley & Sons, 1974), p. 59.

[22] J. Harlan, *Crops and Man* (Madison: American Society of Agronomy and the Crop Science Society of America, 1975), p. 59.

[23] J. Tydings, *Born to Starve* (New York: William Morrow, 1970), p. 4.

[24] P. Ehrlich, "Looking Backward from 2000 A.D.," in E. Odum and B. DeMott, ed., *The Crisis of Survival* (Madison: Scott, Foresman, 1970), p. 239; and H. Brown, *The Challenges of Man's Future* (New York: Viking Press, 1954), p. 56.

[25] J. Mayer, "The Dimensions of Human Hunger," *Scientific American*, Vol. 235 (1976), p. 40.

[26] B. Ferris and P. Toyne, *World Problems* (Amersham, England: Hulton Educational Publications, 1970), p. 212.

[27] R. Robbins, Jr., *Famine in Russia, 1891-1892* (New York: Columbia University Press, 1975), p. 3.

[28] M. Bennett, "Famine," *International Encyclopedia of the Social Sciences* (New York: Macmillian & Free Press, 1968), p. 322.

[29] W. Dando, "Six Millenia of Famine: Map and Model," *Proceedings of the Association of American Geographers*, Vol. 8 (1976), p. 20.

Chapter 5

Famine regions and types

The earth is an unappreciated utopia. Unique within its own planetary system, the earth is in the liquid-water belt, has a suitable rotation period and an orbital eccentricity that inhibits excessive differences in insulation, is not perilously polluted with substances harmful to biological operations, has a stable controlling star and has generated and retained life. Life on earth through time has been able to meet and survive evolving environmental parameters. However, not all life forms had the capability to adjust, and thousands of highly developed organic forms have faded into oblivion.[1] Humans, hominids with a mental capacity sufficiently developed to make possible the deliberate fabrication of implements, have been able to modify physical structures and adapt to changing physical environments. But while humans were evolving and physically changing through mutation, genetic drift, isolation, mixture and natural selection, they were developing value systems, traditions and social organizations—i.e., culture. Culture insured human survival. Cultural unity provided social stability and mutual assistance in times of peril. People, bolstered by other people, expanded their manipulation and inventive skill, along with numbers, and the earth began to be modified by human action.[2]

Crops and domesticated animals are manifestations of human actions, artifacts of ancient and modern cultures, and clues to past, present and future foods.[3] Crops, domesticated animals and man are mutually dependent. This dependency was not a cataclysmic event, it was a gradual process evolving in the last ten millenniums. Before the initial domestication of plants and animals, humans lived as hunters and gatherers. Human population on earth was not large in numbers and was found in areas where food plant and animal diversity was greatest. Diets of hunters and gatherers were excellent, famines unknown and the general health of hunters and gatherers very good. R. Lee and I. De Vore, in their article on problems in the study of hunters and gatherers, concluded that populations of hunter-gatherers were maintained well below the carrying capacity of the area they ranged and:[4]

> Cultural Man has been on earth for some 2,000,000 years; for over 99 percent of this period he has lived as a hunter-gatherer. Only in the last 10,000 years has man begun to domesticate plants and animals, to use metals and to harness energy sources other than the human body.... Of the estimated 80,000,000,000 men who have ever lived out a life span on earth, over 90 percent have lived as hunters and gatherers; about 6 percent have lived by agriculture and the remaining few percent have lived in industrial societies. To

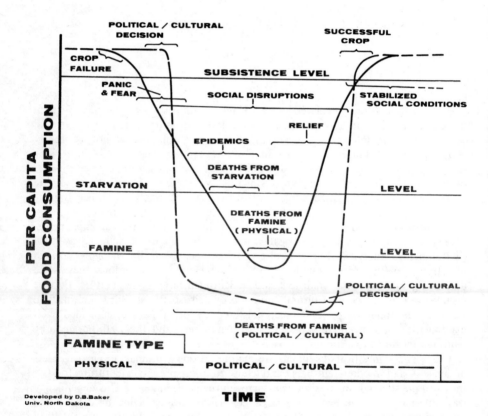

THE FAMINE CYCLE

Developed by D.B.Baker
Univ. North Dakota

Fig. 17

date, the hunting way of life has been the most successful and persistent adaptation man has ever achieved.

More than adequate food led to an increase in population; food problems to an evolution in agricultural activities. The incentive for plant and animal domestication was survival of individuals and entire cultural groups. Farming requires more work, but feeds more people. Diverse forms of agriculture from centers of agricultural origins produced ever increasing food crops and eventual population pressure in such centers led to migration into generally less productive areas of the earth. Hunger, starvation and famine incidents increased in sedentary groups and it was noted that relatively immobile farmers died of mass starvation; famines did not occur among mobile hunters and gatherers. As a manifestation of sedentary agriculture, famines are a facet of the agricultural revolution and cultural biases (Figure 17).[5]

FAMINES OF THE PAST, 4000 B.C. to A.D. 1978

Famines have decreed untimely deaths for at least 6000 years. They were a regular but unexpected calamity dispersed throughout the inhabited world and they varied in severity, location and frequency of occurrence. A famine period in one part of the world in most cases was remembered as a good agricultural year by the inhabitants of another part. A famine is a protracted shortage of total food in a restricted geographical area, causing wide-spread disease and death from starvation. In most instances, a famine cycle (crop failure/food unobtainable, hunger, death from starvation, epidemics, social disruption, relief and a successful crop/food obtainable) was triggered by the failure of food crops in food surplus areas or the restriction of food imports to food deficient areas.[6] The primary natural factors in the creation of situations conducive for famine were drought, floods, frosts, disease and insects; the primary human factors were war, internal disruption, fear, food speculation, panic, politics, poor communications and inadequate transportation. Specific and general locations of high frequency famine regions shifted as civilizations or nations emerged, flourished and declined, and as food demands exceeded food production in certain places. Famines have taken place in the world's best agricultural regions, in all natural zones and have not been restricted to one cultural area or one racial group. The general areas affected by over 800 famines spanning nearly six millenniums, the frequency of the famines, and what are believed to be the primary factors involving famine, were analyzed and then synthesized in Figure 18 showing world famine regions from 4000 B.C. to 1980 A.D. Although famines occurred throughout the world famine regions in *all* time periods, the highest percentage of total famines in each time period occurred in *specific* famine regions. This map identifies the location of five major temporal and spatial famine regions, the location of the "1975–80 Zone of Famine Potential," and the globe-girdling "Future Famine Zone."

WORLD FAMINE REGIONS 4000 BC - 1980 AD

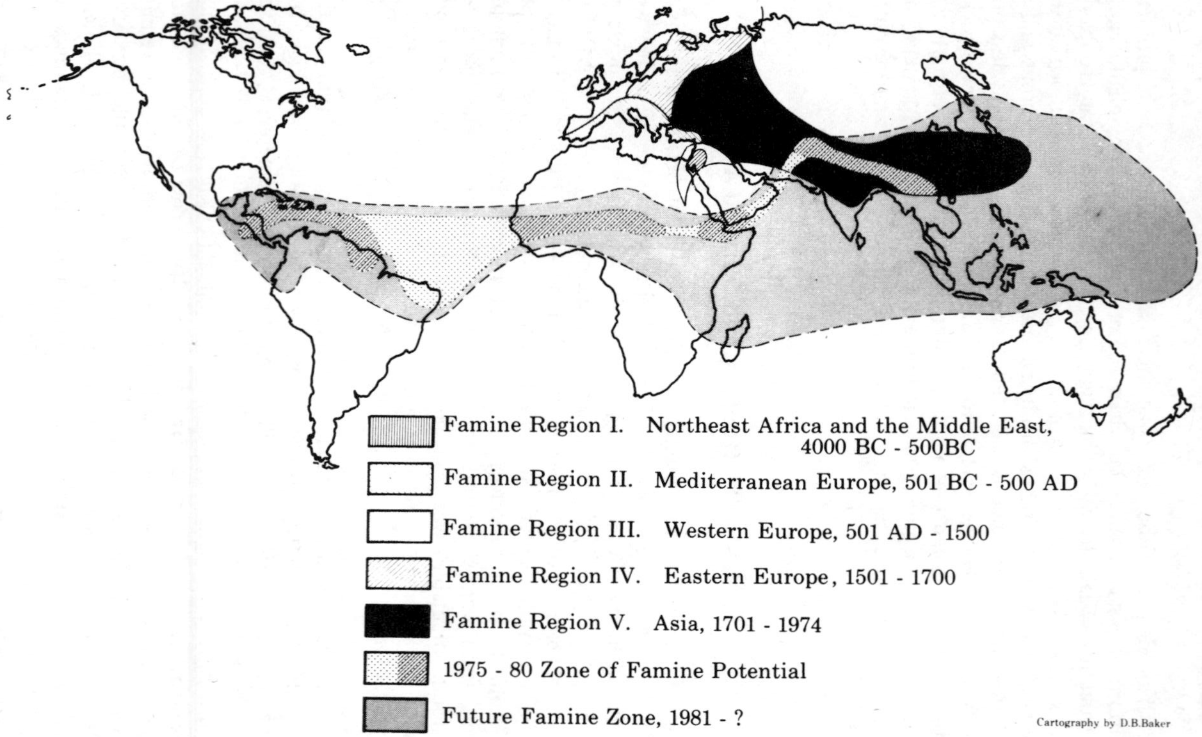

Famine Region I.   Northeast Africa and the Middle East,
                    4000 BC - 500BC

Famine Region II.   Mediterranean Europe, 501 BC - 500 AD

Famine Region III. Western Europe, 501 AD - 1500

Famine Region IV.   Eastern Europe, 1501 - 1700

Famine Region V.   Asia, 1701 - 1974

1975 - 80 Zone of Famine Potential

Future Famine Zone, 1981 - ?

Cartography by D.B.Baker

Fig. 18.

Famine Region I: Northeast Africa and the Middle East, 4000-500 B.C.

Millennia before the birth of Christ, centers of high civilization with advanced agricultural techniques for their time emerged in the valleys of the Nile, Tigris and Euphrates rivers. Broad floodplains and muddy deltas, because of periodic alluvial enrichment, provided people with the opportunity for producing food surpluses and developing economic specializations. Inhabitants of the region were for the most part confined by a harsh, dry and hot physical environment to the floodplains, but these exotic rivers were not tranquil streams and their flows had to be controlled. Great engineering works were constructed to mitigate the capricious mood of the waters and the heavens, i.e., alternating periods of floods and droughts. This task of modifying the physical environment, to insure conditions necessary to support stable agriculture, imposed discipline and special forms of social organization. Although human technological skills enabled those who lived in the floodplains and on the deltas to produce relatively stable and high yielding crops and although at times a proportion of the annual yield was set aside as a reserve to meet the eventuality of a lean year, famines did occur.

Egypt, the eastern tip of the fertile crescent, was a place of haven for those who lived in the Middle East and Northeast Africa suffering from hunger or famine. Its agricultural ribbon along the Nile was better assured against drought than those surrounding areas dependent upon dry farming practice and relying upon rain falling on fields and crops. Agriculture in Egypt was sustained by the overflow of the Nile, a river that received its moisture from monsoon rains in the distant mountains of Abyssinia. A partial or complete crop failure took place when the river did not rise for some reason, and flow into dependent canals and irrigation channels. Yet Pierre Monet wrote:[7]

> The Nile cannot be held solely responsible for the great famines which wrought havoc in Egypt on more than one occasion. The disturbances, which became fairly general during the First Intermediate Period and even more so under the last of the Ramessides, meant that canals and roads were left untended, trade and building operations suspended, and the cultivation of crops brought to a standstill. There was little incentive to sow crops if bandits were likely to make off with the harvest. At the time of the Eleventh Dynasty a man from Thebes wrote to his mother that men and women were being eaten. During a previous period, the inhabitants of Upper Egypt had been reduced to eating their children. During the last years of the Twentieth Dynasty, the price of food continued to rise and people pillaged temples and tombs in order to obtain gold. One year, in particular, was referred to as the year of the hyenas. This was perhaps an exaggeration, yet it may have been literally true. So many people died that there was no time to bury the corpses, which were devoured by hyenas.

One of the earliest authentic records of mankind's suffering in the days of famine was carved on a granite tomb on the island of Sahal (or Sihel), in the first cataract of the Nile. Egyptologists believe that the inscription was chiseled in the time of Tcheser (or Djeser), approximately 4247 B.C. It states:[8]

I am mourning on my high throne for this vast misfortune because the Nile flood in my time has not come for seven years. Light is the grain, there is lack of crops and of all kinds of food. Each man has become a thief to his neighbour. They desire to hasten and cannot walk. The child cries, the youth creeps along, and the heads of the old men are bowed down; their legs are bent together and drag along the ground, and their hands rest in their bosoms. The council of the great ones in the Court is but emptiness. Torn open are the chests of provisions, but instead of contents there is air. Everything is exhausted.

Similarly, the Egyptian prophet Ipuwer commented:[9]

Plague stalketh through the land and blood is everywhere . . . Many men are buried in the river . . . the towns are destroyed and Upper Egypt has become an empty waste . . . the crocodiles are glutted with what they have carried off. Men go to them of their own accord. Men are few. He that layeth his brother in the ground is everywhere to be seen . . . grain hath perished everywhere . . . the storehouse is bare, and he that hath kept it lieth stretched out on the ground . . .

Somewhat later Ankhtifi, a resident and patriarch of Hierakonopolis and Edfu, had inscribed on his tomb (ca. 2000 B.C.):[10]

I kept alive Hefat and Hormer . . . at a time when . . . everyone was dying of hunger on this sandbank of hell. . . . All of Upper Egypt was dying of hunger to such a degree that everyone had come to eating his children, but I managed that no one died of hunger in this home.

The famine in Egypt of Joseph's day, 1708 B.C., is well documented. An interesting translation of this incident is found in the new *Good News Bible*:[11]

The seven years of plenty that the land of Egypt had enjoyed came to an end, and the seven years of famine began, just as Joseph had said. There was famine in every other country, but there was food throughout Egypt. When the Egyptians began to be hungry, they cried to the king for food. So he ordered them to go to Joseph and do what he told them. The famine grew worse and spread over the whole country, so Joseph opened all the storehouses and sold grain to the Egyptians. People came to Egypt from all over the world to buy grain from Joseph, because the famine was severe everywhere.

Food scarcity, endemic in unproductive early Palestine, was a result of wars, pestilence and deficient or erratic rainfall. The literature of this portion of the Near East is studded with accounts of famine. An ancient Atra-hasis Epic and the Hebrew "Deluge Story" tell of a many year famine which preceded the great flood. In Genesis 12:10 is described the vast famine in Canaan which sent Abraham to Egypt; Genesis 26:1, the famine in which Isaac had an experience similar to Abraham but was advised not to go to Egypt for food; Genesis 41:27-53, the horrible famine of the Joseph saga; Ruth 1:1, the Judean famine which led to Elimelech's migration to Moab; II Samuel 21:1, the three year famine in Palestine whose cause was attributed to King Saul's killing of the

Gibeonites; I Kings 18:2, the Samarian famine in the era of Elijah and Ahab; Luke 4:25, the three and one-half year famine in Israel in the days of Elijah; II Kings 6:24, the famine during the siege of Samaria by the Syrians where, in verse 29, is the first act of cannibalism recorded in this region "... so we cooked my son and ate him"; II Kings 25:1, the famine during the siege of Jerusalem by the Babylonian Nebuchadnezzar; and Jeremiah 52:4-6, the famine during a siege of Jerusalem (possibly the same as above).[12]

This region provided the roots of Western civilization and here emerged some of the first towns and cities, professional classes, standing armies, economic and political social stratification, writing and distinct useful forms of agricultural technology. Northeast African and Middle Eastern civilization were based upon agriculture. Once humans became dependent upon cultivated crops for most of their food, famine caused severe suffering and high mortality.

Famine Region II: Mediterranean Europe, 501 B.C.–A.D. 500

Around the city of Rome coalesced an immense empire, which eventually numbered some 80 million subjects, all of whom bore the same seal. The Romans covered portions of Europe, Asia Minor and North Africa with an admirable network of roads and their waterways still remain the great economic arteries of Europe. Agricultural surpluses and specialties of many diverse geographic regions moved freely throughout the empire. The Roman fondness for food is an historic fact and fortunes were squandered on food. Miriam Lowenberg and her co-authors noted:[13]

> During the Empire, Vulgarians (as Seneca called them) were fascinated mostly by gourmandism and boasted about the expense and origins of the dishes they served guests. Some of the emperors, such as Tiberius Caesar, who wrote a cookbook in which he discussed 17 ways to cook a suckling pig, were evidently gourmets; some even called Tiberius a "wealthy glutton." He is said to have committed suicide after spending 100 million sesterces on food and having only 10 million left. One wealthy Roman spent 10 million sesterces for one dinner party. Historians say, however, that the cost of a dinner party also included gifts for the guests. One sad note about the dinner parties was that the guests sometimes fought over their gifts even frightening the women, because the gifts often were *the women*. Atticus, who spent only 3,000 sesterces per month on household expense, is reported to have spent 200,000 on one meal at which Pompey and Cicero were entertained. Rare and very expensive fish, one of which Cato said cost as much as a cow, were used at these feasts in the second century A.D.

And yet famines were quite common in the empire. The emperors monopolized for their own use large amounts of grain. This grain was used to supply the army and the city of Rome. Land confiscated from the senatorial aristocracy or from those condemned was taken by the emperors, and the emperors became the greatest landowners of the Roman Empire. Grain produced on these domains rarely appeared on the open market. Also, the means of transport were under the direct control of the state. The sea was made safe from piracy and a system of roads was constructed. Cities endeavored to build district roads and to connect their territories with the main roads, the rivers and the sea. The Land transport was exceedingly expensive, as compared to transport by sea and river, and for this reason almost all inland cities of the Empire had from time to time food crises and famine.[14] Samuel Dill cites an example of one food crisis created by transportation problems:[15]

> The African corn ships ceased to reach Ostia with their wonted regularity, and the terror of famine spread among the mob of Rome. The masses were becoming sullen and dangerous. There were all the signs of a coming storm. Numbers of the higher families were flying to the safe seclusion of their country seats . . . The distress was temporarily relieved by an "oblatio" of twenty day's supplies made by the Senate.

The peasantry were an oppressed class and in periods of food shortages they were the first to suffer. In times of famine, they flocked to the towns for bread and were often fed from stocks held by the government or landowners. Rome became so crowded with those seeking food during famines, decrees were issued to expel all non-residents. Enlightened aristocrats once protested and commented ". . . if so many cultivators are starved and so many farmers die, our corn supply will be ruined for good: we are excluding those who normally supply our daily bread."[16] A similar situation occurred at Antioch in 384 A.D., "Famine has filled our city with beggars, some of whom have abandoned their fields, since they had not even grass to eat, it being winter, and some had left their cities."[17] When peasants were reduced to eating grass or dying, food was available in the urban centers, either in the government granaries or in private hands.

No substantial food reserves were maintained from year to year. A bad harvest within the empire immediately sent prices rocketing upwards, only to descend to normal equally as suddenly if the next year produced an average crop. Land transport was inadequate to move surpluses from one inland area to another experiencing a food deficit. Food prices thus might be at famine level in one area and cheap in another area at the same time; or a famine might be taking thousands of lives in one area while food was rotting in the fields of another.

To the people whom she subjugated and to all countries which she conquered, Rome provided the prime example of an organized civilization—yet Mediterranean Europe at the time of the empire experienced at least 25 famines. Although famines were recorded prior to 450 B.C., on this date began a famine which endured for more than 20 years and in 436 B.C., thousands of tormented people committed suicide by throwing themselves into the Tiber River to escape the pain of starvation. Approximately 50 years later, raids and siege by the Gauls brought famine within the walls of the city of Rome. Thousands died in the famine of A.D. 6 and there was great suffering between A.D. 79 and A.D. 88 when a devastating drought encompassed the entire Italian peninsula. During this famine period, 10,000 people died on one day in Rome alone. A century later, locusts destroyed all crops and thousands of peasants perished daily along the roads as they fled from famine; the famine eventually reached the city of Rome, and for a brief period 5,000 city dwellers also died each day. Many more famines were recorded in Rome, Judea, Greece, Antioch, Syria, Constantinople, and other sections of Asia Minor.[18]

Famine Region III: Western Europe, A.D. 501–1500

As a result of Imperial Roman internal conflicts and decadence in the third and fourth centuries, the center of European cultural development shifted from the Mediterranean rimland to northwest Europe. Germanic tribes conquered Rome. Their barbaric customs merged with aspects of Roman life to form a new socioeconomic pattern much different than before and after the close of the medieval period. The Roman Empire was divided into many small kingdoms and the strong, unifying central government of the Romans disappeared. Roman law, which protected citizens and provided some measure of security, was replaced by barbarian superstition and "trial by ordeal". General insecurity, absence of an all-encompassing organized state, lack of trade and use of money as a medium of exchange and disruption of transportation mediums and networks led to cultural isolation and economic stagnancy. Western Europe, according to Germanic land-use practices, was divided into large estates and manors. Each estate or manor attempted to be self-sufficient. Towns as central places and nodes of commercial activity became less important and some were abandoned. Education and art were neglected for individual and group survival became paramount. Disruptive cultural differences, isolation, regional antagonisms and marked variations in social organizations reduced human interaction to a minimum. The Christian Church became the main civilizing, hope-providing and even governing force in many areas. Although many regions were brought together into one administrative entity from the mid-700's till 987, most of the kings were unable to control their kingdoms let alone provide relief in times of food shortages or famines. Vassals with titles of prince, baron, duke, count, etc., ruled their independent fiefs through a feudal form of government. Lack of communication, fear, prejudice, jealousy and mistrust nurtured wars and perpetuated horrible famines.

Eighty to 90 percent of West Europe's population could be classified as serfs. Many were actually slaves, without hope or ambition, living only to survive or to serve as instruments of their lords. Defenseless against violence and the risks of a crop failure, they lived in a world bounded by neighboring fields. Transportation and communication had regressed so much that the poor perished by the thousands in time of famine. Rodgers, an Englishman, was convinced:[19]

> . . . the condition of the English peasant was in marked contrast to the lot of the French roturier and the Teutonic bauer. There was but a small surplus population quartered on the products of the soil. The labour of the husbandman was not constrained, as in later times, to support a mass of idlers and consumers. But in other respects his condition was far less satisfactory. His diet, owing to the lack of winter food and nearly all vegetables, was unwholesome during half the year, when he was constrained to live on salt provisions. Leprosy and scurvy were common diseases in medieval England.

England and the other political entities which make up the British Isles suffered at least 95 famines in this time period. Unless the written statements of the chroniclers are inaccurate, in 1314:[20]

> ...notwithstanding, the statutes of the last Parliament, the Kings Writtes & c., all things were sold dearer than before, no fleshe coulde be had, Egs were hard to come by, Sheepe died of the rot, Swine were out of the way; a quarter of wheat, beanes and pease were sold for 20 shillings, a quarter of Malte for a marke, a quarter of Salt for 35 shillings. ...Horse flesh was counted a great delicates; the poore stole fatte Dogges to eate; some (it is said) compelled through famine, in hidde places, did eate the flesh of their own Children, and some stole others which they devoured. Theeves that were in prisons did pluke in pieces those that were newli brought amongst them and greedily devoured them half alive.

France experienced more than 75 famines between 501 A.D. and 1500. Life of the French peasant did not command the attention of many chroniclers. Peasant life had little splendor, they had no feuds or wars, and most endured monotonous poverty. Class consciousness was omnipresent, and the obligation of the servile class was to furnish food and raiment for the clergy and the seigiurs. Although life was hard for the peasants and they suffered severely from undernutrition and malnutrition, few hoped or dreamed of being anything but villeins. William Davis, in his interpretation of medieval history, wrote that at times:[21]

> ...the poor devoured grass, roots, and even white clay. Their faces were pale, their bodies lean, their stomachs bloated, 'their voices thin and piping like the voice of the birds'. Wolves come out of the forest and fed on children. Strangers and travelers were liable to be waylaid in solitary spots and killed simply that they might be eaten. Near Macon a 'hermit' at last was seized who had lured wayfayers to share the hospitality of his cell. The skulls of forty-eight victims were there discovered ... human flesh at times was sold in markets, ... starving children were lured by the offers of a bit of food to places where ghouls could kill and feast on them...

Henry Bennett, in his *Life on the English Manor: A Study of Peasant Conditions, 1150–1400*, also contended starvation and famine were not as frequent nor as severe in England as in France. Bennett quoted A. Luchaire as stating in France "...men died of hunger, on the average, one year in every four" and that forty-eight famine years were recorded in the 11th century alone.[22] Famine and pestilence, not rare before, became frequent with accessories of cannibalism which revealed the seriousness of the food shortages of the age.

Famines were not confined to England and France. They were recorded by national chroniclers in Ireland, Scotland, Wales, Germany, Denmark, Sweden, and at times, famine blighted all of Western Europe. Deaths per famine ranged from tens of thousands to one hundred thousand and more. When it seemed that Western Europe was awakened from the sleep into which it had lapsed after the fall of the Roman Empire, the Black Death and accompanying famine killed from one-fourth to three-fourths of the population or, conservatively, some 40 million individuals. Recovery from the Black Death was slow, but in time, the old system of feudal place and area self-sufficiency gave way to a geographically arranged division of labor and homogeneous cultural groups. Western Europe began to tingle with vitality and the number of recorded famines declined.

Famine Region IV: Eastern Europe, A.D. 1501–1700

While Italy entered and passed through a period of economic progress, Portugal and Spain gathered in the wealth of new trade routes and a New World. France became the leading land power of the world and Eastern Europe struggled to rid itself of the Ottomans and/or the legacy of the Mongol-Tatars. Ignorance of one another was abysmal, although contact between Western Europe and Eastern Europe was not altogether lacking. Eastern Europe was not indifferent to the religious controversies which shook the Christians of the West to their foundations, and was hardly susceptible to the enticements of trade which were felt strongly in Western Europe. The elective throne of Poland became the stake in a long battle between religious denominations. Russia seemed to belong to another world. She looked at the Europe of the Reformation as a place of lunatics while, in return, Western Europe regarded her as a nation of barbarians. The Ottomans were the masters of the Balkans from the Adriatic to the Black Sea. Eastern Europe, an area of great physical and cultural diversity, was caught between the ambitions and demands of Sweden from the north, Prussia and Austria from the west, the Ottomans from the south and, at times, from the Muscovite princes or nomadic hordes from the east. Eastern Europe experienced more than 150 famines in a 200-year period.[23]

An example of the shatter-effect, which destroyed small Eastern European nations that were caught between the great powers, was the plight of Poland. The first dismemberment of the Polish territory by neighboring powers was accomplished in 1773. The second partition was violently affected by Russian and Prussia in 1793; and in 1796, the Polish Republic, which had existed for nearly 10 centuries, was erased from the list of European nations. Rationalization for Austrian, Prussian and Russian territorial aggrandizement was epitomized in publications such as Josiah Conder's *A Dictionary of Geography, Ancient and Modern*, published in London in 1824. Conder wrote "... the fall of the republic, and the extinction of the Polish name, leave no cause for regret, except at the perfidy and violence by which they have been accomplished".[24] He also described rural life in Poland shortly after the emancipation of 1791 in a very biased manner:[25]

> Each family has a cabin or hut, with 13 acres of ground, on the condition of labouring for the owner three days a week. The cabin, which is roofed with thatch or shingles, consists in general of one room with a stove, round which the tenants and their cattle crowd together, amid every kind of filth. The common food is cabbage, potatoes, sometimes pease, black bread, and gruel without either butter or meat. Their chief drink is water, and their only luxury the cheap whiskey of the country, of which, when they can obtain it, they take enormous potations. Their clothing is coarse, ragged, and filthy; they are

for the most part illiterate as their neighbours the Russians, and extremely superstitious and fanatical, neithering remembering the past, nor caring for the future.

Companions of poverty in Eastern Europe included hunger, sickness, robbery, murder, suicide, plague and famine. Famine drove Hungarian parents to eating their children in 1505 and 1586, at the beginning of this time period. Laws were passed to exile the fleeing poor and hungry from municipal precents during famine. Michael Roberts noted:[26]

> The position of the peasants under Swedish rule in the Baltic provinces has provoked some discussion. The general trends of agricultural development in this part of Europe entailed the consequence that their position became increasingly servile, and their freedom of movement grew less. Towards the end of the 17th century there were various attempts at reform which have received a good deal of attention; but other matters intervened, and they did not lead to any result. It is worth emphasizing that peasants on the estates of Swedish noblemen were not any better off than the others. At the turn of the century the population was hard hit by famine. The king could give no help, and some of the measures taken by the government—as for instance its shipping of grain to Finland and Sweden—aroused criticism. Some modern Soviet historians have contended that the population now rose in revolt against Swedish rule in consequence of the harsh measures of the government . . . against Swedish colonialism . . . .

The three year famine of 1600, in the nations of Eastern Europe which bordered Russia and focused upon Livonia and extreme western Russia, claimed at least 500,000 lives. Food substitutes were employed to the detriment of the human body when ". . . people ate straw; hay; dogs; cats; mice; all kinds of dead material . . ."—including human flesh.[27] Bohemia's 1770 famine and pestilence killed 168,000 people. No accurate figure of those who starved to death has been recorded for the horrible Polish famine of the same year. Famines did not simply occur in Eastern Europe and portions of Novgorodian-Muscovite Russia: they were created and prolonged by war, political decisions or indecisions, non-recognition of starvation and famine and refusal to provide aid. Food was a political weapon.

Famine Region V: Asia, A.D. 1701–1974

For the past two and three-quarter centuries, Asia has been the paramount famine area of the world. Three nations, in particular, have suffered the famine cycle to such a degree that they are now somewhat synonymously linked with the term famine, i.e., India, China and Russia/USSR. Each of these nations had or have a dense and impoverished rural population, and each contains significant subsistence agricultural regions where rainfall is limited and highly variable. In India, famine frequency is highest in the northwest and the Deccan Plateau; in China, the valley of the Yellow River; and in Russia/USSR, the Volga Basin.

India, China and Russia/USSR also have excellent subsistence and commercial agricultural regions with ample rainfall and where droughts rarely occurred—but famines did.

Two hypotheses have been articulated in reference to the cause and effects of famines in India. One, the number, severity and extent of Indian famines in this time period, are a direct consequence of English rule and two, famines constitute a natural check on Indian population and must not be tampered with lest population increase more than the means of subsistence. Legends and records mention more than 90 famines in the past 2500 years; 66 percent took place after 1701. Caution must be taken with famine citations, of course, for mention of famine is related to the precision and accuracy of those recording famines. Indian legends cite almost continuous famines between 504–433 B.C. and a severe famine in A.D. 297. A. Loveday, in his study of Indian famines quoted a translated ancient account of the 917–18 Kashmir famine:[28]

> One could scarcely see the water of the Vitasta (Jehlam), entirely covered as the river was with corpses soaked and swollen by the water in which they had long been lying. The land became densely covered with bones in all directions, until it was like one great burial-ground, causing terror to all beings. The king's ministers and the Tantrins (guards) became wealthy, as they amassed riches by selling stores of rice at high prices.

The famine of 1769-70, however, was the first great Indian famine to attract worldwide attention. Many Indian nationals have stated that pre-British rule days were the golden age of India; other Indian scholars are not quite so positive. According to a report published by the Bengal Publicity Board:[29]

> There was grim and grinding poverty when the country came under British rule. The condition of the people, millions of whom went through life on insufficient food, was aggravated by the inevitable decay of the indigenous industries due to economic causes. The famine which visited the unhappy land in 1770 yet stands as a spectre on the threshhold of British rule in India. The suffering was terrible. The effects of this famine aroused the attention of the British people to the defects of the East India Company's administration. The famine was followed by the Regulating Act (1774), Pitt's India Act (1784) and the Permanent Settlement of Bengal (1793). Every one of these measures was adopted with a view to improve the administration of India by the East India Company and enable the people to combat famines more effectively. The disaster formed the keynote to the history of Bengal during the succeeding forty years.

A principle was laid down by British administrators that no human beings would be allowed to perish for lack of food. This principle was carried out in combating all famines since 1770 and up to Indian independence. Still, both in respect to the populations affected, areas impacted and numbers of deaths, the 19th century was the time of India's most terrible recorded famines. India's great population and spiraling population growth rate, religious limitations on food sources and underdeveloped transportation and communication network placed tremendous pressures on locally produced food sources. Devastating famines occurred and millions starved to death. There was adequate food for all in every famine situation; the fault was gross maldistribution of food.[30]

The sages of China have talked about and the scribes recorded 1,829 famines between 108 B.C. and A.D. 29, or 90 famines each 100 years. Primarily seeking a good life within delimited China and not conquest, neglecting idea-exchange and science but encouraging the arts, the population of China increased continuously. Population pressure forced people into marginal agricultural areas and existence here became a perpetual struggle for food. The smallest deviation from a maximum yield eliminated the margin of safety between having barely enough food and starvation. Edgar Snow, a writer with great insights into modern China, quoted F. W. Williams as remarking, "It is notable that in the history of China no great upheaval has occurred without it concomitant of famine".[31] Snow agreed and wrote:[32]

> Many dynasties have been overthrown by hungry mobs, notably those of Wang Mang (9 B.C.–A.D. 23), The Sui (A.D. 589–618), the T'ang (A.D. 618–906), and the Ming (A.D. 1368-1644). . . . Although many factors have contributed to famines, drought and flood have been the most important. Statesmen and able rulers have long recognized this fact; they know that the preservation of peace and order depends upon the prevention of famine.

A constant companion of Chinese famines was typhoid fever. Typhoid fever was spread by the migration of fearful, hungry and sick people who choked the roads out of the famine area in search of food and succor. Banditry and pillage, into which hungry and diseased, crazed men were driven in times of famine, was checked only by harsh governmental action. Paul Bohr depicted the plight of the Shantung famine victims in 1876 as follows:[33]

> Organized pillage was everywhere. Hungry mobs stripped cloth from corpses, robbed merchants and raided homes in search of money to buy grain. In the market places, children and women were sold for a few chash. In time, families were forced to break up and search for food independently. Starving children were often killed by desperate parents who subsequently took their own lives. Roving packs of hungry dogs and wolves not only ate the flesh of the dead but attacked the living as well. The most shocking consequence of famine was the rapid spread of cannibalism. At first the people ate only the rotting flesh of the dead. But later they began butchering the living. Despite strict governmental injunctions, human flesh was sold openly in the markets.

As in India, the 19th century was the century of China's most devastating famines. Four famines (1810, 1811, 1846, and 1849) were reported to have claimed nearly 45 million lives. Nine million died in the famine of 1875–78. This famine occurred in four provinces of north China, about the size of France, called the "Garden of China". Drought, floods, locusts, hurricanes and earthquakes are a few of the natural disasters which enduced crop failures or destroyed crops in the fields. In 1920, a crop failure followed by a drought, lead to an acute shortage of food which was not supplied when the situation was known. An estimated 500,000 people starved to death and approximately 20 million Chinese were made destitute in this famine. Walter Mallory recorded in

China: Land of Famine (Figure 19):[34]

In some of the worst affected districts not only was the entire reserve of food consumed but also all other vegetation. A house-to-house canvas revealed the following bill of fare: k'ang, mixed with wheat blades, flour made of ground leaves, fuller's earth, flower seed, poplar buds, corncobs, hung ching tsai (steamed balls of some wild herb), sawdust, thistles, leaf dust, poisonous tree bean, kaoliang husks, cotton seed, elm bark, bean cakes (very unpalatable), peanut hulls, sweet potato vines ground (considered a great delicacy), roots, stone ground up into flour to piece out the ground leaves. Some of the food was so unpalatable that the children starved, refusing to eat it. Everything of any intrinsic value was sold by the poorer people, even including the roof timbers; and interest rates rose until even 100 per cent was considered not unreasonable in some places. There was extensive migration of the people from the dry regions in some localities whole villages moving out (Figure 20).

Fig. 19. Transportation problems contributed greatly to acute food shortages in the 1921 Chinese famine; grain was transported to famine areas in many ways (Photo by L. M. Mead, China Famine Relief, from the Prints and Photograph Section of the Library of Congress).

Fig. 20. A Chinese woman, during the Chinese famine of 1922, forag-
ing for food-weeds (Photo by L. M. Mead, China Famine Relief, from
the Prints and Photograph Section of the Library of Congress).

There were promising developments in agriculture, education and in transportation-communication in the late 1920's. But the Chinese people suffered terribly
at the hands of ambitious politicians and war-lords. At least 2 million lives were
lost in the Hunan famine of 1929. Famines have occurred in China since 1929,
but the scope and the number of people killed are not comparable to the
famines of the 19th century.[35]

A long list of famine years is recorded in the literature of Russia and the
Soviet Union; famines there have generally been considered as visible
manifestations of deep-rooted internal conflicts and exploitative systems. For

centuries, peasants and industrial workers lived in fear of institutional or natural factors which might disturb the uneasy balance between food production and food consumption. Periodic limitations to the traditional diet, both quantitative and qualitative, had many causes which lay deep in the physical and cultural geography and the economic-administrative history of the country. Any slight variation or fluctuation in food production led to hunger and at times to famine. At least 100 hunger years and 121 famine years have been recorded in Russia between 971 and 1974, giving one year of hardship in every five (Figure 21).

The high frequency of institutional crises and natural events which adversely affected agriculture was not unnoticed by the agricultural producers, and accumulations of stocks or large yearly carryovers of grain were practical goals in order to minimize their effects on local food supply. Yet the ability to accumulate food reserves depended on the possibility of saving out of meagre incomes or limited production. In most regions of grain surplus, a year's stock was the maximum peasant households could afford; in the majority of regions deficient in grain, peasant stocks were minimal. Serf owners or large landowners did not normally maintain substantial grain stocks specifically for famine relief. Prior to emancipation, the propensity of serf owners to consume or squander led them to prefer short-term monetary gains rather than long-term protection of their capital assets, the serfs. Following emancipation, a weak sense of moral obligation was replaced by a wishful sense of charity on the part of former serf owners in times of peasant distress. It became mandatory for the government to provide actual rural and urban famine relief.[36]

Systematic governmental relief activities began in the 15th century and eventually included accumulations of food and cash reserves in urban and rural areas with a high frequency of famine; loans in grain or money to areas most affected by famine; public works in famine-stricken areas; restrictions on grain exports and procedures to expedite internal flows of grain to stricken areas in famine years; and solicitations for assistance and relief funds from the public and abroad. The governmental approach, formalized during the 18th and 19th centuries, viewed famine relief in administrative terms. Free grain trade became a central principle and public works an important supplement to the regular procedures for aiding those in need. A three-tier system of famine relief, organized and codified in the era of the great reforms, created a nationwide capital fund and put the task of relief on a national, provincial and local footing. Organs of local self-government (zemstvos) were given the responsibility of managing the local operations to secure supplies of food. A pernicious defect of the governmental relief program, however, was the lack of coordination between the agencies involved in the struggle to save lives during famine.[37]

Famine occurrence in Imperial Russia increased gradually, reaching a high point in the 19th century, then declined. During the 19th century, rural population growth and rural food requirements equaled production in an average year. In poor agricultural years, local self-sufficiency came into conflict with national and international food commitments. Still the Soviet period, after the October Revolution in 1917, was the era of the great famines. In 1921–22,

Fig. 21. Peasants feeding thatch to animals during the Russian famine, 1891–92 (from a wood-engraving printed in the *Illustrated London News*, and secured from the Prints and Photograph Section of the Library of Congress).

approximately 9 million starved to death; in 1933–34, between 4 and 7 million died; and in 1946–47 nearly 2 million died.

Only one European nation has experienced a famine since the end of World War II. The Soviet famine of 1946–47 claimed the lives of 2 million people. Yet the Soviet government has never officially admitted that this famine occurred. American and English studies on Russia occasionally mention a famine in the northern Ukraine and in Belorussia, but provide few or no details. Previous famines were acknowledged by the Imperial Russian government and by Lenin in 1921. However, the famine of 1946–47 was similar to the famine of 1933-34 in that it was man-made and could be classified as a "political" famine. A decision to rigorously restore the provisions of the collective farm charter which was relaxed during World War II, coupled with a drought and the use of scarce grain in other segments of the world to promote party goals, produced the last famine recorded in Russian-Soviet history.[38]

Overpopulation in marginal agricultural regions, drought, floods, revolution, religious taboos and cultural food constraints, war and political decisions worked simultaneously to produce senseless deaths for millions in Famine Region V, Asia. Throughout India, China and Russia/USSR, for the greater part of the last three centuries, cultural changes and technological innovations did not keep pace with population and market pressures on food resources.

TYPES OF FAMINES

A spatial analysis of approximately 800 famines, spanning 6,000 years, has led to the identification of five basic famine types: physical, transportation, cultural, political, and overpopulation.

(1) Physical (or Egyptian) famines in regions where the physical environment was naturally hostile to intensive forms of sedentary agriculture but man developed techniques which enabled him to temper natural hazards in all but their extreme form.

(2) Transportation (or Roman) famines in highly urbanized, commercial or industrial food deficit regions dependent upon distant food sources and supplied normally by a well developed transportation system.

(3) Cultural (or West European) famines in food surplus regions induced by archaic social systems, cultural practices and overpopulation.

(4) Political (or Eastern European) famines in regions that are nominally self-sufficient in basic foodstuffs but where regional politics or regional political systems determine food production, food distribution and food availability.

(5) Overpopulation (or Asian) famines in drought-prone or flood-prone, overpopulated, marginal agricultural regions with primitive agricultural systems, whose inhabitants' perennial food intake was only slightly above starvation levels.

THE POTENTIAL FOR FAMINE

A decade ago, the world food problem was perceived as a food-population problem. It was argued that the human race did not reach its first billion people until A.D. 1830. Only a century later, in 1930, the second billion was reached; 30 years later, in 1960, the third; and it was estimated that in 2000, mankind would add the sixth billion. Relentlessly, human numbers were growing by 80 million or more each year. If man were to avert famines, particularly in developing countries with high population growth rates, world food production had to double and this was thought unlikely. To the dismay of many concerned demographers, growth in world population exceeded the most pessimistic expectations.[39] Yet in developed nations, food production rose by three percent a year while population increased only one percent. Food production also increased in developing nations by about three percent, barely keeping ahead of a 2½ percent population growth. Gross world food production has kept pace with population growth, and per capita food production is now higher than in the 1960s (Figure 22).

Alarm about world food supplies and reserves in the late 1970s is more than just a concern for a rapidly increasing world population; it is a concern for the modern famine triad of population growth, world affluence and revolutionary dietary expectations. The most recent world food crisis was triggered by bad weather in the early 1970s; this reduced agricultural production in the USSR, China, India, Australia, Sahelian Africa and Southeast Asia. World food production declined for the first time in 30 years. Concomitantly, world grain stocks were at their lowest level since 1952. The food situation was aggravated by the unprecedented scale of USSR grain purchases, inflation, monetary instability, speculation in commodities and the energy shortage. World demands for food would have remained stable or experienced growth had not this unique spatial distribution of bad weather occurred.

A famine would have taken place in 1972 or 1973 in the USSR, China and India had not the national affluence and the changing dietary expectations of most citizens in these nations forced the government to make massive food purchases not only to maintain people but also to provide food for animals. National food priorities and diets of nations change. As societies become wealthier, their consumption of animal products increase. This means that a greater proportion of basic foodstuffs, such as grain and soybeans that could be fed to humans directly, is converted into feed for poultry or large farm animals. Diets composed of wheat, rice, potatoes or cassava are being replaced by diets dominated by meat, fats, oils, sugar, vegetables and dairy products.[40] Not even the most totalitarian government would attempt to reverse such a trend in dietary improvement.

Through education, propaganda and political action, the common man throughout the developing world has come to believe and expect marked economic progress and a sound basic diet for his family. There is a world revolution in consumer expectations and failure to meet these expectations in food and nutrition is more explosive than failure to reach nonfood consumption

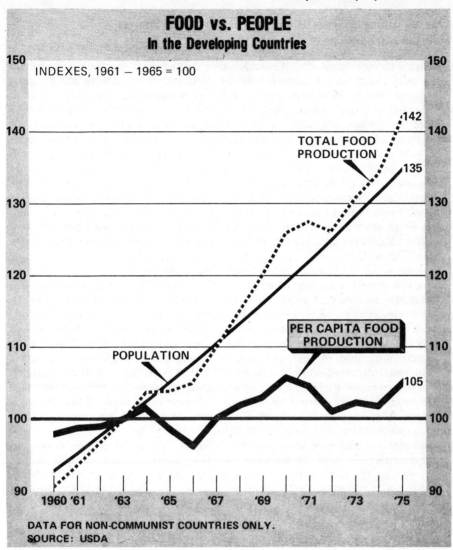

FOOD vs. PEOPLE
In the Developing Countries

INDEXES, 1961 – 1965 = 100

TOTAL FOOD PRODUCTION 142

135

PER CAPITA FOOD PRODUCTION

POPULATION

105

1960 '61 '63 '65 '67 '69 '71 '73 '75

DATA FOR NON-COMMUNIST COUNTRIES ONLY.
SOURCE: USDA

Fig. 22

goals. Hundreds of millions have felt the pangs of hunger, have seen their children go hungry, have been taught that malnutrition and hunger increase their susceptibility to infectious disease, sickness and possible death. Workers know from personal experience that it is difficult to labor in the fields when one is weak from lack of food. Expectations differ from person to person, but most people want immediate relief from the fear of hunger and want a richer, more healthful diet.[41] If the common man in developing countries fails to receive food and economic progress, then agitators are there to tell them that a better diet, increased economic production, fairer distribution of income and a higher level of living can be achieved in their lifetime if they follow the Marxist model for national development. Relative deprivation of expectations leads to social change; persistent deprivation of expectations leads to revolution.

Barring a major catastrophy, food production in most of the developed nations of the world should be more than adequate to provide each citizen a rich and varied diet in the 1975–80 period. Elsewhere, despite increasing total food production, per capita food production will remain low or decline slightly. Within the "1975–80 Zone of Famine Potential," delineated on the map comprising Figure 18, five areas are experiencing food problems today and are areas of high famine potential. These areas are: (1) the Caribbean; (2) the Sahel; (3) Ethiopia-Somalia-Yemen; (4) Trans Jordan-Syria; and (5) portions of South Asia (northern Pakistan, northern India, Bangladesh, Burma and Laos). Cultural factors which inhibit increased agricultural productivity combined with the world's highest percentage of natural increase, create serious food-population problems in the Caribbean area. Transportation and communication problems in the vast drought-prone Sahel and also in Ethiopia-Somalia-Yemen have inhibited agricultural development and relief efforts in time of crop failure in the past and will do so in the 1975–80 period. Political activities by external groups and power struggles among various internal groups in the Trans Jordan-Syrian, as well as the Ethiopia-Somalia-Yemen areas, have created an environment conducive for famine. Overpopulation in marginal agricultural segments and areas of severe natural hazards in Pakistan, India, Bangladesh, Burma and Laos have reached a point where only immediate resettlement, stringent birth control and comprehensive development programs can avert an acute population-food imbalance in the 1975–80 period. With tremendous population growth in areas experiencing great nutritional difficulties, inequality in food production and utilization and the revolution in expectations that have swept the developing world, mankind is running a desperate race with famine.

FUTURE FAMINES, 1981–?

The world food problem of the future will be similar to that of the past, namely, the problem of poor countries. Return to relative abundance and inexpensive food in developed countries will not remedy the problem of chronic food shortages in the developing world during the last twenty years of the 20th century. Despite the gradual improvement of per capita food supplies over the past century, the situation in many developing nations will continue to be grim. Figure 18 delineates a globe-girdling tropical "Future Famine Zone." Thirty-nine nations and northeast Brazil, all within this zone, will have very serious food problems and, possibly, famines by 1985 or 1990. These nations and other poorer countries within this zone contained two-thirds of the world's population in 1978, produced only one-fifth of the world's food and accounted for four out of every five births.[42] The current world population of 4 billion will double in 40 years if the present growth rate continues. Population in the "Future Famine Zone" will account for nearly 80 percent of the growth.

Short-term natural events, such as droughts or floods, which cause local crop failures, can occur in the 1980s and 1990s as they have in the past, and a benevolent world climate can no longer be taken for granted. With the use of improved technology, superior seed, more fertilizers, new hybrids, improved insecticides, novel sources of food, reduction in waste, improved transportation and communication networks and assistance from the developed nations of the world, these short-term events, which in the past contributed to starvation or famine, should only at the most lead to food rationing in restricted areas.[43] The world of the 1980s and 1990s will have the capability to cope with short-term crop failures, but the problem of the future may be long-term shortages of total food.

The developing nations of the world within the "Future Famine Zone" have only a few short years to evolve from food deficient nations to nations which are self-sufficient in basic food products. These nations do not have time for trial and error, discovery or invention; know-how must be transferred and aid made available. Developing nations with food problems must accept change in social and institutional patterns, land and/or animal ownership, birth control and even food preferences. Famines can only be thwarted by all the nations of the world supporting massive agricultural development programs in those areas where the greatest potential for increased food production is located and where the greatest need for food exists.[44]

CONCLUSIONS

Famines in the past were short-term events, confined to restricted geographical areas and taking the lives of limited numbers of people. No famines were recorded in North America, South America (except northeast Brazil), Central and South Africa, Australia and New Zealand; and no nationwide famine has been recorded in even India, China or the USSR. However, future famines will last for extended periods of time, cover broad geographical areas, encompassing many nations and will involve tens of millions. Future famines will undoubtedly be man-made and will be of a transportation, cultural, political or overpopulation type. Famines can be averted by reducing population growth, modifying cultural food preferences and practices, changing social and political environments, improving world communications and transport and by creating a world food bank. The solution to the man/food problem in the last two decades of the 20th century will necessarily require changes in the traditional behavior of most of the world's people.

NOTES

[1] H. Shapley, "On Climate and Life," in H. Shapley, ed., *Climatic Change* (Cambridge: Harvard University Press, 1970).

[2]W. Howells, *Mankind in the Making* (Garden City, N.Y.: Doubleday, 1959), pp. 341–346.

[3]J. Harlan, *Crops and Man* (Madison, Wis.: American Society of Agronomy and Crop Science Society of America, 1975).

[4]R. Lee and I. De Vore, "Problems in the Study of Hunters and Gatherers," in R. Lee and I. De Vore, eds., *Man the Hunter* (Chicago: Aldine Press, 1968), pp. 3–12.

[5]W. Dando, "Man-Made Famines: Russia's Past and the Developing World's Future," *Proceedings of the Association of American Geographers*, Vol. 7 (1975), pp. 60–63.

[6]J. Mayer, "Coping with Famine," *Foreign Affairs*, Vol. 53 (Oct., 1974), pp. 99–101.

[7]P. Monet, *Eternal Egypt* (New York: The New American Library, 1964), p. 77.

[8]Cited in W. Aykroyd, *The Conquest of Famine* (New York: Reader's Digest Press, 1975), p. 25; and R. Graves, "Fearful Famines of the Past", *National Geographic*, XXXII (July, 1917), pp. 69–71.

[9]See A. Erman, *The Literature of the Ancient Egyptians* (New York: E. P. Dutton, 1927), for this and many other commentaries of famine and related problems.

[10]B. Bell, "The Dark Ages in Ancient History. I. The First Dark Age in Egypt," *American Journal of Archeology*, Vol. 75 (1971), p. 3.

[11]"Genesis 53:57," *Good News Bible* (New York: American Bible Society, 1976), p. 50.

[12]M. Cepede and M. Lengelle, *Economie Alimentaire Du Globe* (Paris: Librairie de Medicis, 1953), p. 16.

[13]M. Lowenberg et al., *Food & Man* (New York: John Wiley & Sons, 1974), p. 43.

[14]M. Rostoutzeff, *The Social & Economic History of the Roman Empire* (Oxford: Clarendon Press, 1926), pp. 528–529, 590.

[15]S. Dill, *Roman Society* (London: Macmillan Ltd., 1933), p. 148.

[16]A. Jones, *The Later Roman Empire, 284–602* (Norman: University of Oklahoma Press, 1964), pp. 795, 810.

[17]Jones, op. cit., note 16, p. 810.

[18]A. Keys et al., *The Biology of Human Starvation*, 2 vols. (Minneapolis: University of Minnesota Press, 1950), Vol. II, pp. 1248–1249.

[19]J. Rodgers, *The Economic Interpretation of History* (London: G. P. Putnam, 1938), p. 16.

[20]W. Cunningham, *The Growth of English Industry and Commerce During the Early and Middle Ages* (Cambridge: University Press, 1905), p. 388.

[21]W. Davis, *Life on a Mediaeval Barony* (New York: Harper & Bros., 1923), pp. 255–256.

[22]H. Bennett, *Life on the English Manor: A Study of Peasant Conditions, 1150–1400* (Cambridge: University Press, 1938), p. 237.

[23]S. Krasovec, *Clovestvo, Kruh in Lakota: Vceraj, Danes, Jutre* (Ljubljana: Drzavna Zalozba Sloveniji, 1970), pp. 393–396; and M. Tikhomirov, *Novgorod: k 1100 Letuu Goroda* (Moskva: 1964), pp. 299–309.

[24]J. Conder, *A Dictionary of Geography, Ancient and Modern* (London: Thomas Tegg & Son, 1834), p. 530.

[25]Conder, op. cit., note 1, p. 529.

[26]M. Roberts, *Sweden's Age of Greatness, 1632–1718* (New York: St. Martin's Press, 1973), pp. 46–47.

[27]"Hunger," *Entsiklopedecheskii Slovar* (St. Petersburg: I. A. Efrona, 1893), p. 103.

[28]A. Loveday, *The History & Economics of Indian Famines* (London: G. Bell & Sons, Ltd., 1914), p. 11).

[29]Bengal Publicity Board, *Famines in India* (Calcutta: B. G. Press, 1933), p. 5.

[30]"Famines," in the *Cyclopaedia of India* (1888 ed.), Vol. 1, pp. 1072–1076.

[31]E. Snow, *The Other Side of the River: Red China Today* (New York: Random House, 1962), p. 457.

[32]Snow, op. cit., note 30, p. 457.

[33]P. Bohr, *Famine in China and the Missionary* (Cambridge: Harvard University Press, 1972), pp. 20–21.

[34]W. Mallory, *China: Land of Famine* (New York: Books for Libraries Press, 1926), p. 2.

[35]J. de Castro, *The Geography of Hunger* (Boston: Little, Brown & Co., 1952), p. 29.

[36]A. Kahan, "Natural Calamities and Their Effect Upon Food Supply in Russia," *Jahrbucher Fur Geschichte Osteuropas*, Vol. 16 (1968), pp. 353–377.

[37]W. Dando, "Imperial Russia's Conflict With Famine," *Journal of Historical Geography*, Vol. 3 (1977), pp. 69–70.

[38]W. Dando, "The Soviet Famine of 1946–47," *The Great Plains Rocky Mountain Journal*, Vol. 5 (1976), p. 15.

[39]B. Terris and P. Toyne, *World Problems* (Amersham, England: Hulton Educational Publications, 1970), pp. 212–213.

[40]C. Kellog, "World Food Prospects and Potentials: A Longrun Look," in *Alternatives for Balancing World Food Production Needs* (Ames, Iowa: University of Iows Press, 1967), p. 99.

[41]G. Borgstrom, *The Hungry Planet* (New York: Macmillian, 1972), p. vii; and I. Brown and E. Eckholm, "Choices," *War on Hunger*, VIII (Nov., 1974), pp. 1–3.

[42]D. Halacy, Jr., *Feast and Famine* (Philadelphia: Macrae Smith Co., 1971), pp. 138–155.

[43]K. Brandt, "Famine Is Not Inevitable," in *Can Mass Starvation Be Prevented* (New York: The Victor Fund, 1967), p. 25.

[44]L. Blakeslee, *An Analysis of Projected World Food Production and Demand in 1970, 1985, and 2000*, Vol. 1 (Ann Arbor: University Microfilms, 1969), pp. 452–462; G. Bridger and M. de Soissons, *Famine in Retreat?* (Letchworth, England: Aldine Press, 1970), p. 193; and G. Borgstrom, *Too Many: A Study of Earth's Biological Limitations* (London: Macmillan, 1969), pp. 316–340.

Chapter 6

Conflicting interpretations of the contemporary world food problems

The dimensions of undernutrition, malnutrition and starvation in the world are not well defined. Undeniable signs exist that an every-increasing number of people in both developed and underdeveloped nations will live out their brief span of life on earth on diets incapable of sustaining a productive, contributing life. For more than 30 years, humans have lived through a unique period in world history as well as in the annals of world food production. There have been few periods in the records of agriculture of similar sustained production and expansion, yet millions have died of starvation and famine. In 1972, more than 40 countries reported to FAO they were having internal food production problems and might not be able to provide food for their citizens until the next harvest. Limitations to the world's food reserves, food production, food processing, food transportation, food storage and people's abilities to purchase food have innumerable ramifications. These limitations are worsened by the explosion of world population and the continued upsurge in consumption of all resources by a dwindling population minority. In a paper presented by George Borgstrom at the World Food Symposium in Chicago, he stated:[1]

> Few seem to realize the nature and magnitude of our calamity. Mankind is facing a situation unprecedented in history by adding more than one billion in the next ten years (currently more than 80 million a year), i.e., a new Europe each sixth year, a new U.S. in less than three years. Asia is adding a new Japan each second year. Latin America is, however, growing most rapidly. Brazil is currently increasing with more people per year than the USSR, Mexico with more than the United States. Africa is not far behind, Nigeria growing more

95

than the U.S. The Philippines grow annually with as many as Japan. Both China and India are at current rates each adding a new U.S. in numbers prior to 1987; so is Africa.

In the same presentation Dr. Borgstrom noted that man's living domain is not limited to the numbers registered in population statistics. He calculates the carrying capacity of the world is five times larger or 19 billion (if livestock were not fed a diet that could be used by humans) and concludes trade is a chief way of removing limitations in regional food supplies. There are conflicting interpretations of the contemporary world food problems and eight different perspectives will be examined: (1) Overpopulation in Marginal Agricultural Areas, (2) Political Decisions or Indecisions, (3) Cultural Bias and Fossilization, (4) Transportation Failures, (5) Climatic Change, (6) Eco-Catastrophes, (7) Soil Death, and (8) Man vs. Man.

OVERPOPULATION IN MARGINAL AGRICULTURAL AREAS

Since 1798, when Thomas Malthus published *An Essay on the Principle of Population*, there have been warnings that the world's population would overtake food supplies. The world's population was 2 billion in 1930, 3 billion in 1960, 4 billion in 1975 and may exceed 6 billion by the year 2000. Man's reproductive capacity and behavior are atypical. Human beings bear smaller litters, are fertile for a long period and survive longer after the reproductive years than most mammals. Human females are usually capable of childbearing for approximately thirty years, and the male is potent for an even longer period. A woman can produce 20 or more children before menopause and the survival rate is unusually high by mammalian standards. History is replete with examples of exploding human groups, and eventual imbalances between people and resources have tested man's ability to survive. However, only in the last quarter of the 20th century have population-food imbalances reached such great numbers and excessive densities that national and international famines are a possibility; only recently have such great numbers aspired to higher levels of existence and looked covetously at the wealth of the United States of America. Virtually no outlets exist in other parts of the world for those who might want to emigrate. Grave are the barriers to progress presented by population-food imbalances.[2]

Modern day Malthusians emphasize the geometric or exponential character-istics of growth rates. They conclude there will be a dramatic moment when the world's population will outstrip food supplies. To emphasize their point of view they have employed an analogy of a pond which will be covered by lilies in 30 days by a species which doubles in number each day. If water lily growth rates in this pond are indeed geometric, then on the 29th day the pond will only be half-covered with plants. Modern day Malthusians thus believe world population today is similar to the 29th day at the pond.[3] One day soon there will suddenly be too many people and the world will be faced with a population that exceeds world food supplies. Possibility of altering the world's food production capacity,

Fig. 23. Children sitting on the bare earth in the courtyard of the Niger Clinic in Port Harcourt being fed a mixture of stockfish and beans. Civil war had torn them from their families and they were suffering from an early stage of malnutrition (UNICEF photo by Paul Larsen, 1970, ICEF 5996).

in their mind, is limited for they cannot imagine food production equaling the anticipated population explosion. Scarcity of prime agricultural land is, in their opinion, a major constraint to greater food production. When fertile land is plentiful food production can keep pace with the growth in population. Once the most productive and most accessible fertile agricultural land is placed under cultivation, additional food production can only be secured by using increasingly marginal land. As long as soil resources are finite, a time will come when it will be impossible to support the increasing population. Poverty, starvation and social inequity are natural characteristics of society, concluded Malthus and his modern day disciples, and beyond the control of humans. Malthusians argue that it is more humane to let poor hungry people and nations succumb to their inevitable destiny. A natural relationship between the human race and the natural world must be maintained; starvation and famine must be allowed to perform their population control functions (Figure 23).

Scientific humanists retort, to the apocalyptic predictions of the world population running out of food, that the dynamic nature of agriculture and the positive experiences of developing countries to date are reasons for optimism about the world's long-term ability to feed itself. According to their data, the potential exists to adequately feed vastly larger population numbers than now exist on the earth. Based upon a diet of 2,500 calories per day, many scientific-humanists estimate the carrying capacity of the earth is ten to twelve or more times the predicted world population in the year 2000, or 6 billion people. This diet includes high-quality proteins, fruits and vegetables. If the calorie content of the diets increases to 4,000 to 5,000 per person per day, Roger Revelle estimates the world could support 38 billion to 48 billion people or over ten times the present human population of the earth.[4] They assume that economic development will continue and population growth should decrease with the process of urbanization, industrialization and modernization. Affluence, literacy and improved health in developing nations tend to induce a change in priorities and values, which in turn result in smaller families. Decreased family sizes should occur for there will be diminishing potential value of children's labor, increased costs and difficulty of raising children and more effective governmental birth control programs. Scientific humanists conclude that land is only one factor in agricultural production, and only about 10 percent of the land area of the earth today is cropland. With incentives to improve the land, whether good or marginal, the food producing capacity would be increased in almost all agricultural regions of the world.[5] The most productive agricultural land today was once considered marginal, harsh, raw land but people made investments in time and energy to enhance the natural productivity of cropland.

POLITICAL DECISIONS OR INDECISIONS

Regional food scarcities in the next few decades will precipitate a crisis greater than any the world has recorded in its collective memory. Before the crisis resolves itself, countless millions will perish.[6] Yet there is no world food scarcity today nor will there be in the future. There is a maldistribution of food resources on the surface of the earth. Whether food will be shared is doubtful and a "Food Triage" has developed in international political circles. Food deficient nations are being grouped into: (1) those whose people and government will survive without massive food aid; (2) those whose people and government will only survive with food aid and (3) those whose people and government will probably not survive even with massive food aid. Food is power; it is not a weapon. The denial of food with resultant famine is the weapon.[7] Repeatedly, in the first 79 years of the 20th century, nations have used food as a political tool for controlling internal dissidents and for subjugating (either economically or politically) other nations. Twice Germany attempted to humble the United Kingdom through a food blockade and during World War II, utilized famine as a weapon on mainland Europe. Stalin used food as a means of controlling "socially obstinate" peasants within the USSR and induced massive famine in 1933–34 and again in 1946–47. As producers of the bulk of the world's exportable grain, the United States government may soon be forced to make the decisions of whose people and government will be afforded aid and will survive. Political decisions and indecisions by American politicians may lead to a brutal pragmatic food policy, for many politicians contend food is now one of the principal tools in America's negotiating kit.

Political power and political decisions and economic powers and economic decisions go together, merge and blend into a system. "Social" politicians and "new" economists argue that hunger and famine are not a result of current population pressures on land that will not support a given population, but an aspect of political and economic processes within and between nations which produce social and income disparities. Uncontrolled population growth, hunger and famine are reflections of a weak, insensitive political system.[8] Political and ideological support systems maintain the present high level of living enjoyed by the elite within wealthy and poor nations. Currently, the single most important cause of world hunger and contributing factor to famine is poverty. To many social politicians and new economists, famine is the extreme form of poverty. Poverty is intentional, necessary and legislated to preserve the welfare of those who are rich or at least very affluent. They argue that malnutrition, undernutrition, hunger and starvation affect only certain groups within any society, not all groups—even within the United States. Both note that North American agricultural wealth holds the key to world famine relief operations. Faced with a deficit balance of payment crisis in part related to energy problems and cost of imported oil, both the United States and Canada have attempted to increase one of their most lucrative gold securing export items—food. The use of food as an instrument of national foreign policy, to shore-up the dollar and to influence internal politics of foreign nations, has been wielded by the United States. Examples of recent political decisions or indecisions by the United States government to employ food as an instrument of foreign policy include denying critical supplies of wheat to the Marxist Chilean government of Allende, then granting wheat to Chile after Allende was overthrown and wavering but eventually terminating foreign aid to India during its war with Pakistan.[9]

"Progressive" politicians, many "populists" and "Marxists" predict the elite and the affluent segments of all societies will be threatened by the ramifications of the world's entering a new and decisive stage of its history, an era of definite food limits. Contradictions inherent in a world with conspicuous wealth and prominent poverty will force radical political decisions and destroy the world community's food stability. Abuses in political power have created poverty, overpopulation in marginal areas, hunger and famine. Only decentralizing current world dominating political and economic structures, dismantling multinational corporations and national agrarian reforms can prevent famine.[10] Wealthy developed nations must make the political decision to economically compensate exploited former colonies for past wrongs, for it is in their self-interest; they must create a basis for world social and economic security or be seriously threatened by a potential world food war. Most Marxists believe population growth creates wealth, for expanding populations provide labor and markets. Only in rare cases of excessive population explosion in very marginal agricultural areas combined with energy resource exhaustion can social disruptions and famine be attributed to population. Problems posed by population growth, energy depletion and food scarcity are too great to be solved within the capitalist form of political-economic social organization. In capitalist nations, the only solution to the life-threatening crisis of massive world hunger is replacement by a political system more concerned about the world community as a whole, and stronger social control over the use of food for the benefit of mankind.

CULTURAL BIAS AND FOSSILIZATION

Culture encompasses an amalgamation of learned behavior, attitudes and ideas that controls the greater part of mankind's thought and actions. No two cultures are identical but certain cultural practices are almost universal. Religion, costume, diet, architecture and other artifacts, settlement patterns, folklore, art and social organization are cultural traits. Each culture is closely associated with a particular economic pattern. What is the intelligent way to use land, forests and other resources; which occupations are held in esteem and which are odious; what is a socially acceptable business practice; and what can one eat, can only be understood in the full cultural context of a group. Also, the way a group accepts economic or dietary innovations is based upon cultural traits. The distain for farming by the cattle-obsessed elite of East Africa, absence of beef-cattle culture in India, negligible importance of vineyards in Islamic cultural areas and the low esteem held by the urban proletariat for collective farmers in the Soviet Union are examples of cultural biases. Taboos against selected foods, restrictions on how foods should be prepared, seasonal or weekly prejudices in serving selected foods and cultural preferences in foods and food preservation create qualitative and quantitative variance in diets. Institutional obstacles to agricultural innovations, incentives, marketing, credit, land tenure and fears can restrict expansion of agriculture, the introduction of new crops and agrotechniques and even prohibit alerting the world to a regional food problem or accepting relief. Cultural biases and cultural fossilization will play a significant role in contributing to future famine formation.

Need for alleviating current malnutrition, undernutrition and famine is becoming increasingly serious, as are new demands for food to supply the growing world population. Few cultural anthropologists, cultural geographers and other social scientists have approached the world food problem from the basis of available food resources a group eats and will not eat. Cultural food preferences and food prejudices present major barriers in putting to use available life-sustaining food resources, raising the standards of world nutrition and eliminating famine. Cultural bias and fossilization lead groups to neglect highly nutritious foods that are found locally and consume scarcer foods of less nutritious value.[11] "Food naturalists" note many individuals and groups avoid foods such as beef, chicken, eggs, dogmeat, horse, camel, etc. which are important sources of protein and would substantially reduce widespread protein deficiency. In nations where food animals roam at will and consume scarce calories, there are those who claim that food can be classified as clean or unclean and food preferences symbolize ethnic and religious distinctness. Vegetarians claim that food of animal origin is not essential for proper maintenance of the body. It is true that a diet devoid of animal origin food can be healthful, if non-animal source foods are carefully selected. However, there is danger in a purely vegetarian diet that necessary amino acids will not be supplied in sufficient amounts for body needs. Humans have become dependent upon food plant sources, combined with small quantities of animal foods. Biases do exist for eating wheat, rice, rye, barley, sorghum and countless other life-sustaining plant foods. Food naturalists contend there is adequate food on earth for everyone today and tomorrow if attitudes and customs restricting use of nutritional foods were changing.[12]

New methods of food production advocated by modern "food fabricators" include improvements on conventional agriculture, development of new forms of agriculture and visionary exotic foods produced in factories or by direct synthesis of solar radiation. The main problem in such cases is convincing people to change traditional ways of growing food and modifying traditional diets.[13] New plant breeds, such as IR-8 rice, are not in themselves exotic but the grain produced from new plant breeds may taste different and methods to grow such new plant breeds may be in conflict with aspects of a culture. Hydroponics is somewhat exotic, but irrigation of cropland is now conventional. Direct synthesis of solar radiation to create starches and fats is plausible, however, the economic costs are such that most societies would reject this approach. Chemical foods or pills manufactured in the same way as synthetic rubber or some plastics are invisioned, after the energy problem is solved. Inexpensive foods such as "fava", developed by Swedish nutritionists from chick peas, dehydrated milk and teff, can be marketed cheaply. Fish protein is a major element in the world's food supply. While fresh fish is decreasing as a regular item of human diet, odorless and tasteless fish protein concentrates are now being manufactured. Micro-organisms are being touted as the worldwide staples of the future. Cultural bias, fossilization and inertia will limit improving the nutrition of many cultural groups for people are slow to change dietary habits (Figure 24).

TRANSPORTATION FAILURES

Although the world is fragmented into cultural groups, nations and blocs, advances in modern transportation assisted in reducing the numbers of famine deaths in the past one hundred years. International trade has removed spatial

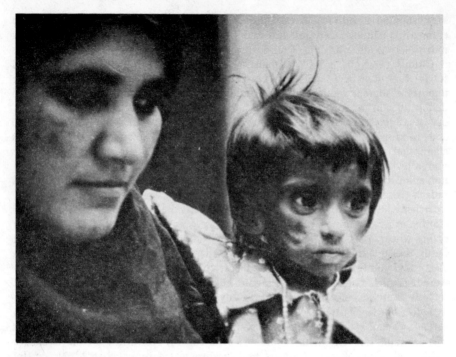

Fig. 24. This one year old Iraqi child suffered from severe malnutrition caused principally by her mother's lack of knowledge about proper foods (UNICEF Photo, ICEF 3010A).

restrictions on food supplies to isolated areas. Yet a frightening crisis looms in the future, for there is great disparity between the highly advanced state of transportation technology and the primitive state of political institutions and human greed. Total world contact can produce a total world war or a multi-national world famine. Transportation breakdowns or blockades can induce famine; transportation of food products from a marginal or deficit food region can produce a famine and transportation of food aid to an area with a crop failure can alleviate famine. The evolution of man's spatial organization from "Spatially Restricted Societies" to "Spatially Restricted Interdependent Societies" has produced qualitative benefits for the less developed nations of the world. Contrary to popular notions, most transfers of food and livestock feed in world trade have been to secure the nutritional affluence in Europe, Japan and since 1972, the Soviet Union.[14] Japan and Europe, which together contain about one-fifth as many people as China and India, import more grain. China's, India's, and most African countries' food imports are modest in relative terms, and are counterbalanced by food exports. Other developing nations, under strong economic and political pressures, export their high quality foods and thus increase internal malnutrition. Affluence and excellent transportation are creating a greater imbalance in the world's maldistributed food base than in any period of man's history.

Good harvests do not present serious problems with nations chronically short of food, but a poor harvest when food reserves are limited can lead to widespread hunger and famine unless food can be transported to the stricken area by some means. Underdeveloped transport facilities or artificial restrictions can create an uneven distribution of human food supplies through space and time. Dramatic incidents of crop failure which have resulted in hunger and famine within isolated regions or communities continue to be reported by the communication media of the modern world. Inadequacy of transportation means and communications produces pockets of poverty and inadequate diets in all nations, including the United States. Many forms of agricultural produce require special modes of preservation in transit, and the capacity, speed and frequency of movement of common carriers influence carrier choice and transport cost. Needless to say, transportation modes must always be evaluated in terms of cost, for if the charge eliminates the anticipated profit there is no incentive to ship food. Transportation means and costs affect the food producer in outward movements of his product along with the inward shipments of seeds, fertilizers and goods required for the unit and household. Total transport costs include freight charges, handling, insurance, customs, packaging costs and storage fees, and are a function of weight, time and distance. Modern patterns of agricultural regions and commodity crops are in a sense the product of changing transport technology. Transporting food is at times restricted or encouraged by tariffs, quotas and import/export controls.[15] There are those who argue that import controls are necessary to protect the home country agriculturalist. Others insist that free trade of food items would benefit less developed nations and would redistribute part of the world's wealth. Political influence determines transportation policies and rates at the local as well as national and international level.[16] Local administrative legislation and land use or zoning ordinances protect local producers at the expense of the consumers, at the expense of third world agriculture and at the expense of total world food production maximation. The world food problem is complicated and distorted by poor transportation facilities in areas with recurring food problems and by political restrictions to international movements of food commodities.

CLIMATIC CHANGE

Despite 20th century man's technological progress, food harvests on the surface of the earth remain at the mercy of the weather. Some areas of the world have climates that are less favorable for food production than others, and much of the world's staple food grains are produced in regions having alternately wet and dry seasons. The major wheat producing areas of the world are confined to the grasslands of North America, South America, eastern Europe, Asia and Australia. The great rice areas of India and southeastern China are largely confined to tropical and subtropical monsoon climates. Such areas are often subject to drought, even in decades of excellent agricultural weather. However, if the earth were to experience a slight climatic change, the possibility for precipitation and temperature deviations would add to the difficulty of growing food for an ever expanding world population.[17] The earth is cooling, and the worldwide atmospheric circulations produced the North African droughts, the lack of penetration of monsoonal rains in India and seasonal delay in the onset of spring rains in the Soviet Virgin Lands wheat area. Small changes in climatic variables produce singificant environmental changes for food production and also reduce North America's ability to provide food relief in times of famine.

For the past 50 or 60 years inhabitants of the earth have experienced a period of benevolent weather, some of the best agroclimatic years recorded in seven or eight centuries. Unfortunately, many climatologists and even declassified Central Intelligence Agency reports contend the earth is entering a period of climatic change. Ramifications of such a change may produce the greatest single challenge humans will face in coming years. It will affect what food is grown, where food is grown, magnitude of crops, what people will eat and even may trigger mass migration and all encompassing international famines. While different climatologists forecast different futures, there is some agreement that plans must be made now lest changing weather patterns result in unimaginable famine. Meteorologist John M. Norman of The Pennsylvania State University stated recently:[18]

> Although climatic prediction is fraught with imponderables, one fact is certain—that changes are taking place. If it is these changes that we are interested in, it is logical to look in the geographical areas likely to be the most sensitive to change; Iceland is considered to be such an indicator area. A thousand-year reconstructed history of Iceland's temperature clearly indicates the well known "little ice age" from 1550 to 1900 and also the recent warm spell. Changes over the most recent 100 years are better documented for the northern hemisphere and the entire world, because of the more extensive data base available. The most recent drop in temperature which is obvious . . . is well documented, and the estimates vary from 0.5°C to 1.0°C for the northern hemisphere since 1945. This drop in temperature is likely to have some climatic effect; for example, the growing season in England appears to have been shortened, perhaps by as much as two weeks prior to 1950. Iceland's per-acre yield of hay has dropped 25 percent, and her ports are having increased problems with drifting ice. Perhaps one of the most interesting observations to be made from the record of the sea temperatures around Iceland is that the past thousand years have been predominantly cooler temperatures with short warm interludes. This might suggest that the last 50 years have been a significant anomaly. It is the anomalous character of the last 50 years' climate that leads climatologists to believe that the most recent cooling trend is a return to a more "normal" condition and, thus, a long-term effect.

Exactly what induced this period of climatic change is not known, but there are three main factors influencing the amount of solar radiation that reaches the surface of the earth and the amount of long-wave earth radiation passed into space: volcanic dust, man-made dust and carbon dioxide. The "cool-earth" school of thought believes that the earth has been cooling for decades, but not noticed for the areas where it might have been observed were areas that human generated heat helped to heat the earth's atmosphere. They point to the curious temperature patterns revealed on maps and state the earth is cooling but people are creating and tempering weather at places. The "hot-earth" school of thought postulates that atmospheric pollution is accelerating natural climatic change by trapping long-wave earth radiation and magnifying the earth's atmospheric heating process from below; a greenhouse effect compounded by pollution. They believe man-made dust and carbon dioxide are helping a process that will eventually conclude with the north and south poles as hot as the equatorial tropics. Whether cold or hot, a change from what humans come to view as a normal climate will have untold effects upon human endeavor. The production of food is of course paramount, but countless other human activities and institutions are dependent upon climatic consistency. Massive food shortages as a result of climatic change would have a grim effect on the world economy, world politics and the chance for world war or world peace.[19] Two billion people were added to the world population during a time of unusually favorable agricultural climate; how will they be fed?

ECO-CATASTROPHES

Since more food will be required to meet worldwide demands in the future, double cropping, increased use of fertilizers and irrigation, planting large areas to individual crops and utilizing high-yielding varieties and effective pesticides will create an agro-environment conducive for eco-catastrophes.[20] Man, when converting land to intensive production of agricultural crops, alters both plant life and other organisms. Weeds, insects, diseases, nematodes, pest birds, rodents and other organisms find conditions much more favorable for their existence. Use of chemicals to increase yields, destroy pests, inhibit disease and reduce tillage required for weed control, can destroy food crops while encouraging the development of new insects and disease problems. Massive irrigation can raise the water table to heights that normal rains lead to floods and evaporation of mineral-charged water at the surface leaves plant-killing saline deposits. Expansion of dry agriculture into marginal areas in order to increase food production can result in massive deflation of soils and vast dust storms. Micro scale modifications of the environment set the stage for macro scale natural occurrences (hurricanes, tornadoes, blizzards or flooding) to not only destroy crops but the environmental matrix for food production.

Insect pests and other creatures which share the planet earth with human beings eat similar foods and compete with humans for the same food. For centuries agriculturalists could do very little to counter insect pests which took a substantial part of the harvest. Once a new chemical was synthesized which killed on casual contact and would continue to kill for weeks, those who produce food used it immediately. This chemical was DDT, and uncountable amounts of food were saved from a multiple of winged and creeping predators. Now DDT is banned in many countries and there are those who call for it to be outlawed everywhere. Environmentalists have fears of its toxicity to man and fears of this and other persistent pesticides have detrimental effects on many species other than those intended to be controlled.[21] More effective than any ban is the observed creation of strains of pests resistant to pesticides. Over 230 species of insects, mites and ticks are known to have developed resistance and their number is increasing. Thinking that approved pesticides are unable to kill pests, agriculturalists spray more often with more potent doses. Excessive spraying pollutes the environment and favors the survival of insects with developed resistance. Destruction of natural enemies, predators and parasites of target pests by pesticide overkill permits pest populations to build up rapidly. Prior to the advent of modern synthetic pesticides, chemicals were used to control pests only when everything else failed; there were natural means for pest control. An integrated pest control program of conserving natural enemies by using conventional pesticides only when crops are severely damaged, would avert a potential eco-catastrophy, concludes the Food and Agricultural Organization of the United Nations (Figure 25).[22]

Crop evolution through time was shaped by complex interactions involving natural and artificial plant selection. Selection was very intense, for the only plants that survived were those man chose to plant. The end products that emerged from thousands of years of selection were food plants, well adapted to the region in which they evolved and to particular diseases, pests or insects within that environment. They were low-yielding but dependable. Most important, they were genetically diverse. After World War II, new, uniform, high-yielding, modern varieties of food plants began to replace the old that had evolved over the millenniums. These plants were susceptible to various races of pathogens and the southern corn leaf blight epidemic in 1970 demonstrated modern hybrids' disease vulnerability.[23] In 1971, the Tungro virus severely reduced the IR-8 rice yields in the Philippines and prevented the use of IR-8 rice in Bangladesh. A replacement, IR-24 rice, was found to be susceptible to both local pests and viruses. A world crop-by-crop analysis reveals an extremely risky dependance on a narrow gene base. More and more people are being fed on fewer and fewer crops and these are becoming increasingly uniform, genetically, and increasingly vulnerable to plant disease epidemics.

Modern agriculture has transformed once varied vegetal regions into monotonous uniform fields. Crop development has moved from the fragmented fields that enabled crops to intermingle to plant breeding stations. Those who produce commodity foods to feed the world's non-agriculturalists depend more and more upon a few highly developed varieties which yield very well and provide a uniform product. Uniformity, however, has brought an end to further food plant evolution. Future food plant development depends almost entirely upon the genetic diversity of what exists now. Once flourishing crop races are lost to the world. Agronomists urge that old crop races be collected and preserved as a source of desired traits needed for future cultivated food plants; some plant breeders do not believe a plant gene bank is so important. There is a potential of major cereal plants, such as rice, wheat, sorghum or corn contracting

Fig. 25. Insect pests destroying the corn crop in southern North Dakota at the time of the Great Economic Depression (Photo from the Prints and Photograph Section of the Library of Congress).

some new and virulent disease and dying. World production of staple foods would be reduced, and plant breeders would have no gene bank to draw genetic materials for resistance characteristics. A world gene bank for crop plants, fruit and forest trees and domestic livestock would insure the human race of food sources in case of an eco-catastrophe never before experienced.

SOIL DEATH

Approximately three-quarters of all human food comes from the world's cropland, yet only 11 percent of the earth's land surface is arable. Millions of acres of high quality agricultural land is lost to highways, urbanization and to areas of waste disposal each year. Soil is also lost to erosion, but it is continuously being formed.[24] Since soil is considered a ubiquitous resource, there is a general lack of concern for soil misuse and erosion. While man is aware of what happens to vegetation as a result of insect attacks, industrial fumes, fire or drought, the soil is regarded as a renewable resource capable of absorbing and decomposing all material developed by man. Soil fungi, bacteria, algae protozoa and arthropods have an enormous capacity to cope with organic materials. However, in the past few decades, the production of materials unknown in nature has overwhelmed the resources of the soil. Plastics and biocides persist in the soil because so few organisms can break these materials down. Chemicalization of agriculture runs the risk of permanently producing a sterile soil that requires continuous application of man-made substances to maintain fertility. Man, by assuming that the soil is lifeless, may change its structure, processes and functions. There is a risk of man killing the life supporting plant matrix, soil.

To provide food for a population projected to increase to more than 6 billion in less than 25 years, production of food must be doubled on available arable land. This doubling includes increased demands attributable to affluence plus population growth. Because land is essential to agriculture, cropland loss and cropland degradation is a serious problem. Unfortunately, the best arable land in the world is already in agricultural production, productivity potential is being reduced by soil erosion, degraded cropland requires increased energy inputs to counter lost soil productivity and substantial cropland is being lost annually to urbanization and transportation facility construction.[25] Land, labor and energy are three prime needs for crop and animal production, and by manipulating these needs one can be partly substituted for another. For example, increasing land use intensity through energy inputs can reduce the cropland needed to produce a set amount of food. David Pimentel and his associates at Cornell University have noted:[26]

> Both arable land and fossil energy are finite resources. The FAO estimates that about 11 percent of world land (1.5 billion hectares) is suitable for cultivation and nearly all of this land is already in cultivation. About 22 percent (3.0 billion hectares) of the world land area is now used for livestock production and is in pastures, ranges and meadows. Forest covers another 30 percent (4.1 billion hectares) of the land area, while the remaining 37 percent is either too dry, too cold or too steep for any agricultural production. Arable land (potential) can be increased by irrigation and the use of other inputs, but these require increased energy or labor (or both). Also, the quality of arable land is slowly being degraded by erosion. For example, in the United States, which has the most modern agricultural technology, about 36 metric tons of topsoil are lost annually per hectare in corn production in Iowa. For the United States as a whole, about 3.6 billion metric tons of topsoil are lost annually, that is, about 31 metric tons per hectare of cultivated land. To replace this annual loss would take nearly 11 years [about 100 years are required to produce 25 millimeters of topsoil or about 2.9 metric tons per hectare per year].

Pimentel and others contend science and technology will help human beings overcome some of the food problem. Lester Brown in *The Worldwide Loss of Cropland* indicates a growing worldwide shortage of productive cropland and most political leaders seem oblivious to this problem. He doubts whether a combination of cropland expansion and yield per hectare increase will satisfy the anticipated growth in world food demand.[27] Experience has shown that augmenting food supplies is not as easy as controlling human or plant disease, building railroads or highways or even providing relief in times of food need. Destruction or loss of life-generating and life-sustaining soil eliminates the very foundation for supporting and elevating the quality of life for those people who inhabit the earth now and in the future.

DISTOPIA: MAN vs. MAN

Mankind has evolved and his culture enhanced in cycles of feast and famine; we are entering the famine phase of the cycle. Famines are man-made. Since 500 A.D. famines have been multi-factored, but cultural in cause. Famines of the future will be contrived. Extreme food-population imbalances in the next twenty or so years will be confined to less developed nations in tropical and subtropical areas. Population pressures and cultural biases here inhibit changes in agricultural techniques, social systems and diets. Political systems in the zone of future famines are unstable and decisionmakers narrow in vision. Transportation networks are inadequate for effective economic development, but adequate for exploitation by more affluent nations. To compound an acute situation, climatic change will reduce the capability of food exporting, mid-latitude nations to provide food assistance in times of acute food shortage. Eco-catastrophes must be planned for, plant disease epidemics will become more common and soils will be made sterile. Man, provided with a space home with capabilities to support life unlike other known planets, has planted the seeds of his own destruction.

NOTES

[1] G. Borgstrom, "Limitations to World Food Supply," a paper presented at the World Food Symposium, June 9, 1975, p. 3.

[2] S. Wortman, "Food and Agriculture," *Scientific American*, Vol. 235 (1976), pp. 503–509.

[3] L. Brown, *The Twenty-Ninth Day* (New York: W. W. Norton, 1978); L. Brown, P. McGrath and B. Stokes, *Twenty-Two Dimensions of the Population Problem* (Washington, D.C.: Worldwatch Institute, 1976), pp. 30–31.

[4] R. Revelle, "The Resources Available for Agriculture," *Scientific American*, Vol. 235 (1976), pp. 164–178.

[5] S. Wortman and R. Cummings, Jr., *To Feed This World: The Challenge and the Strategy* (Baltimore: The Johns Hopkins University Press, 1978), pp. 57–82.

[6] E. Rothschild, "Food Politics," *Foreign Affairs*, Vol. 54 (1976), pp. 285–307.

[7] E. Butz, "Agro-Power," *Saturday Evening Post*, Vol. 248 (1976), p. 37.

[8]F. Lappe, "remarks," in the Transnational Institute Report, *World Hunger: Causes and Remedies* (Amsterdam: Transnational Institute, 1974), p. 37.

[9]J. Douglas, "Confronting Famine," *Science News*, Vol. 105 (1974), p. 322.

[10]F. Lappe and J. Collins, "Food First," in T. Emmel, *Global Perspectives on Ecology* (Palo Alto: Mayfield Publishing Co., 1977), pp. 452–465.

[11]W. Zelinsky, "Food as Foundation of Civilization," in G. Koerselman and K. Dull, *Food and Social Policy, 1* (Ames: Iowa State University Press, 1978), pp. 142–143.

[12]J. Parker, "Affluent Saudis Increase Imports of Some U.S. Foods," *Foreign Agriculture*, Vol. XIV (1976), No. 5, p. 2.

[13]V. Ruttan, "Induced Technical and Institutional Change and the Future of Agriculture," [Reprint] (New York: The Agricultural Development Council, Inc., 1973).

[14]D. Hume, "U.S. Agricultural Exports–. . . 'a National Asset,' " *Foreign Agriculture*, Vol. 7 (1975), pp. 2–3.

[15]G. Fielding, "The Role of Government in New Zealand Wheat Growing," *Annals of the Association of American Geographers*, Vol. 55 (1965), pp. 87–97.

[16]G. Fielding, "The Los Angeles Milkshed: A Study of the Political Factor in Agriculture," *Geographical Review*, Vol. 54 (1964), pp. 1–12.

[17]R. Bryson, "A Perspective on Climatic Change," *Science*, Vol. 184 (1974), pp. 753–759.

[18]J. Norman, "Limits to Land Use-Climate," *Proceedings of the University-Wide Food Symposium, Food and Our Future* (University Park: Pennsylvania State University, 1975), pp. 59–60.

[19]R. Bryson and T. Murray, *Climates of Hunger* (Madison: University of Wisconsin Press, 1977).

[20]D. Pimentel et al., "Land Degradation: Effects on Food and Energy Resources," *Science*, Vol. 194 (1976), pp. 149–154; also D. Pimentel et al., "Energy and Land Constraints in Food Protein Production," *Science*, Vol. 190 (1975), pp. 754–760.

[21]I. Rose, "Ecology Fears Boost Kenyan Phrethrum Exports," *Foreign Agriculture*, Vol. XIV (1976), pp. 9–10.

[22]*Food and Environment: Reconciling the Demands of Agriculture with Global Conservation* (Rome: Christengraf, 1977), pp. 22–27.

[23]D. Harmon, Jr. and M. Chou, "Food Enough for All," *Worldview*, (1975), p. 21.

[24]P. Sanchez and S. Buol, "Soils of the Tropics and the World Food Crisis," *Science*, Vol. 188 (1975), pp. 598–603.

[25]D. Pimentel et al., "Land Degradation: Effects on Food and Energy Resources," *Science*, Vol. 194 (1976), pp. 149–154.

[26]D. Pimentel et al., "Energy and Land Constraints in Food Protein Production," *Science*, Vol. 190 (1975), p. 755.

[27]L. Brown, *The Worldwide Loss of Cropland* (Washington, D.C.: *Worldwatch Institute*, 1978), p. 37.

Part III

Case studies: The past as a key to the future

Chapter 7

Famines in England and the United Kingdom

Famines were common in England, Great Britain and the United Kingdom from 10 A.D. to 1850. Cornelius Walford, in his classic paper, cited 187 famines in this time period and noted two famines out of three were attributed to cultural factors.[1] Famines here were primarily human initiated and human sustained. Tribal antagonisms and Roman military ventures created famines in the 43 A.D. to 450 time period; war, separatism and fear nurtured famines in the 450–1066 time period; social tensions between Anglo-Saxons and Normans along with conflicts between the church and state, plus aspects of climatic change led to numerous famines in the 1066 to 1485 time period; and financial woes, debasement of currency, disfranchised rural poor, along with religious bigotry, produced famines in the 1485 to 1850 time period. In each period, the particular stage of advancement of the island people's culture and the characteristic features of such stages produced different types and intensities of famines. Famines ceased with the Great Irish Famine of 1845–50, for they were culturally based and could be eliminated when the decision-making social class did not want them to occur. The Great Irish Famine was, in essence, years of concentrated holocaust and has been described as a period of cultural murder. British famine relief during the first years of famine was generous, although many claim not enough was done to save lives; famine relief from Great Britain in the last years of the famine period was inadequate. Although the last famine to be recorded in the United Kingdom, the "Great Hunger" planted seeds of hate and distrust that manifest themselves today and will continue to bear bitter fruit for generations

113

Table 1. Walford's List of Famines in England and the United Kingdom, 10 to 1878 A.D.

Date	Place	Physical causes cited	Cultural causes cited	Date	Place	Physical causes cited	Cultural causes cited
10–15 A.D.	Ireland		X	605	England	X	X
54	England		X	625	Britain		X
76	Ireland		X	664	Ireland		X
104	England & Scotland		X	667	Scotland		X
107	Britain	X		669	Ireland		
119	Britain		X	680	Britain	X	
151	Wales		X	695–700	England & Ireland		X
160	England		X	712	Wales		X
173	England	X		730	England, Wales & Scotland		X
192	Ireland		X	746	Wales		X
228	Scotland		X	748	Scotland		X
238	Scotland		X	759	Ireland		X
259	Wales		X	768	Ireland	X	
272	Britain		X	772	Ireland	X	
288	Britain		X	774	Scotland	X	
298	Wales		X	791	Wales		X
306	Scotland		X	792	Scotland		X
310	England		X	793	England		X
325	Britain		X	803	Scotland		X
439	Britain		X	822–23	England & Scotland		X
466	Britain		X	824–25	Ireland		X
480	Scotland		X	836	Wales		X
515	Britain		X	856–859	Scotland		X
523	Scotland		X	863	Scotland	X	X
527	North Wales	X		872	England	X	X
531	South Wales		X	879	Universal		
535	Ireland		X	887	England		X
537	Scotland & Wales		X	890	Scotland		X
576	Scotland		X	895–897	Ireland	X	
590	England	X		900	England		X
592	England	X					

Table 1. (cont'd)

Date	Place	Physical causes cited	Cultural causes cited
931	Wales		X
936–939	Scotland		X
954–958	England, Wales & Scotland		X
962	England	X	
963–64	Ireland		X
968	Scotland		X
969	England	X	
975	England		X
976	England		X
988	England	X	
989	England	X	
1004–5	England		X
1008	Wales	X	
1012	England		X
1025	England	X	
1031	England	X	
1042–48	England		
1047	Ireland	X	
1047–48	Scotland		X
1050	England	X	
1053–54	England		X
1068	England	X	
1069	England		X
1073	England		X
1086	England	X	
1087	England	X	
1093	England		X
1096	England	X	
1099	England	X	
1106	England	X	

Date	Place	Physical causes cited	Cultural causes cited
1111	England	X	
1116	Ireland		X
1117	England	X	
1121–22	Scotland	X	
1124	England	X	X
1125	England	X	
1126	England	X	
1135–37	England		X
1141–1152	England		X
1153	Ireland		
1154	England	X	X
1162	Universal		
1175	England	X	X
1176	Wales		
1183	England & Wales		X
1188	Ireland		X
1193–96	England		
1200	Ireland	X	
1203	England & Ireland	X	
1209	England	X	
1224	England	X	
1227	Ireland		X
1235	England	X	
1239	England		X
1248	England		X
1252	England	X	
1257	England	X	
1258	England	X	
1262	Ireland		
1271	England & Ireland	X	
1286	England		X

Table 1. (cont'd)

Date	Place	Physical causes cited	Cultural causes cited
1289	England	X	
1294	England		X
1295	England & Ireland	X	
1297	Scotland	X	
1298	England		X
1302	England, Scotland & Ireland		X
1314	England & Ireland	X	
1316	England & Ireland		X
1317	Ireland		X
1321	England		X
1332	Ireland		X
1335	England	X	
1336	Scotland		X
1339	Ireland		X
1341–42	England & Scotland		X
1353	England		X
1355	England		X
1358	England	X	
1369	England	X	
1390	England		X
1392–93	England		X
1410	Ireland		X
1427	Scotland	X	
1429	Scotland		
1433	Ireland		X
1437–39	England	X	
1440	England & Scotland		X
1447	Ireland		X
1486	England		X
1491	Ireland & England		X
1494	England		X
1497	Ireland		X
1521	England		X
1522	Ireland		X
1523	England		X
1527	England		X
1545	England		X
1549	England	X	
1556–58	England	X	
1563	England (London)		X
1565	British Isles		X
1586	England & Ireland		X
1588–89	Ireland		X
1594–95	England		X
1601–03	Ireland		X
1630	England		X
1649–50	Scotland & Northern England	X	
1649	England (Lancashire)		X
1650–51	Ireland	X	X
1690	Ireland	X	X
1694–1700	Scotland & England	X	
1709	Scotland & England	X	
1727–29	Ireland		X
1739–40	Ireland	X	
1740–41	England	X	
1741	Scotland	X	
1748	England		
1765	Ireland		X
1766	Scotland		X
1795	England		X
1801	England		X
1812	United Kingdom		X
1822	Ireland	X	
1831	Ireland		X
1845–50	Ireland	X	X

Source: Cornelius Walford, *The Famines of the World: Past and Present* (New York: Burt Franklin, 1970), pp. 4–16. Of the total famines listed 40% were recorded in England 33% in Ireland 15% in Scotland 8% in Wales 4% in …

to come. Famines in England and the United Kingdom are classic types associated with emerging western cultural patterns and exploitive capitalism (Table 1).

ROMAN PERIOD (43 A.D. to 450)

Prior to the invasion of Britain by Claudius in 43 A.D., the Celtic inhabitants were divided into tribes and led by tribal princes. Constantly warring, the Celts lived in defensible hill forts, fortified villages of isolated marsh hamlets. Tribal biases, wars and an underdeveloped transportation network created and/or perpetuated hunger, starvation and famine. Roman conquest of the divided Celtic tribes in the lowlands of southeastern Britain was rapid, but hill tribes offered fierce resistance. More than four decades were needed to solidify Roman control and a grievous famine in 54 A.D. was attributed to this campaign. Although Wales and Yorkshire were brought under Roman domination, indigenous inhabitants constantly revolted. To protect the rich agricultural lands of south Britain from social disruption, Emperor Hadrian constructed a continuous rampart across the island from the North Sea to the Irish Sea. Roman designed towns and villages were constructed in the productive lowlands of the south, midlands and east. Roman culture and aspects of Roman agriculture spread rapidly in the protected region, but in Wales and northern Britain few towns flourished and industry was nonexistent. By the fourth century, Romanization reached its apex. Strategic roads were constructed to facilitate control and commercial activities. London, a focal point for an integrated sea, river and road transportation network, became an important commercial center. Agriculture provided a base for prosperity. Wheat and wool were exported to Rome. Twenty famines were recorded during this period of Roman control. The most serious were the famines of 54, 192, 228, 306 and 310 when 40,000 English perished. An emerging Romano-British culture group was unable to resist Celtic domination when the Roman legions were withdrawn between 375 and 400 A.D. Although hindered by repeated uprisings, Romanization of Britain provided the unifying force which tempered the effect of severe food shortages in the 43 to 450 time period.

ANGLO-SAXON PERIOD (450 to 1066)

Social disruptions created great hardships for the peoples of Britain in the 450 to 1066 period. After the departure of Roman troops, the Picts and Scots conducted devastating raids that forced the Romano-British remnant to seek Saxon military aid. Once the Saxons were victorious they turned against those who had sought their assistance. A long period of warfare was terminated when the entire island was conquered and divided into many kingdoms. Social organization was changed and a society with many distinct social classes emerged. Slavery became important and constituted a major export item. Agricultural innovations were introduced, such as their plow, and aspects of Romano-British animal husbandry retained. The basis for a prosperous society existed, however, incessant wars between the sixth and ninth centuries hindered economic development. Extreme jealousies existed between the many small kingdoms. Particularism, separatism, fear and distrust nurtured and isolated famines; 62 famines were recorded in this time period. Lack of a social organization that would lay aside part of a good harvest for use in time of a bad harvest led to weather playing a clear and direct role in people's lives. For example, in 680 a three-year drought provided the setting for a horrible famine in parts of Britain. Bishop Wilfrid observed:[2]

> No rain had fallen in that province [Sussex] in three years . . . whereupon a dreadful famine ensued, which cruelly destroyed the people. In short, it is reported, that very often forty or fifty men, being spent with want, would go together to some precipice, or to the sea-shore, and there, hand in hand, perish by the fall, or be swallowed up by the waves.

Weakened by internal strife, the Vikings began to compound the problems of a disrupted society by raiding England (Engla land, or the land of the Angles) in the early 800s. Danish armies permanently settled the land between the Tees and Welland in 865, and Norwegians threatened all of northwest England. Britain became an island of distinct cultural groups, each independent and distrustful of the others. Eventually England became a segment of a large Danish empire that included Norway and the Baltic Slavs. Divided and exploited, the peoples of Britain suffered many periods of hunger and famine.[3] The most serious famines were the Irish famine of 664; English famine of 695 when people ate human flesh; England, Scotland and Wales in 730; Ireland in 759; England in 822–23 when thousands starved; Scotland in 936 when people devoured each other; England, Wales and Scotland in 954; England in 976, the great famine; England in 1004; and England in 1042. Beyond all doubt, the worst privation of the British peasant was famine.[4]

NORMAN PERIOD (1066 to 1485)

William the Conqueror seized England in 1066. He ruled by force and distinctions between petty kingdoms had little meaning to him. William unified England and made his court the center of government. Those who opposed him were terrorized or killed and famine was employed as a tool for social control. Simeon of Durham wrote:[5]

> In consequence of the Normans having plundered England—in the preceding year [1068] Northumbria and some other provinces, but in the present and following year [1069–70] almost the whole realm, yet principally Northumbria and the adjacent provinces—so great a famine prevailed that men, compelled by hunger, devoured human flesh, that of horses, dogs and cats, and whatever custom abhors; others sold themselves to perpetual slavery, so that they might in any way preserve their wretched existence; others, while about to go into

exile from their country, fell down in the middle of the journey and gave up the ghost. It was horrific to behold human corpses decaying in the houses, the streets, and the roads, swarming with worms, while they were consuming in corruption with an abominable stench. For no one was left to bury them in the earth, all being cut off either by the sword or by famine, or having left the country on account of the famine. Mean while, the land being thus deprived of anyone to cultivate it for nine years, an extensive solitude prevailed all around.

By his shrewd distribution of confiscated estates, William prevented the appearance of powerful provincial nobles and avoided the difficulties which delayed for so long the unification of France and Germany. Norman administrative machinery, which had operated effectively on the continent, avoided conflict between the church and state. The Church of England was remodeled along continental lines and only years later was there an ecclesiastical challenge to the authority of the king. It was Thomas Becket's murder in 1170 that destroyed Henry II's plan for a unified English civil law and gave the clergy immunities which complicated legal activities for centuries. Henry's successor, Richard I, used England as a source of funds to support his military adventures and crusades. His financial demands, disaffection produced by his long absences from England and open rebellion created food shortages. After Richard I, each king's personality and whims became the prime factor in English economic and political life. Although the Magna Carta in 1215 constrained absolutism, the wars which followed disrupted the administration of the nation and inhibited aid to famine victims. Local failure of crops might have been relieved if there had been a deep concern for individuals, better roads and unrestricted movement of food and people. Unfortunately, food shortages were aggravated by the exploitive policy of the feudality. Nobles refused to abate tolls and "cornered" grain in times of shortages to raise food prices.

Caring more for administrative efficiency than for the welfare of his subjects, Henry III manipulated state funds to provide more cash to support his ambitious role in European politics. A famine was created in 1258 and this famine gave rise to a party which opposed the king. J. Penkethman wrote:[6]

A great dearth followed this wet year past, for a quarter of wheat was sold for 15s. and 20s., but the worst was in the end; there could be none found for money when—though many poor people were constrained to eat barks of trees and horseflesh; but many starved for want of food—20,000 (as it is said) in London.

A civil war ensued and the king was captured. Parliament administered England until royal power was re-established by Edward I. Edward used food as a weapon, and in 1277 a contrived famine compelled the Welsh rebel Llewelyn to surrender. England prospered during Edward's reign, but there were famines in Scotland. His death in 1307 ushered in a period of agrarian depression which lasted approximately 200 years. Famines in 1314 and 1316 were so severe that Edward II's household felt the effects. George Homans observed:[7]

A severe famine in 1315 was only the beginning of misfortune. The plagues of the middle of the century followed . . . . Peasants' revolts were characteristic of the time of disequilibrium after the shock. They were brutally put down by an upper class still so unshaken by change or by the agitation of intellectuals that it was ready to use force to the utmost to preserve the form of society of which it was the apex. Worst of all, the marchings and counter-marchings of the Hundred Years War devastated France and exhausted England. Except for wars on the borders and the revolt against the weak king Henry III, led by Simon de Montfort, Earl of Leicester, the thirteenth century was a time of relative peace for Englishmen. In the fourteenth and fifteenth centuries, the state of war either at home or abroad was nearly continual. Much of the stagnation of economic life can be blamed on these disasters, coming so to speak, from without. More of it came from developments within the structure of society.

The Hundred Years War sapped the vitality of the medieval English monarchy and disrupted public order. Trade in wool and agricultural products declined, Edward III went bankrupt, wheat prices fluctuated greatly, arable land was taken out of production and rural villages abandoned. The Black Death claimed one-third of the nation's population in 1349 and harsh social conditions led to a peasant revolt in 1381. Richard II, who reigned from 1377 to 1399, was unable to cope with the strain of office and abdicated his throne. Henry IV lacked political acumen and funds to continue the French wars. Aristocratic cliques led to a period of civil disturbances, called the Wars of the Roses, which hampered agriculture, industry and trade. Campaigns were brief and normally confined to the summer months. A usual way to harm an enemy and his supporters was to damage crops, so that even a short campaign might mean a year of hunger or starvation.[8]

Sixty-eight famines were recorded from 1066 to 1485. The most serious were the English famine of 1069; England in 1093; Scotland in 1116 when "people ate each other"; England in 1124; England and Wales in 1183; England in 1193–1196 when common people perished from lack of food; Ireland in 1227; England in 1235 when 20,000 died in London; England in 1258; England in 1294 when thousands of the poor died; England, Scotland and Ireland in 1302; England in 1314; England in 1321; England and Scotland in 1341; England in 1353; England in 1392; Ireland in 1410; England in 1439 and Ireland in 1447.

MODERN PERIOD (1485–1850)

Henry VII, 1485–1509, enriched and strengthened the crown's financial position at a time when a number of famines were attributed to "great scarcity and high prices". He was able to suppress a rebellion in Yorkshire and Cornwall, reinforce common law, confiscate monastic lands, expand the export trade, encourage shipbuilding and design a successful English foreign policy. His successor, Henry VIII, aggravated social conditions by permitting the growth of large land holdings which employed few farmers. A class of landless rural laborers was created. High unemployment rates, debased currency and inflation contributed to hunger and starvation. Many famines were recorded, and in 1527:[9]

> Such scarcities of bread was at London and throughout England that many dyed for want thereof. The King sent to the Citie, of his own provision 600 quarters; the bread carts then coming from Stratford towards London were met at the Mile End by a great number of citizens, so that the maior and sheriffes were forced to goe and rescue the same, and see them brought to the markets appointed, wheat then at 15s the quarter.

A social revolution fermented as a result of poor national leadership, agrarian unemployment and industrial problems; agriculture as a critical facet of the national economy was neglected. Edward IV, 1547-53, in an attempt to finance a Scottish war, also debased the coinage and induced a program that led to doubling of basic food prices. As a result, uprisings and civil disturbances broke out in all corners of the kingdom. Religious leaders and social critics claimed that English yeomen were being converted into paupers or slaves by actions of the King and of landlords. According to Scory, Bishop of Rochester, the extent of land thrown out of cultivation was two acres in three.[10]

> A great number of people are so pined and famished by reason of the great scarcity and dearth that the great sheep masters have brought into this noble realm, that they are become more like the slavery and peasantry of France than the ancient and godly yeomanry of England.

Mary I failed to improve the status of the poor and hungry, and a severe three-year famine capped her reign. Elizabeth I, 1558-1603, restored unity and some economic vitality to England. New industries were developed, commercial activities expanded and a Poor Law designed to assist those unable to find work was passed in 1563. Unfortunately, the financial burden of the Spanish War led to increased taxation, closing of important continental markets for English manufactured goods and social unrest among the hungry poor. In order to fund state programs, agricultural products were exported to the detriment of the indigenous poor:[11]

> By the late Transportation of graine into forreine parts, the same was here grown of an excessive price, as in some parts of the Realme, from 14s. to 4 markes the quarter, and more, as the Poore did feele; and all other things whatsoever were made to sustain man, were likewise raysed, without all conscience and reason. For remedie whereof our Merchants brought back from Danshe much Rye and Wheat, but passing deere; though not of the best, yet serving the turn in such extremities.

James of Scotland succeeded Elizabeth to the English throne and the new political unity of England, Wales and Scotland was officially titled Great Britain. Although the 1603-1625 reign of James was noted for inflation, corruption in government and discontent, no famines plagued Great Britain. His successor, Charles I, advocated an unpopular ecclesiastical policy which led to national revolt and famine in Lancashire, parts of northern England and Scotland in 1649. He was tried and executed in the same year.

   J. Penkethman, in his work subtitled *A true relation or Collection of the most remarkable Dearths and Famines which have happened in England since the comming in of William the Conquerour, as also the rising and falling of the price of wheate and other Graine, with the severall occassions thereof*, attributed famines in England and Great Britain from 1066 to 1638 to:[12]

(1) War, whereby both corn and land was wasted, as also people destroyed.

(2) Unseasonable weather, extremes of cold and frost or rain, of winds, thunder, and lightning, tempest and such like.

(3) The abasing of the coin.

(4) Excessive consumption and abuse of wheat and other victuals in voluptuous feasts.

(5) The uncharitable greediness or unconscionable hoarding of corn-masters and farmers.

(6) The merchants over-much transporting of grain into foreign parts.

He concluded that the most critical factors necessary to eliminate famine from the island kingdom were:

(1) Peace, whereby men have liberty to till the ground and reap the fruit thereof.

(2) Seasonable and kindly weather.

(3) Great store of fine gold and silver.

(4) Moderate use of the creature and sparing diet.

(5) The corn-masters and farmers Charitable bounties or conscionable exporting of grain to sale.

(6) The importation of grain from foreign parts, through careful control.

Penkethman's "famine factors" were not only significant in the time prior to his published work in 1638, but also in years to follow. Cromwell's Irish campaign, after the death of Charles I, led to famine throughout the country. His puritanical standard of conduct and his internal governmental policies resulted in Charles II returning to Great Britain in 1660 and assuming the throne. Charles' reign was a healing one but James II's devisive rule resulted in his being replaced by William of Orange in 1689. William's reign and that of Anne improved the economic status of Great Britain, but there were famines. Smout, in his history of the Scottish people noted:[13]

> Of all the famines which afflicted Scottish society at different times that of the 1690s is the best documented, and it was also the one that burnt itself into the memory of the people much as the Great Hunger of the 1840s did in Ireland. A hundred years afterwards, when the ministers of Scotland were compiling the Statistical Account, vivid stories could still be told about it in parishes as far apart as Mull, Aberdeenshire, Inverness-shire and Fife, and it was also very serious in the south west. The minister of Torryburn said that the number of burials in the parish rose from an average of about 21 a year to 114 in 1697 and 81 in 1699. Elsewhere it was said that a third or even a half of the population died or emigrated, and if the overall mortality for the whole country was nothing like as bad as that it was still very serious.

Smout in the next paragraph of his work quoted Robert Sibbald's description of what Sibbald had seen in 1699:

For want some die in the wayside, some drop down in the streets, the poor sucking babs are starving for want of milk, which the empty breasts of their mothers cannot furnish them. Everyone may see Death in the face of the poor that abound everywhere; the thinness of their visage, their ghostly looks, their feebleness, their agues and their fluxes threaten them with sudden death if care be not taken of them. And it is not only common wandering beggars that are in this case, but many householders who lived well by their labour and their industry are now by want forced to abandon their dwellings. And they and their little ones must beg, and in their necessity they take what they can get, spoiled victual, yea, some eat these beasts which have died of some disease which may occasion a plague among them.

There are many descriptions of famines in this time period, of dead bodies with grass or human flesh between their teeth and of people struggling towards graveyards so that they could have Christian burials.

The 1714–1820 period was a time of prosperity, internal peace, external wars and the acquisitions of new markets. Sound financial and commercial administration and growing trade laid the foundation for industrial growth years later. Unfortunately, the American War for Independence, the Irish problem and war with France retarded internal development in Great Britain. George III's 60-year reign dominated this segment of history. He was not an ideal leader and internal social discontent plus harvest failures created unrest early in his reign. Internal solidarity was gained with the threat of French invasion and the agricultural boom resulting from the need for home-produced foodstuffs to carry out the war. Industry expanded as war contracts were awarded and London became the financial capital of the world. Still, for the urban poor and disfranchised rural yeomen there were dearth and scarcities of the necessaries of life. John Mitchell in 1767 stated:[14]

Causes of the dearth of provisions in England does not proceed from any temporary accidents of the seasons, but from three permanent causes. First, the great increase of towns; second, the want of husbandmen and laborers in the country; and third, the great number of horses.

The first and most manifest cause of this dearth appears to be, a great increase of the trading and manufacturing towns . . . neither the number of people in the kingdom, nor its agriculture limited and confined as it is to one or two particular products of the earth, are sufficient to support such an extensive trade and commerce, which takes the people from their employment in agriculture to plow the seas instead of the land. . . .

The next cause of this dearth is a decrease of people in the country, at least in proportion to the cities and trading and manufacturing towns; . . . a great neglect of tillage, and the turning of arable lands into grass grounds in order to maintain the great flocks of all kinds, and particularly of horses. . . .

In towns, to which the people of England so much resort, they cannot maintain and provide for a family, as they do upon farms in the country, which supplies everyone with the necessaries of life from their own labor and industry. Upon land, people can only want through negligence, but in towns they starve for want of employment, which they often cannot get.

The heavy taxes, and especially those upon articles of daily consumption, affect the price not only of provisions, but of every thing else in the kingdom . . . . And the lands are engrossed by opulent farmers who consume most of the superfluities of life, they raise the price of provisions accordingly, and the poor are obliged to pay the duties on wine, tea, and sugar, and in their bread.

> The number of horses is so much increased among the people of all ranks, that they appear to consume as much as would maintain the greatest part of the people in the kingdom.
> The very best of the lands are kept in grass for horses, and the people are thereby deprived of their chief employment in tillage, which affects not only their substance, but their very existence .... Horses consume from two to three bushels of corn a week, that is from 104 to 156 bushels a year; whereas ten bushels of corn a year maintain the people.

Speculation on the relations between population, food supply and national prosperity resulted in considerable literature generated on the topic. Theorists had observed the role war, pestilence and famine played in controlling population growth. Their efforts were accelerated by inflation, bad harvests and the credit crisis in 1795 which induced a severe scarcity in foodstuffs and a mild famine in southern England. Malthus's *Essay on Population* (1798) was to many Englishmen of his time a critique of the Poor Laws, a system of relief adopted in 1795, to meet the distress created by low wages and inflation after the outbreak of war with France in 1793. Under the influence of Malthus:[15]

> ... poor relief came to be regarded by educated people as a main, if not the principal, influence behind the contemporary rise of population. It was argued that it cheapened subsistence to the poor and encouraged large families. Propounded in this narrow way, the thesis never squared with the development of numbers in Scotland and Ireland, where the English system of poor relief did not prevail. It broke down completely upon the continuing increase revealed by the census long after the giving of out-relief in aid of wages had been curbed in 1834. But throughout the first half of the nineteenth century the idea was a political force and swayed powerfully the opinions of the governing classes.

In 1801, when the Act of Union unified England, Scotland, Wales and Ireland into one United Kingdom, a great scarcity and famine led Parliament to investigate means of supplying more food to the nation. George IV, 1820-1830, was faced with an economic depression and a severe Irish famine when he assumed the throne. Subsequent bad harvests and high food prices, along with considerable rural unemployment, let to food riots and.civil protests. Economic and social unrest continued during William IV's 1830-37 reign. Middle-class and working-class demands were made to modify or repeal the Corn Laws, Poor Laws and Currency Laws. Reforms were made in existing programs created to help low income people faced with rising food prices, and Parliament provided aid for relief of the Irish famine in 1831. Still, many serious domestic problems had not been addressed by the reigning monarch or by Parliament. Economic and social conditions in the United Kingdom at the inception of Victorian reign, 1837-1903, were exemplified by a series of economic recessions and bad harvests. Social disintegration and class-struggles during the "hungry 1840s" led to agitators advocating open class war and political revolution. The Irish famine of 1845-47 was considered by many Englishmen to be a national disgrace. It led to the repeal of the Corn Law which was initially designed to maintain high rents and high internal grain prices, and efforts were made to improve the quality of life in Ireland. English reformers agitated actively to redress Irish grievances. But as Herman Ausubel, in his book, *In Hard Times*, stated:[16]

> The years of the Great Famine were a traumatic experience for the Irish people; even traumatic is too mild a word to convey the severity of the impact on them of funerals, funerals, funerals, to say nothing of the hunger and disease that preceded death .... Even more important, the explanations of the Famine that were set forth in the late forties had tremendous staying power, and they shaped Anglo-Irish relations for the rest of the Victorian age .... The truth about the Famine quickly came to matter less than the mythology that gathered about it, and the essence of this was that the other island was responsible for Ireland's greatest misfortune. The English emerged as monsters who preached and acted on the inhuman doctrine that the best thing for Ireland was to permit the Famine to wipe out a large section of its population. The steps that the English took to deal with the unprecedented and baffling disaster were ignored. And the efforts of the dedicated English friends of Ireland were overlooked.

Ausubel stressed "emigration", despite the dangers it involved, as the English solution to the Irish famine. This one famine was so severe that it is considered a turning point in Irish-English history, a crisis of uncomparable magnitude and a traumatic setback that reversed the Irish population trend and initiated a decline that continued into the last decades of the 20th century.[17] Six years of incredible horror reduced the population of Ireland from nearly 9 million in 1845 to 6.5 million in 1850. In a compassionate piece of work, Cecil Woodham-Smith detailed the failure of the Irish potato crop, shortsightedness of English policy-makers, callousness of landlords, prejudice of British officials, the desperate migration and the effects of *The Great Hunger* upon Irish history. Her stunning work contributes to the documentation of one of the great human disasters in modern times.[18] No famine has been recorded in England or the United Kingdom since the Irish famine(s) of 1845-50. This social catastrophe led to changes in attitudes and reforms that produced a "great" Britain.

In total, 37 famines were recorded in the Modern Period, 1485 to 1850. The most severe famines were the intolerable Irish famine of 1497; the English famine of 1521; England in 1527 when many died from lack of daily bread; England in 1549 from neglect of agriculture; England in 1586 from excessive grain exports; Ireland in 1588-89 when people consumed human flesh; England in 1595; Ireland in 1650-51 occasioned by war; England in 1740-41 created by hoarding; Scotland in 1766 as a result of massive exports of food grains; Ireland in 1822 produced in part by a potato crop failure; and Ireland in 1846-47 which claimed the lives of an estimated 1,029,552.

NOTES

[1] C. Walford, *The Famines of the World: Past and Present* (New York: Burt Franklin, 1970), pp. 4–16.

[2] *Ecclesiastical History of England* (London: G. Bell, 1881), p. 194.

[3] P. Clemoes and K. Hughes, eds., *England Before the Conquest* (Cambridge: The University Press, 1971), p. 227.

[4] J. Thompson, *Economic and Social History of the Middle Ages (300-1300)* (New York: Frederick Ungar, 1966), p. 762.

[5] W. Hassall, *How They Lived: An Anthology of Original Accounts Written Before 1485* (New York: Barnes & Noble, 1962), pp. 297-298.

[6] J. Penkethman, *Artachthos or a New Book Declaring the Assise of Bread* (London: R. Bishop & Edward Griffine, 1638), p. 13.

[7] G. Homans, *English Villagers of the Thirteenth Century* (New York: Russell & Russell, 1960), pp. 33-34.

[8] D. Waley, *Later Medieval Europe* (New York: Longmans, 1964), pp. 99-101.

[9] Penkethman, op. cit., note 6, p. K2.

[10] J. Froude, *History of England from the Fall of Wolsey to the Death of Elizabeth* (New York: Ams Press, 1969), p. 116.

[11] Penkethman, op. cit., note 6, p. K3.

[12] Penkethman, op. cit., note 6, p. K3 (6).

[13] T. Smout, *A History of the Scottish People, 1560-1830* (New York: Charles Scribner's Sons, 1969), pp. 154-155.

[14] J. Mitchell, *The present state of Great Britain and North America, with regard to agriculture, population, trade and manufacturers, impartially considered* (London: T. Becket, 1767), pp. 1-39.

[15] W. Court, *A Concise Economic History of Britain, from 1750 to Recent Times* (Cambridge: Cambridge University Press, 1967), p. 8.

[16] H. Ausubel, *In Hard Times: Reformers Among the Late Victorians* (New York: Columbia University Press, 1960), p. 267.

[17] T. Freeman, *Ireland: A General and Regional Geography* (London: Methuen & Co. Ltd., 1969), p. 6.

[18] C. Woodham-Smith, *The Great Hunger* (New York: Signet Books, 1964).

Chapter 8

India, 297-1943 A.D.

For the purpose of this study, India is a geographical area or subcontinent that at this time includes the political entities known as India, Pakistan, Bangladesh, Nepal, Bhutan and Sri Lanka. This descriptive geographic term was applied to the subcontinent by the ancient Greeks and it meant to them "the land of the Indoi or Hindu." Civilizations flourished here in the third and second millenniums B.C. and the subcontinent's wealth attracted many invaders. India's racial composition includes Caucasoid, Mongoloid and Negroid, plus many remnant groups. Physically and culturally, the peoples of this subcontinent are not homogeneous. Society has traditionally been composed of many separate fragments reflecting almost every basis of social differentiation, i.e., ethnic affiliation, language, religion, area of origin and a very complex complement of castes. Mutual tolerance and acceptance of the status and functions of various groups provide a basis for the underlying diversity, yet unity of the subcontinent. By far the most important social unit was and is the family; the most important political-economic unit, the village and the most important control of social structure among the dominant ruling group, the caste system. A large fraction of India is suitable for agriculture. Approximately two-thirds of the land is topographically-edaphically usable, but climatic limitations reduce cultivation to about two-fifths of the total area. It is impossible to overestimate the importance of the monsoon in the lives of the inhabitants for in a traditional, spatially restricted, agrarian society life depends upon what is accomplished during the monsoon rains. Years of drought are interspersed with more frequent years of average or bumper crops. Underlying many of India's famine problems has been

Table 2. Loveday and Bhatia's List of Indian Famines, 297–1943 A.D.

Date	Place	Physical causes cited	Cultural causes cited
297	Magadha	?	?
445	Kashmir	?	?
917–18	Kashmir	?	?
1033	Hindustan	?	?
116–19	Deccan and Burhanpur	?	?
1200	Bombay	?	?
1259	Bombay	X	?
1291	Delhi and Siwalik	?	?
1305	Delhi	?	?
1343–45	Delhi	?	?
1351–1363	Kashmir	?	?
1396	Deccan	X	?
1423	Deccan	?	?
1471–72	Bahmini and Bombay	?	?
1494	Delhi	?	X
1500	Delhi	?	X
1520	Bombay	?	X
1527	Sind	X	?
1540–43	Sind	?	?
1540	Coromandel Coast	?	?
1554–55	Delhi, Agra and Bajana	?	?
1556	Hindustan	?	X
1576	Delhi	?	?
1577	Kutch	?	?
1592	Sholapur	?	?
1594–98	Central India and Hindustan	?	?
1613–15	Punjab	?	?
1623	Gujarat and Ahmedabad	?	?
1628–29	Hoozoor	?	?
1629–30	Deccan	?	?
1650	Ahmedabad	?	?
1660	Aurangzib's dominions	?	?
1676–77	Hyderabad	X	X
1685	Deccan and Hyderabad	?	?
1702–04	Bombay and Deccan	?	?
1709	Bombay	?	?
1718	Bombay	?	?
1737	Bombay	?	?
1739	Bombay	?	?
1746–47	Bombay	?	X
1759	Bombay	?	?
1770	Bengal	?	?
1781	Madras		X
1782	Bombay and Madras		X
1783	Bengal, Bellary, Kashmir and Rajputana		X
1787	Mahratta	X	?
1790–92	Bombay, Hyderabad, Gujarat, Madras, Kutch and Orissa	X	
1799–1804	North West Provinces, Bombay, Central India and Rajputana	?	?

Table 2. (cont'd)

Date	Place	Physical causes cited	Cultural causes cited
1806–07	Carnatic	?	?
1812	Bombay, Agra and Madras	X	
1819–20	Rajputana, Deccan and Broach	X	
1820–22	Upper Sind	?	?
1824–25	Deccan, Bombay and Madras	?	?
1832–33	Sholapur and Madras	?	?
1833–34	Gujarat, Kandish and Deccan	X	
1853–55	Bellary, Madras, Deccan, Rajputana and Bombay	X	
1860–61	Punjab, Rajputana and Kutch	?	?
1862	Deccan	?	?
1866–67	Orissa, Behar, Ganjam, Bellary, Hyderabad and Mysore		X
1868–70	Punjab, Gujarat, Deccan and Rajputana	?	?
1873–74	Behar, Bundelkhand and Bengal		X
1876–78	Madras, Bombay, Mysore and Hyderabad	?	?
1877–78	Kashmir		
1888–89	Ganjam and Orissa		X
1896–97	Bengal, Bombay, Central Provinces, Behar, Madras, Delhi, Hyderabad and Rajputana	X	
1899–1900	Baroda, Kutch, Kathiawar, Central Provinces and Punjab	?	?
1900–02	Gujarat	X	
1906–07	Darbhanga	?	?
1907	United Provinces	X	?
1943	Bengal	?	X

Sources: A Loveday, *The History and Economics of Indian Famine* (London: G. Bell and Sons, Ltd., 1944), pp. 135–137; and B. Bhatia, *Famines in India* (Bombay: Asia Publishing House, 1967), p. 363. Of the famines listed, 50% were recorded in the period of British Conquest (1707–1815) and British India (1815–1943).

its population growth, combined with economic and subsistence pressures on the food produced with the aid of life-giving rains. Seventy famines have been recorded by Loveday and Bhatia in the 297 A.D. to 1943 time period, and only 11 percent were directly attributed to a physical factor (Table 2).

W. R. Aykroyd, in his book, *The Conquest of Famine*, mentioned factors which he believed brought about famine in India since early times. He concluded:[1]

> The extreme poverty of the mass of the population allows no margin of safety, economically or physical. The source of food is agriculture of a simple kind dependent on uncertain rainfall. Until recently the great size of the country and lack of communications have hindered transport of grain from one area to another. The obtaining of food for famine relief obviously does not depend on the mere distance between the famine area and the areas where food is available; it depends on the communications between these areas. An abundant harvest in Madras would be of no use in a famine in Rajputana when the only means of transportation was by bullock cart.
>
> Apart from natural causes, a most potent factor has been the disruption of life by civil wars. Throughout most of history India has suffered from unending strife between emperors, rajahs and invaders. Wars have often converted mere scarcity into famine. Armies may not directly destroy crops and livestock, but their mere presence is a heavy burden on the peasant, since soldiers have to be fed and have to be paid, and unless they are fed and paid will ravage the countryside. Further, war may not only cause famine but prevent efforts to relieve it.

A number of the most terrible famines known in world history occurred in India during the 19th century. Pre-European famines were a state of extreme hunger in a region as a result of a deficiency in the accustomed food supply. Families, at this time, subsisted primarily on food raised either by themselves or by immediate neighbors. Limited transportation means and communication networks required people to depend upon local food reserves or to leave the famine area in search for food. All socioeconomic groups within a famine region suffered alike. Although a complete account of every famine that occurred in the pre-European period of Indian history is nonexistent, evidence suggests a major famine took place every forty years. Post-European famines claimed more lives, covered broader areas and were transformed into a social calamity. British conquest and British control of India produced marked changes in the Indian economy and many famines were triggered by the consequences of these changes. Famine frequency increased in the period of British conquest, 1707–1815, to one famine every seven years. More striking than the increase in famine frequency and magnitude of famine deaths was the change in the nature of famine, from a shortage of food in pre-European India to the lack of the ability to buy food in British India. A direct relationship was established between those who lived in poverty and those who died in a famine. B. Bhatia, in his remarkable study of *Famines in India*, equated catastrophic famine with British colonialism. He wrote:[2]

> The economic transition in India was bound to be accompanied by hardship for those who failed to keep pace with economic progress or take advantage of the

opportunities that it offered. England had a similar experience in course of the Industrial Revolution. The Poor Law of 1834 was a recognition not only of the existence of economic distress among destitutes and paupers amidst all-round rapid economic progress, but also of the State's responsibility for relief to the poor. But the magnitude of hardship was much greater in India than in England. In England, the changeover was rapid and people thrown out of employment in the rural areas were soon absorbed by the new industries. In India, on the other hand, the process of industrialization was retarded by the compulsions of colonial economy. The entire population was, therefore, increasingly thrown on agriculture as the principal source of livelihood. Thus in India the normal economic process was reversed. In England and other European countries, in the nineteenth century, labour was released from agriculture to provide wage labour to the expanding industries; in India, manufacturing industry threw out labour to be absorbed in stagnating agriculture.

Bhatia believed that instead of an absolute shortage of food in a geographic area, food shortages under the British were magnified and intensified by tremendous increases in the price of food grains. Food grain price increases led to death by starvation for the rural poor were unable to purchase food to feed themselves—even when food was available. Economic and social factors were more important in British India than natural scarcity in causing distress and starvation. A diametrically opposite view of famine during British rule was presented in a publication of The Publicity Board of Bengal in 1933. The author addressed the question "Were the pre-British days a golden age in India?" and came to the conclusion that the British were the only rulers of India who even attempted to pursue a policy to eliminate famines or formulate a system of national famine relief:[3]

> There was grim and grinding poverty when the country came under the British rule. The condition of the people, millions of whom went through life on insufficient food, was aggravated by the inevitable decay of the indigenous industries due to economic causes. The famine which visited the unhappy land in 1770 yet stands as a spectre on the threshold of British rule in India. The suffering was terrible. The effects of this famine aroused the attention of the British people to the defects of the East India Company's administration. The famine was followed by the Regulating Act (1774), Pitt's India Act (1784) and the Permanent Settlement of Bengal (1793). Every one of these measures was adopted with a view to improve the administration of India by the East India Company and enable the people to combat famines more effectively. The disaster formed the keynote to the history of Bengal during the succeeding forty years.
>
> The famine of 1770 was followed by famines in 1784, in 1803 in Bombay Presidency, in 1833 in Madras Presidency and in 1861 in the North-West Provinces. This succession of famines touched the heart and roused the conscience of the British administrators. They had tried a policy of piecemeal relief like their predecessors in India and had found it wanting. During the Orissa famine of 1866, they evolved a concerted policy to provide against the recurrence of such tragedies. The principle was laid down that human beings must not be allowed to perish for lack of food.

FOOD, VILLAGE AND LAND USE:
FACTORS IN INDIA'S FAMINE EQUATION

The peoples of India have been and are, for the most part, vegetarians. Their diet consists mainly of wheat, rice, millet, barley, beans, pulses, spinach, mustard, radish greens, eggplant, okra, cucumbers, etc. Foods derived from animals, such as fowl, mutton, buffalo and goat, are restricted to a small segment of the population—principally Christians, Muslims and Parsis (Hindus eat no beef and Muslims eat no pork). Fish is consumed by non-vegetarians and especially those who live along coastal regions or major water bodies. Physiographic diversity and cultural preferences have led to wide variations in the types of foodstuffs raised and eaten in different parts of India. Wheat, served as baked or fried cakes, is a staple in northern and western India. Rice is the staple in eastern and southern India. Millet is the prime source of human energy in the dry upland areas. Barley, and now corn, is served as a supplement to rice or wheat dishes. Green pulse, chick-pea and pigeon pea are a primary source of protein. The subcontinent is well endowed with a large variety of fruits. Mangoes are prized, as are various sweets and special milk products. Various Hindu castes have distinctive food laws, food customs and food preferences. Famine relief historically has been complicated by religious food taboos and cultural biases.

Most people in India live in nucleated villages and here is where the caste system is most carefully observed. The village structure, with a stable division of labor and a well defined system of obligations and rights, remains a dominant social entity in India. Most are agricultural villages and the yearly cycle of agricultural activities provides the basis for most social and many religious festivals. Agricultural villages are inhabited primarily by those who own land around or near the village, those with tenancy rights, lesser tenants and landless agricultural laborers. Land-holdings are small and are usually owned by a joint family. Along with farmers, each village contains carpenters, barbers, blacksmiths, sweepers, weavers, etc. Villages have clearly defined social areas, including one for the lowest castes. Isaiah Bowman, in 1923, made the following observation in his book on world problems in political geography:[4]

> The society of India has its basic feature in the village organization. Through all the long and complicated history of India, varied by conquest, by interstate rivalries, by famines, by calamities such as plagues of locusts and epidemics of disease that carried off millions, the village organization and confederations of village communities have been maintained. These confederations have been the most durable organization in India, and the improvement of Indian conditions can be carried on only if attention is paid to the. value of the village community as the basis of self-government.

Land use before the advent of British power was decided, for the most part, by customary patterns enforced by self-perpetuating village elites. Land use relations and norms were rooted in usage rather than statutes. Rights to till the soil and harvest what was produced was unquestioned as long as the farmer paid what was demanded of him by the local ruler or administrator. British conquest led to drastic change in land use, partly as a direct result of the emphasis upon commercial crops. Agricultural exports and tax revenues were needed by the British to finance the conquest and consolidation of the conquest. Tax revenue was secured either through the landowner-landholder or directly from those who worked in the fields. This dual system, employed from 1793 to 1947, led to the farmers supporting a large number of middlemen and speculators plus a growth in the economic power of absentee landlords, and moneylenders. Older regional land use systems were weakened by British methods of collecting revenue and shattered by the spread of commercial agriculture. Need for tax money stimulated planting of industrial crops and specialty items rather than planting food crops for family, village or regional consumption. Wheat was exported from Punjab cotton from Bombay and jute from Bengal. Industrial crops commanded a higher price than food crops so many farmers shifted to cotton, sugar cane and tobacco. Reserves of grain traditionally kept for poor harvest years were sold and rural inhabitants were less prepared to survive a drastic decrease in yields. Bowman commented:[5]

> Pressing upon the people of India in a manner to produce great distress is the land tax, in addition to which is the water tax in the irrigated areas. The land tax keeps the mass of the population in a state bordering on slavery. Millions cannot get sufficient food. At the end of his year of labor, the farmer finds his crop divided between the landlord and the government. He has to go into debt to the village shopkeeper, getting credit for food and seed in the ensuing year. Since 240,000,000 people in India are connected directly or indirectly with agriculture, this means that a large majority of them, probably two thirds, are living in a state of squalor.

Tenants, crop sharers and hired agricultural laborers without any incentive to increase productivity, or on the other hand, incentive to improve soil fertility for future tenants, took little interest in improving the land. Agricultural innovations ceased and, in most cases, crop production practices remained time-honored ones. Yields per unit area of traditional crops stagnated and increase in industrial crop output was achieved at the expense of food grains.

FAMINES IN INDIA, 297-1707

Since time immemorial, those who have inhabited India have suffered and died from famine. Their pain and their sorrow is revealed in legends and later attested by historic events. References are made to famine in one of the first Indian economic treatise, the *Arthasastra* written by Chanakya, Minister of Chandragupta, between 322-289 B.C.:[6]

> In the month of Bhadrapada, when the fields in the land were covered with the autumnal rice—a crop which was just ripening—unexpectedly there fell heavy snow. Under this (snow) which resembled (in its whiteness) the grim laughter of Death bent on the destruction of all beings, there sank (and perished) the rice crops, together with the people's hope of existence. Then came a terrible famine, which resembled a kind of hell with the masses of starving people (moving about) like ghosts. Tormented by hunger, everyone thought only of his belly, and forgot in his misery love for his wife, affection for his children and tender regard for his parents. . . .Uttering coarse words, emaciated by hunger, terrible to look at, and rolling his eyes in all directions, each person strove apart to keep himself alive at the cost of (all other) living being.

Lacking a well developed means of communication and a unified transportation network, people subsisted on food raised by them or by others in the village. In times of poor crops or a crop failure, individuals looked only to the immediate neighborhood to make up the deficiency in food supplies. Frosts, floods, locusts, droughts or unseasonable rains contributed to many crop failures and were principal factors in creating food shortages in the less densely populated and relatively dry Deccan Plateau area. Few crop failures were recorded in the densely populated Indus River valley for water was available for crops from the river and there is evidence of extensive provisions for grain storage in all central places.

The "Golden Age" of India, according to many historians, extended from about 320 to 500 A.D. during the Gupta dynastic period. Art, medicine and education flourished at this time. One major famine was recorded in this Golden Age, and that famine occurred in Kashmir in approximately 445. Other dynasties thrived in various areas of the subcontinent at the same time as the Gupta and enjoyed prosperity along with peace. Relative internal stability was shattered by a series of invasions by Huns, Persians, Afghanistans and Tatars from 450 till the late 1400s. War and plague contributed to many serious food shortages and famines. Ibn Batuta, a famous Arab geographer, wrote a vivid account of famine horror in the early 1300s and food shortages were so universal in 1344–45 that the Emperor Muhammad was unable to obtain adequate food for his household. Data is not available to synthesize a true picture of the impact almost continuous wars between various Hindu and Moslem dynasties in the next two centuries had on yearly food production, but famines were frequent. In many instances, all famine relief was prohibited by military decree. The Mogul (Mongol) invasion in 1526 created a social and economic environment that yielded many terrible famines, including a famine that claimed the lives of two-thirds of the inhabitants in the Hindu kingdom of Vijaynagar. A scorched earth policy, banning the planting of fields and forbidding all food imports into various areas in order to prevent invading forces from securing food supplies, became a standard tool of war and a creator of famine. Mogul emperors were able to solidify and expand their land holdings but they too were continuously attacked and their empires endangered. Cannibalism, during the Mogul invasion-consolidation period, became a survival necessity for many. Emperor Shah Jahan, the fifth ruler of the Mogul Empire in India, assumed the throne in 1627 and during his reign the Moguls reached their golden age. Although best remembered for the perfectly proportioned Taj Mahal and the splendor of his public works, he is also remembered by many for the famine of 1629–30 when:[7]

> ... the number of the dead exceeded all computation or estimate. The towns and their environs and the country were strewed with human skulls and bones. Instead of seed men ate each other; parents devoured their children. Bakers ground up old bones, or whatever else they could get, and, mixing the dust with a little wheat, sold the cakes as valuable rarities to the wealthy. Human bodies, dried in the sun, were steeped in water and devoured by those who found them.

Shah Jahan was unable to mitigate this severe famine and ubiquitous hunger for too much money was spent on luxuries and too much effort wasted in war or intrigue. Other Mongul emperors were able to successfully reduce famine casualties and were pioneers in famine relief techniques.

FAMINES DURING THE BRITISH CONQUEST, 1707–1815

European incursion into India began in the early 1500s with the Portuguese seizing ports on the continent's west coast. Other European nations, the Dutch, English and French, fought the Portuguese and each other for control of the lucrative spice trade. Not to be denied a share of India's mineral and agricultural wealth, Queen Elizabeth formed the British East India Company by royal charter and the Company built trading facilities at Bombay, Calcutta and Madras in the 1600s. Strong Mogul (Mongol) rulers were able to inhibit European territorial aggrandizement for many decades. The British East India Company, after the death of Aurangzeb in 1707, capitalized upon the lack of internal cohesion and began a series of campaigns and political maneuvers that enabled them to gain control of much of India by 1757. India thus came under the control of a private profit-seeking company concerned primarily with trade. Returns on investments and operating capital for expansion were more important than the individual inhabitant of a geographical entity with a long and rich history. Bhatia, in his discussion of British colonialism and famines, maintained:[8]

> The burden which Indian agriculture was called upon to bear increased for another reason. The expenditure of the Government was on a lavish scale and quite out of proportion with the economic conditions of the people of the country. Besides, the country had to bear the cost of Imperial wars . . . .

As a result of grinding poverty and omnipresent internal food shortages aggravated by wars, the territory controlled by the British East India Company seethed with rebellion and bitterness. Constantly in economic and social turmoil, any slight variations in factors which contributed to food production or distribution resulted in famine. A catastrophy of enormous magnitude was triggered in 1770; it defied description and shocked the world. A famine so devastating that perhaps 10 million people starved to death drew to the attention of the British people the defects of the East India Company's administration of the subcontinent. So all-encompassing and so disastrous was this famine, it created the keystone to the economic and social history of many parts of India for nearly half a century. Surgeon General Edward Balfour, in his *The Cyclopaedia of India*, wrote:[9]

> Bengal suffered in the year 1770 from famine more widespread and terrible than any which had ever befallen any other British possession, and which Colonel Baird Smith deemed to have been the most intense that India had ever experienced, and one-third of all Bengal lay waste and silent for twenty years.
>
> The crops of December 1768 and August 1769 were both scanty, and prices became very high; and throughout the month of October 1769 hardly a drop of rain fell. The usual refreshing showers of January to May also failed in 1770, in which year until late in May scarcely any rain fell. The famine was felt in all the northern parts of Bengal as early as November 1769, but by the 4th

January 1770 the daily deaths from starvation in Patna were up to 50; and before the end of May, 150. The tanks were dried up, and the springs had ceased to reach the surface, and before the end of April 1770 famine had spread desolation. In Murshidabad, at length, the dead were left uninterred; dogs, jackals, and vultures were the sole scavengers. Three millions of people were supposed to have perished. It is also said that within the first nine months of 1770, one-third of the entire population of Lower Bengal perished for want of food. According to Grant, one-fifth of the entire population perished; according to Mill, five-eights; while Ward and Marshman state one-third. The year 1770 corresponds to the Bengali year 1276, and it is known to this day amongst the people as the Che'hattar Saler Durbhikya Manwantara. It was during the governorship of Mr. Carter; his government did nothing to help the people and the Company's servants trafficked in grain.

Newspaper accounts and reports by British government officials aroused the world to the callousness and ineptitude of the East India Company's administration. Measures were taken by Parliament to improve the Company's governance of India and to provide effective relief of famine. Measures passed included the Regulating Act of 1774, Pitt's India Act of 1784, and the Permanent Settlement of Bengal Act of 1793. These attempts to improve facets of life in India were helpful but did not solve the deep rooted problem and the 1770 disaster was followed by famines in 1781, 1782, 1783, 1787, 1790-92, 1799-1801, 1802-1804, 1806-1807, and 1812. Decision making within the East India Company was confined to a limited number of highly educated or trained British administrators and indigenous officials. Of great interest was the influence of Thomas Malthus upon those he lectured as professor of history and political economy in the college of the East India Company from 1805 until his death in 1834. Aykroyd contended that the text book or tea room philosophy of leading British authors and public officials was transmitted into action policy in India. He cites the dreadful Gujarat and Marwar famine of 1812 as a classic example of relief being denied by governmental policy.[10]

Adam Smith's book, *The Wealth of Nations*, influenced famine relief in India as in Ireland. In 1812 the Government of Bombay, faced with an episode of food shortage partly due to locusts, refused to interfere in any way with private trade. The Governor recorded in a special minute his adherence to the principles of political economy as expressed in *The Wealth of Nations* and his conviction that unassisted trade could do more to relieve such distress as existed and to effect an equable distribution of supplies than the government could do with all its resources. This dogma discouraged the control of prices, the prohibition of the export of food from famine areas, and its procurement and import into these areas by government action—methods of famine prevention and relief which seemed common-sense in earlier and later times. Another dogma which affected governmental action against famine was that giving anything away for nothing—even giving food to the starving—demoralized the recipients and led to "pauperism". Such convictions sometimes proved as disastrous in India as in the Irish famine of the 1840s.

Although the peoples of India were considered among the most frugal in the world and in places where most people lived the land among the most fertile, famines became more frequent during the period of British conquest and consolidation. Misery and poverty, a common aspect of the cultural landscape, were expanded and magnified—not because of worn out soils or overpopulation but because of an attitude. There was inadequate utilization of both India's human and natural resources combined with defects deeply ingrained within the East India Company's administration. A great number of famines killed millions of people when there was no real crisis in food production.[11]

FAMINES IN BRITISH INDIA, 1815-1943

Poverty, hunger, famine and British cultural insensitivity nurtured discontent against the East India Company. Attempts were made by Parliament and the Crown after the end of conquest in 1815 to improve the governance of India, fashion a new order and ameliorate perennial food problems. Still, famines killed hundreds of thousands in 1819-20, 1820-22, 1824-25, 1832-33, 1833-34, and 1853-55. The Company attempted to provide famine relief when the death toll in 1833 reached over 100,000, but no definite policy was formulated. Cash was given, public work programs started, granaries opened and revenues remitted or never claimed during various famines but people continued to die from chronic malnutrition or starvation. The Company's insensitivity and lack of administrative skills were revealed, in 1857, to the world in dramatic fashion when the Bengal Army revolted against their British officers. Before the Sepoy Mutiny was finally crushed in 1859, it spread over a large part of northern India. As a result of this revolt, the power to govern in India was transferred to the British government. The first serious famine after India was taken over by the Crown occurred in 1860. A free trade principle was maintained by British authorities as well as a policy of "no work, no assistance." Those who were incapable of work were placed in poorhouses and fed. Grain was transported into the famine area on newly-constructed railways and Great Britain subscribed £ 108,090 for famine relief. Piecemeal uncoordinated relief assisted in tempering human mortality but the new administrators in India found it unsatisfactory. Unfortunately, no formalized famine relief policy was devised immediately after the 1860 famine and this oversight contributed to the estimated 10 million deaths in the fearsome Orissa famine of 1866-67.

The Governor-General of the stricken area had no set procedure to follow in 1866-67 and did not attempt initially to provide famine relief. Although advised that rice should be imported for stocks had been exported to meet the demands of the cotton growers near Bombay, the Governor-General followed what he believed to be the teaching of Adam Smith and rejected the idea of importing grain. Even the grain from a ship that had run aground and whose cargo was rotting in the holds, was not permitted to be taken ashore for use in famine relief. Millions starved to death while the "laws of supply-and-demand" failed to provide food and while merchants hoarded remaining stocks to take advantage of rising prices. When the Governor-General finally recognized the magnitude of deaths and ordered rice into the famine area, torrential monsoon rains obstructed relief activities. The following year a famine claimed hundreds of thousands of lives in Rajputana, the most calamitous event ever recorded there. Those who could escape from the famine began to flock into known areas where food was available. British relief was better organized and district officers were made responsible for all deaths in their districts. So disturbed was the colonial government, that a policy of saving human lives at all costs was promulgated. This policy helped reduce mortality during the "Panic Famine" of 1873-74, but cost the government about nine million sterling. Relief expenditures for the famine of 1873-74 were exorbitant and resulted in aid for the 1876-78 Madras, Bombay, Mysore and Hyderabad famine being delayed until it began to claim hundreds of thousands of lives. In areal extent, population affected, duration and intensity, the 1876-78 famine was the most grievous since the beginning of the century. Balfour stated:[12]

> In the beginning of 1878, a trial census was taken of the districts of N. Arcot, Bellary, Chingleput, Coimbatore, Cuddapah, Kistna, Kurnool, Madrastown, Madura, Nellore, and Salem. In these, in 1875-76, the deaths were 340,545; but in 1876-77 they increased to 925,103, or 67 per thousand of the population of 13,765,165. According to the estimated population at the end of 1876, the losses were in Bellary 21 percent; Kurnool, 27 percent; Cuddapah, 26 percent; Nellore, 21 percent; Coimbatore, 17 percent; Chingleput, 10 percent. The Salem district estimated population in 1876 was 2,129,850. Actual population on the 14th of March 1878 was 1,559,876—that is, there were 569,956 souls in this one district, or nearly 27 percent of the people unaccounted for. And in this Salem district the famine distress was not then over.
>
> In Mysore the January census showed that about 25 percent, or one-fourth, of the population had melted away, equal to 1,250,000 souls.
>
> In Bombay the average deaths had been 32,909; but in the year 1876-77 the mortality was 149,053, and there were 32,054 diminished births. In Oudh, the N. W. Provinces, the Punjab, and Central Provinces, the deaths were abnormally great.
>
> Great efforts were made to relieve the famine-stricken. The people of Great Britain subscribed about £ 800,000; the Government of India laid out about £ 10,000,000; and private individuals and the public servants in India vied with each other in efforts to save life.

This famine made it clear to all concerned that the government lacked basic insights into the socioeconomic conditions of the affected area and the extent of famine. Although there was great loss of life and much bitterness vented against the British, their dominance throughout the subcontinent was not threatened. Government officials became preoccupied with Imperial Russian activities along the northwest frontier and neglected to formulate a comprehensive famine relief policy based upon what had been learned. Kashmir became a scene of many battles and the social havoc reduced agricultural production to a degree that resulted in a famine. This 1877-78 famine in Kashmir was the first recorded there in a century. A commission was appointed after this famine to determine what action might be taken to diminish the severity of famines in India. *The Report of the Famine Inquiry Commission of 1880*, produced under the direction of General Richard Strachey, became the basis of an Indian Famine Code in the 1890s.[13] Measures adopted to combat famine in this code included a famine insurance fund, detailed famine relief guidelines, construction of protective railways and expansion of irrigation works. Strachey's commission determined India regularly yields a surplus of food, more than necessary to compensate for a crop failure in any region. Unfortunately, from agriculture was derived the funds to pay for the cost of administrating the subcontinent. Food grain exports showed a rapid and remarkable increase from 1870 on, in spite of increasing frequency of starvation and famine. Three to four severe famines per decade claimed millions of lives from 1880 till 1910. Human and institutional factors were blatantly more important than floods, droughts or locusts in causing hunger and famine in British India.

A struggle between the financial needs of the state and the people's need for a concerted policy to eliminate the constant threat of famine continued through the late 19th and early 20th century famine years. Governments at various scales implemented conflicting programs and negated, at times, the good being done to relieve suffering and death. A distinct change in governmental attitude and adverse world publicity of each famine led to improvements in famine aid. This enlightened attitude and sound programs saved many lives during the famine of 1907–08. It was a turning point in British colonial India and no incidence of famine was recorded until the infamous Bengal famine of 1943. The Bengal famine, during World War II, cracked the foundation of British rule in India. Akhter Hameed Khan, a witness to and participant in the horrors of this famine, claimed in ordinary language it was a man-made disaster.[14]

> Nature was not the chief culprit of the Bengal tragedy. Even the official experts admitted that it was a man-made disaster. Bengal was blessed with abundant rainfall. Extensive crop failure was very rare. Contrary to recent newspaper stereotypes, floods or cyclones, though frequent, were mostly limited in extent. Nature no doubt was sometimes over-exuberant, but usually generous. Neither was it her fault that men, in the Malthusian manner, had matched their fertility with that of the land. In the thirties rice used to be exported from Bengal, though in diminishing quantities. The loss caused by bad weather was made good by imports from Burma or other parts of India. Since the end of the first world war, rice prices had been stable. A fatal shortage was considered improbable. It was commonly said that Bengal's food problem could be solved by one good monsoon. In those ancient days such a remark seemed a sensible appraisal, not a joke.

A "Denial Policy" designed by the British military command in anticipation of a Japanese landing in the Ganges-Brahmaputra delta upset established patterns of production and distribution. Akhter Hameed Khan, as a participant, contended that this denial policy was much less ruthless, but similar, to the Russian scorched earth policy during World War II. All transportation equipment was removed along with all stored rice. Rice planting was prohibited to deny potential food sources to the enemy. Very little food remained and none was returned when the Japanese did not invade. Between one and two million Bengalis died as a result of this denial policy. A program of food aid, price control, regulated trade, rationing, plus an appeal to grow more food eventually ended this contrived food crisis. Anxiety and hardship prevailed in the area after the famine and the question of food became a public obsession. Freedom from the British yoke was a set goal even though Indian troops and resources were employed by the British to defeat the Japanese and Axis Powers. After the defeat of the Japanese, the British government began making plans for their withdrawal from India. A firm decision to pull out by June 1948 prompted intense political activities which culminated in the announcement of a plan to partition British India into two independent nations. The British Parliament passed An Indian Independence Act in 1947, and the British Indian Empire ceased to exist. When the British departed they left a legacy of difficult situations and imperfect food policies. Although poverty and hunger exist, famines have been contained. The peoples of the subcontinent have declared war on large-scale famine and won.

NOTES

[1] W. Aykroyd, *The Conquest of Famine* (New York: Reader's Digest Press, 1975), pp. 49–50.

[2] B. Bhatia, *Famines in India: A Study in Some Aspects of the Economic History of India, 1860–1965* (Bombay: Asia Publishing House, 1967), pp. 21–22.

[3] Anonymous, *Famines in India* (Calcutta: B. G. Press, 1933), pp. 6–7.

[4] I. Bowman, *The New World: Problems in Political Geography* (New York: World Book Co., 1923), p. 48.

[5] Bowman, op. cit., note 5, p. 92.

[6] *Famines in India*, op. cit., note 3, p. 4.

[7] *Famines in India*, op. cit., note 3, p. 5.

[8] Bhatia, op. cit., note 2, p. 22.

[9] Surgeon General Edward Balfour, *The Cyclopaedia of India* (1880), pp. 1072–1073.

[10] Aykroyd, op. cit., note 1, p. 53.

[11] J. de Castro, *The Geography of Hunger* (Boston: Little, Brown & Co., 1952), pp. 180–182.

[12] Balfour, op. cit., note 9, p. 1075.

[13] "Famine Administration in a Bengal District in 1896–7," *The Economic Journal, Vol. X* (London: Macmillian & Co., Ltd., 1900), pp. 421–424.

[14] A. Khan, *A History of the Food Problem* (Ann Arbor: Michigan State University, Asian Studies Center, 1973), p. 2.

Chapter 9

A millenium of Russian famines

A long list of famine years are recorded in Russian geographic and nongeographic literature, and famines are a visible manifestation of deep rooted internal conflicts and an exploitative system.[1] Russian peasants and workers for centuries lived in fear of institutional or natural factors which might disturb the uneasy balance between food production and food consumption. Any slight variation or fluctuation in food production within the Russian system led to hunger and at times famine. Limitations to the traditional Russian diet, both quantitative and qualitative, were multifactored in cause and lay deep in the physical and social geography and economic history of the country. Traditional agricultural practices, i.e., prior to collectivization, included three-field rotation of crops, paucity of draft animals, use of a wooden plow, limited use of fertilizers, reliance upon a single type of crop, sowing by hand, reaping by hand sickle and threshing with a flail. Almost 90 percent of the sown area was seeded to grains such as rye and wheat with some buckwheat. Good farming practices, by West European standards, were rare and yields were very low.[2]

In the 19th and early 20th centuries when the greatest number of recorded famine and hunger years occurred, the peasant, even when harvests were below average or even if there was a crop failure, would still sell grain for he was dependent on the cash earned from the sale of grain to pay his taxes, buy salt, cloth, some tools, etc. Famine catastrophes were greater in this crude form of commercial agriculture than in the previous subsistent agricultural system. Granted, this change in basic rural economics, growth of markets and commercialization of agriculture would not have been a serious problem if

141

production had been such as to provide adequate grain for the peasant and for market. However, an examination of crop yields throughout Russian history and, particularly when Russia was a major exporter of agricultural products reveals that yields were unbelievably low. Thus, an archaic agricultural system, perpetual undernourishment nurtured by a cruel social environment and a complex combination of recurring events and situations not all related to natural factors made Russian famines inevitable.

Conjoined with a harsh social environment, a multifactored physical system (with climate playing a leading role) limited the sown area, types of crops grown and yields. Heat and moisture, the basic climatic resources of agriculture, were inadequate or in various states of imbalance in most of Russia. In northern Russia, yields of traditional Russian crops are primarily determined by heat since this is an area of moisture surplus in relation to heat. While in southern Russia, an area of moisture deficiency and heat surplus, yields or crop productivity are determined greatly by the moisture available to the plant in its life cycle. Only in limited parts of Russia are the agroclimatic resources adequate to produce surpluses in sufficient amounts that would warrant great investments of time, capital or labor. Yet climatic aberrations in the best agricultural areas of a particular stage in the evolution of the Russian state were common: protracted dry spells were and are frequent phenomena and, for most of Russian history, statistical averages of annual precipitation have limited value. In the past as is the case today, droughts sporadically affect large sections of Russia and last from a week or months to a year or to a succession of years.[3] Nevertheless, the whole history of Russian agriculture has been one of continuous field experiment with the ill-defined variables of a limited agroclimatic resource base. Through time, bad practices were discarded and acceptable agrotechniques prevailed. Errors in judgment, mistakes and unsuccessful innovations were eliminated by the brute force of hunger and famine.

FAMINE AND HUNGER YEARS

Famines have been recorded in Russian history since the first chronicles were written but securing details about each of these famines is extremely difficult. It should not be assumed that every famine or hunger year has been noted in this exploratory study for although famines were a regular but unexpected calamity, they were dispersed over an area larger than all of western Europe and they varied in severity, location and frequency of occurrence. Centuries of underdeveloped transportation modes created a custom-sustained rural community life that was isolated and was almost independent of the city and/or the nation. A famine year in one section of Russia may be, and in most times was, remembered as a good agricultural year by the inhabitants of another.

Understandably, hunger years are more difficult than famine to identify, verify and near impossible to map for hunger in one form or another has always plagued Russia. Under normal occidental dietary conditions, hunger and appetite cannot be sharply separated. However, they are not concomitant under duress arising from war, disease and/or pestilence, panic or crop failure engendered by natural factors. Hunger, as recorded in Russia history, is not simply the lack of food to satisfy an appetite: nor is hunger a severe shortage of food for a short period of time. Hunger is the paucity of any of the necessary food constituents needed to maintain health, i.e., "hollow hunger" or undernutrition resulting from an inadequate supply of food for an extended period of time, and "hidden hunger" or malnutrition resulting from a poor, improperly balanced diet. The lack of any of the necessary food constituents needed to maintain health could and did lead to premature death although the body of the decedent many times did not appear emaciated. Chroniclers could not and did not identify all types of hunger but they did record severe shortages of food for extended time periods which covered broad geographical areas and affected large numbers of people. Hunger years as recorded in Russian history are entitled to confidence for although hunger years are extremely difficult to define, they are vividly conspicuous and grossly obvious when seen, experienced and survived.[4]

Pre-harvest hunger, the paucity of a particular food or dish or even the shortage of a specific vitamin or mineral was not a famine. A Russian famine, historically, was a protracted shortage of total food over a large geographical area causing widespread disease and death from starvation. Gradual disappearance of food and food substitutes first produces emaciated, listless, weak individuals; then inactive, skeletonized, animal-like creatures sometimes waiting and many times hoping for death. Regardless of the socioeconomic level, the young, the small, the nervous or highly active perish first; less nervous or less active, larger and older individuals perish last. Concomitant with starvation is the weakened body's lack of resistance and its susceptibility to disease which can and has led to horrendous epidemics.[5]

But survival in a period of scarcity or complete unavailability of food for any period of time was dependent upon an individual's general health, which in itself was a resultant of many factors including food consumption in non-hunger, non-famine periods. It appears that the food habits developed on the basis of experience and survival through successive generations provided an adequate, balanced diet. However, serfdom and then commercial agriculture led to less freedom of choice in foods and reduced dietary variety. The standard peasant diet in the 19th and part of the 20th century could be described as protein deficient—not all proteins, however, but primarily those amino acids that the body cannot synthesize, a series of essential amino acids. Foods containing the highest protein content and all eight essential amino acids (including meat, eggs and milk) were the most expensive to produce or purchase and too valuable for most peasants to eat. Peasants were forced to consume less and less relatively high-cost complete protein foods and rely heavily upon low-cost grain. A diet comprised primarily of grain invariably lacked one or more of the essential amino acids which resulted in a vast segment of the population regularly receiving less protein than that considered necessary for their body's growth, energy and maintenance.[6] Thus, occasional acute quantitative diet limitations which produced hunger and famine in the first 800 years or so of this millennium evolved into persistent quantitative diet limitations (undernutrition) compounded by serious qualitative diet limitations (malnutrition).

Table 3. Famine Years in Russia: 971–1970

Year(s)	Location	Cause
971[e]	Belobereg	War
997[e]	Belgorod	War
1024[a, e, f, g]	Suzdal'	Fear and panic (Women?)
1070–71[a, e, f, m]	Rostov-Volyn'	
1092–93[a, e, f]	Kiev	War and drought
1127[d, m]	Novgorod	Frost and floods
1128[a, d, f, x]	Polotsk, Novgorod, Pskov, Suzdal' and Smolensk	Excessive rain and floods
1137[d, m]	Novgorod	Frost and rebellion
1161[d, m, x]	Novgorod	Frost and drought
1188[d, m, x]	Novgorod	Frost
1193[e, m]	Southern Russia	?
1215[a, d, f, h, m, x]	Novgorod and Suzdal'	Frost and transportation
1230–31[a, d, f, g, m, x, a1]	Most of Russia except Kiev	Frost
1279[a, f]	Many regions of Russia	?
1308[d]	Novgorod	Epidemics, mice, grain speculation
1309[a, f]	Most of Russia	?
1332[a, b, f, x]	Southern Russia	Drought
1364–65[b]	Central East-European Plain	Drought
1366[b]	Land of Novgorod	Drought
1371[b]	Moscow and most of the Central East-European Plain	Drought
1421–22[a, d, f]	Land of Novgorod	Snow, rain and floods
1442–43[a, b, f]	Tver	Drought
1445[d, I]	Novgorod	Internal disruptions and bandits
1468[b]	Lands north and south centered on Pskov	North–heavy rains, floods South–drought (poor crops?)
1512[a, f]	No recorded indication of location	Poor crops
1525[b, v]	Most of Moscovy	Drought and transportation
1553[a, f]	No recorded indication of location	?
1557[a, f]	Trans-Volga	?
1570[a, f, o, s, t]	Moscovy, especially Novgorod	Political and massacre
1601–03[a, f, g, j, k, o, u, z, a1, d1]	Most of Moscovy	Mist, rain, frost and anarchy
1608[a, f]	Central East-European Plain	Anarchy
1630[a, f]	No recorded indication of location	?
1636[a, f]	No recorded indication of location	?
1650[a, f]	Pskov	?
1660–61[a, h]	Tobolsk, Solikamsk and other locations	Food speculation

Table 3. (cont'd)

Year(s)	Location	Cause
1820–22[a, f]	Vilno, Kherson, Belorussia, St. Petersburg, Novgorod, Tver, Pskov, Smolensk, Orlov, Kursk, Ekaterinoslav and Chernigov	?
1827[a]	Tavricheskaya	?
1830[f, h]	Volyn' and Pskov	?
1833–34[a, f, i, a1]	Novorussiya, Bessarabia, Vitebsk, Poland, Smolensk, Pskov, Orlov, Tambov, Ryazan' and Chernigov	Drought
1839–41[a, f, i, a1]	Tula, Ryazan', Kursk, Chernigov, Kostroma, Saratov, Vitebsk, Perm, Arkhangelsk and Liflan	?
1843–45[a, f, h, i, d1]	Pskov, St. Petersburg and Novgorod	?
1846[h, d1]	Bessarabia, Kharkov, Voronezh, Saratov and Orenburg	?
1848–50[a]	Novorussiya and in many other sections of Russia	?
1851[h, d1]	Moscow, Kaluga, Chernigov, Tver, Yaroslav, Tula, Kazan, Riga, Kharkov, Voronezh, Saratov and Vyatka	?
1855[h, d1]	No recorded indication of location	?
1863[a]	No recorded indication of location	?
1867–68[a, h, d1]	Finland	?
1873–74[a, f]	Samara and Orenburg	(Crop failure?)
1877[d1]	No recorded indication of location	?
1879–80[a, f, g]	Saratov	?
1883–84[a, f, h, a1, d1]	Kursk, Kazan', Kharkov and Vyatka	Drought
1891–93[a, b, c, f, h, j, z, d1]	Kazan', Vyatka, Perm, Tobolsk, Simbirsk, Samara, Saratov, Orenburg, Nizhniy Novgorod, Moscow, Tver', Penza, Ryazan' and other locations in Russia	Drought and political
1897–98[b, c, h, b1, c1, d1]	Western East-European Plain	Drought
1901[b, c, g]	Ukraine and areas along the Volga	Drought
1905–06[b, c, g, h, j, k, d1]	Ten provinces along the Volga and in Ukraine	Drought
1911–12[b, c, g, h, j, d1]	Along Volga and Eastern slopes of the Urals	Drought
1921–22[b, c, g, h, o, w, b1, d1]	Ten provinces along the Volga and in Ukraine	Drought, war and transportation
1933–34[b, c, h, n, q, w]	Ukraine, North Caucasus, along the Volga and in Kazakhstan	Political and "antisocial obstinacy"

Table 3. (cont'd)

Year(s)	Location	Cause
1941–43[p, b1]	Leningrad and in many parts of the USSR	War
1946–47[b, c, g, n, e1]	Ukraine and Central Industrial Region	Political and drought

Note: Information regarding year, location and cause of Russian famines is extremely difficult to secure; it is fragmentary and, in many instances, questionable. Undoubtedly, many Russian famines were not included in this table simply because they were not recorded. In a number of instances, the location was not indicated and the causes (or what was believed to be the causes of famine) not recorded unless unfavorable meteorological conditions directly attributed to a crop or a series of crop failures. Chroniclers of the distant past did take particular note of extraordinary natural phenomena and, in particular, droughts. The most valuable single source of famine data was F. K. Stefanovskiy's doctoral dissertation in medicine which noted and footnoted the major Russian famines from 1024 to 1892. This remarkable dissertation, published in Kazan' in 1893, is significant not only for its excellent bibliography and for the author's use of primary source material, but also because of Stefanovskiy's observations regarding food substitutes, farming conditions in the late 19th century and rural poverty. Although subject to error and revision, Table 3 comprises the most complete list of Russian famines that is available in the literature.

Sources: [a]F. K. Stefanovskiy, *Materiyaly dlya Izucheniya Svoisty Golodnogo Khleba* (Kazan', 1893); [b]I. E. Buchinskiy, "O Zasukhakh na Russkoy Ravnine za Posledneye Tysyacheletiye," from B. L. Dzerdzeevskiy, ed., *Sukhovei, ikh Proiskhozhdeniye i Bor'ba's Nimi* (Moskva, 1957), pp. 23–28; [c]A. I. Rudenko, ed., *Zasukhi v SSSR* (Leningrad, 1958), pp. 162–165; [d]M. N. Tikhomirova, *Novgorod: k 1100 Letiyu Goroda* (Moskva, 1964), pp. 299–309; [e]S. H. Cross and O. P. Sherbowitz-Wetzor, *The Russian Primary Chronicle: Laurentian Text* (Cambridge, 1953), pp. 90, 123, 134–135, 146, 150, 173, 178–179; [f]"Golod," *Entsiklopedicheskii Slovar' (Tom IX)* (Moskva, 1893), pp. 102–104; [g]"Golod," *Bol'shaya Sovetskaya Entsiklopediya (Tom 11)* (Moskva, 1952), pp. 623–626; [h]A. Keys, J. Brozek, A. Henschel, O. Mickelsen and H. L. Taylor, *The Biology of Human Starvation, Vols. I and II* (Minneapolis, 1950), pp. 1249–1251; [i]Baron von Haxthausen, *The Russian Empire* (London, 1968), pp. 68 & 439; [j]G. T. Robinson, *Rural Russia Under the Old Regime* (New York, 1932), pp. 18, 116, 152, 245; [k]V. O. Kluchevsky, *A History of Russia* (New York, 1960), pp. 55, 345, 265; [l]A. Rambaud, *The History of Russia; From the Earliest Times to 1877, Vol. I* (New York, 1890), pp. 85, 158–159; [m]G. Vernadsky, *Kievan Russia* (New York, 1948), pp. 315–316; [n]V. Kubijovyc, ed., *Ukraine: A Concise Encyclopaedia* (Toronto, 1963), pp. 200–201, 820–822, 898; [o]E. Seeger, *The Pagent of Russian History* (New York, 1950), pp. 148–149, 162, 340; [p]L. Goure, *The Siege of Leningrad* (Stanford, 1962); [q]S. and B. Webb, *Soviet Communism: A New Civilization, Vol. II* (New York, 1936), pp. 258–272; [r]S. Graham, *Peter the Great* (New York, 1929), p. 322; [s]J. Koslow, *Ivan the Terrible* (New York, 1961), p. 192; [t]H. von Staden, *The Land and Government of Muscovy* (Stanford, 1967), p. 29; [u]S. Graham, *Boris Godunof* (New Haven, 1933), pp. 145–146; [v]H. Lamb, *The March of Muscovy* (New York, 1948), p. 107; [w]P. N. Miliukov, C. Seignobos and L. Eisenmann, *History of Russia* (New York, 1968), Vol. 2, p. 55, and Vol. 3, pp. 362, 381–382, 410; [x]M. Tikhomirov, *Towns of Ancient Rus* (Moscow, 1959), pp. 69, 101, 102, 146; [z]M. T. Florinsky, *Russia: A History and an Interpretation* (New York, 1953), Vol. 1, pp. 225, 485, 601, and Vol. 2, pp. 474–481, 1159; [a1]P. I. Lyaschenko, *History of the National Economy of Russia, to the 1917 Revolution* (New York, 1949), pp. 101, 197–198, 364, 468; [b1]J. de Castro, *The Geography of Hunger* (Boston, 1952), pp. 50, 277; [c1]E. P. Prentice, *Hunger and History* (New York, 1939), pp. 112–113; [d1]H. H. Fisher, *The Famine in Soviet Russia, 1919–1923* (Stanford, 1927), pp. 475–480; [e1]N. S. Khrushchev, "Report to the Central Committee of the Communist Party of the Soviet Union," *Pravda*, Dec. 10, 1963, p. 5.

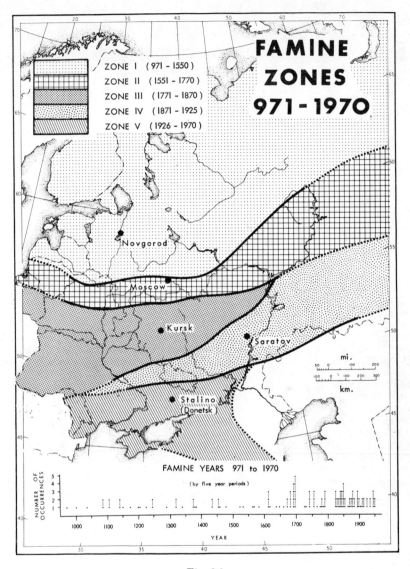

Fig. 26

Table 3 which details famine years in Russia from 971–1970, lists in excess of 100 famine years in this millennium—one famine year out of every 10 since 971. This table implies that Russian agriculture for a thousand years has been subject to natural or institutional factors so adverse to food production for Russian consumption that famine and hunger were endemic. A glance at the figure in

Fig. 27. Villagers fleeing from the Russian famine of 1892 slowly trudge towards St. Petersburg in hope of relief (from a wood-engraving printed in the *Illustrated London News*, and secured from the Prints and Photograph Section of the Library of Congress).

Table 3 for total famine and hunger years (and also the graph, *Famine Years 971 to 1970*, at the bottom of Figure 26) reveals that the number of instances increased gradually, reaching a high in the 1800-1899 period, then declined. Famines, in the period between 971 and 1599, were recorded only one year in every 17. This increased to approximately one famine year out of every five in the 1600 to 1799 period and one out of every three in the 1800 to 1899 period. Most disturbing is that in the 19th century the unbearable institution of serfdom, then pseudoemancipation and exploitative commercial agriculture were combined with intolerable and inept administrative tyranny, giving rise to a habitually hostile total environment where the ugly combination of famine and/or hunger presented itself two out of every three years (Figure 27).

LOCATION OF FAMINES

An attempt to locate the general area affected by famines and their primary causes led to the compilation of Table 3 which is by no means complete. However, the general location of 90 percent of the cited famines as well as the location of all famines in which a crop failure was directly attributed to drought has been noted. From this, three significant observations can be made at this time:

(1) The geography of Russian famines reflects the changing spatial dynamics of Russia's major agricultural regions from 971 to 1970. Specific and general locations of famines moved as the Russian state expanded to its present size and famines have appeared throughout a millennium in Russia's best agricultural regions.

(2) Droughts were not the primary factor in the creation of situations which eventually led to famine. Buchinskiy, while studying climatic change in the Ukraine, gathered statistics on droughts recorded by chroniclers for over a thousand years. He lists 60 droughts from 994 to 1954 and less than 25 percent of these droughts could possibly be considered a significant factor in famine formation. When Buchinskiy's statistics are collated with others and then compared with Table 3, a myth is shattered: when droughts occurred in Russian history a famine did not necessarily follow, i.e., drought and famine were not synonymous. Droughts were a primary factor in not more than 15 to 16 percent of the total Russian famine years since 971.[7]

(3) There seems to be unity in the diverse locations of famine which when mapped and analyzed form famine zones varying in time and space from 971 to 1970.

Five different zones (or linear combinations of regions) are delimited on the map comprising Figure 26. Famines occurred in these five zones in five different time periods:

Zone I (971-1550): Centered on Novgorod (a spatially interdependent enclave in a food deficit area) but including most of the northwest segment of the

Baltic-North Russian Plain, this zone recorded 32 famine years. Novgorod, in this time period, emerged as the largest city in Russia and a major cultural and commercial center. A pattern of trade developed in which most of the cash income was derived from exporting or trans-shipping raw materials or finished manufactured products. Novgorod, because of its location, was strongly influenced by the West and was able to remain apart from the contemporary Russian trend towards a spatially restricted, agricultural, neofeudal society. The changing of the primate city from the boundary between the forest-steppe and mixed forest (Kiev) to the taiga or the northern coniferous forest (Novgorod) should have reduced the possibility of drought occurrence.[8] However, an examination of the famines recorded in this zone revealed that drought was considered a primary factor in one out of four instances. This figure is very high and does not seem to be in accord with the climate of this zone today nor the climate of this zone as noted by the chroniclers during this period. Nevertheless, since this zone did not produce sufficient food in good years to supply its population, a crop failure was extremely serious and famine could only be averted by importing food. When the main routes of communication were closed for any reason, a famine of serious proportions took place in Novgorod.[9]

Zone II (1551-1770): Centered on Moscow but including segments of Zone I, this zone recorded 34 famine years. Not one famine in this zone was directly attributed to drought or drought as the primary factor—there is a political character to famines in this zone. As the center of Russian power and culture shifted from Kiev (located on the boundary between forest-steppe and mixed forest) to Novgorod (taiga) to Moscow (mixed forest) and as the center of Russian population also shifted, so did the famine zone. Moscow, in this time period, became an almost sacred center of a world power—by persuasion, marriage, annexation, financial manipulation, guile and force. As a central place it functioned as the hub of Russian secular and religious activities, as the major focus for the exchange of goods and finally as the heart of nascent processing and industrial activities. Here, a galaxy of Muscovite leaders shrewdly exploited the complete spectrum of social stratification to pursue a policy of national unification and growth regardless of loss of life and devoid of sentiment. Muscovite Russia's agricultural base was adequate for the feeding of its people. Famines did not simply occur in Zone II, they were created and, in many instances, prolonged by political decisions or indecisions.[10]

Zone III (1771-1870): Centered approximately on Kursk, south of Moscow in the forest-steppe, Zone III recorded 29 famine years with only three or four attributed to drought. As Imperial Russia expanded its borders south and westward at the expense of the Poles and Turks, Russian agriculturalists and invited foreign settlers poured into the newly acquired areas. Colonists moved out of the moist taiga and mixed forest vegetal zones into the deciduous forest and forest-steppe. The potential for drought increased as the settlers moved farther south and east. However, the number of settlers was limited, agricultural land was plentiful and yields of crops by Russian standards were considered good, yet 29 famine years were recorded in one hundred years. Famines in this time period were not a resultant of natural factors. An institutional factor, serfdom and the extension of serf bondage in a more brutal form, led to a severe aggravation of the peasants' alimentary resources.[11] Agricultural surpluses beyond the needs of a family were small but there developed an aggregate demand for the exchange (local and regional) of grain and animals or animal products primarily to meet legal and social obligations. The transition between a spatially restricted, extensive subsistence agricultural society to a spatially interdependent, extensive semi-commercial agricultural society came too quickly and without advances in agrotechniques or crops that would make it possible to support a large rural population. Thus, problems associated with the development of productive yet exploitative agriculture within the framework of serfdom played a major role in the creation of famine in this zone.

Zone IV (1871–1925): Centered on Saratov, south and east of Kursk in the steppes of southeastern European Russia, Zone IV recorded 19 famine years. At first, the settlers who moved from the moist forest and humid forest-steppe into the subhumid, flat, immense, grassy steppe were not overly cognizant of a decrease in total precipitation coupled with increased variability of annual receipts. However, it soon became cruelly apparent that severe droughts can and do occur here once every four or five years. Drought was a primary contributing factor in two out of every three famine years between 1871 and 1925.[12] This zone was an agricultural frontier into which land-hungry Russian people moved in response to some improvement in agrotechnology, overpopulation in certain rural areas and the desire for agricultural exports by the Imperial Russian Government. Grain from this zone played a major role in setting the price of Russian wheat on the world market yet one out of every three years was recorded as a famine year (Figure 28).[13]

Russian famines at the end of the 19th century and the beginning of the 20th were not *specifically* caused by drought, although a crop failure in an afflicted area without food reserves or food relief could lead to a famine.[14] Famines in this zone were created primarily by economic controls rather than the intimate relations of an agriculturalist to the land he tilled. Eventual overpopulation on marginal agricultural land, merciless taxation and an emphasis on heavy exports on grain *all* imposed upon a backward agricultural system in a habitually hostile environment contributed to abject rural poverty, hunger and famine. Extended rural-urban interaction which mushroomed in this spatially interdependent, extensive commercial agricultural society created an extreme form of regional specialization and abandonment of certain critical facets of regional self-sufficiency. To most of the peasants of Russia, and particularly those who survived the numerous famines which took place in Zone IV, commercial agriculture became commensal agriculture, i.e., an association beneficial to one partner.[15]

Zone V (1926–1970): Included in this zone is a sizable portion of the major Soviet winter wheat producing agricultural region, and it extends to the southern boundary of non-irrigated farming (excluding the Caucasus and selected parts of Soviet Central Asia). Zone V, centered on Stalino (Donetsk), encompasses steppe, dry-and-salt steppe, semidesert and finally merges with sandy deserts on the east. Spatially interdependent, extensive socialist planned agriculture is possible

Fig. 28. Cossack patrol near Kazan preventing the peasants from leaving their village during the Russian famine of 1892 (from a wood-engraving printed in the *Illustrated London News*, and secured from the Prints and Photograph Section of the Library of Congress).

Fig. 29. A cartload of dead children who died at a collection station in Samara Province during the Soviet famine of 1921 (Photo by Dr. Hill, American Red Cross, and secured from the Prints and Photograph Section of the Library of Congress).

153

without artificial irrigation but is subject to periodic droughts and excessive variability of harvests. Droughts occur here on the average of one out of three or four years.[16] In the 1926–1970 period, seven famine years were recorded, four in the dry, droughty zone and three elsewhere. Not one famine which took place in this zone in 44 years can be attributed solely to drought. However, in each of the famine instances, a drought occurred and there was a sharp decrease in total grain consumption but not so drastic a reduction as to produce famines which claimed millions of lives. The famines which have been recorded here were not caused by natural factors—man caused the famines in the 1926 to 1970 period (Figure 29).

The radical transformation from spatially interdependent, extensive commercial agriculture to centrally planned, spatially interdependent, extensive socialist agriculture unquestionably disrupted food production in the Soviet Union for decades. Agriculture under socialist central planning did not reap the presupposed benefits of increased efficiency, additional capital, new technology and the dissemination of information. Instead planning errors and administrative misjudgements were canonized and rigidly applied throughout the Soviet Union with dreadful repercussions. Political expediency, the desire to eliminate the recalcitrant segment of peasant class stratification which produced 50 percent of the commercial output of grain, the need to finance industrial expansion and national defense, collectivization and then an unfavorable agricultural year *created* the famine of 1933 and 1934.[17] And in 1946 and 1947, a decision to rigorously restore the provisions of the collective farm charter which was relaxed during World War II, coupled with the use of scarce grain in other segments of the world to promote Party goals, produced the last major famine recorded in Russian history.[18]

FACTORS CONTRIBUTING TO THE DEVELOPMENT OF FAMINES

The sequence of events which produced famine in every time period was complex and multifactored. It would be extremely difficult if not impossible to specifically identify the *one* cause of most famines. The primary natural factors in the creation of situations conducive for famines to develop, as outlined in Table 3 were climate, disease, rodents, insects and floods. The primary human factors recorded were war, political decisions, transportation, serfdom, communications, incompetence, perennial rural poverty, disease and/or pestilence, panic and food speculation. But food shortages resulting from any one or a number of natural factors should not have led to hunger, starvation or famine. In every instance, there appears to have been adequate foodstuff for everyone in the country and more than enough to carry the stricken area or areas through their time of troubles. The suffering which resulted from acute food shortages and famine in Russia was in large measure man-made, i.e., the failure of man to accord relief. In essence then, all of the famines which have occurred in Russia from 971–1970 can be predominantly attributed to human factors.

CONCLUSIONS

To conclude this exploratory study of the geography of Russian famines, it must be remembered that: (1) famines are as much a part of Russian history as are tyranny and oppression; and (2) droughts were not the primary cause of famines recorded in Russian history. Famines were not restricted, historically, to areas along the subhumid-semiarid boundaries (refer to Figure 26); famines have repeatedly taken place in the best agricultural regions of Russia at a particular time period. A detailed examination of the literature revealed that there has been little reason for famines to have emerged in the past and no reason why a famine should ever occur in the future. But it must be remembered that the failure of a government or a nation to alleviate hunger cannot be divorced from the general attitude of the privileged group a government serves. The problem of hunger and famine is not new in this world and neither is man's inhumanity to his fellow man, at times, to preserve a way of life, group ambitions or national goals.

NOTES

[1] Read S. A. Klepikov, *Pitaniye russkogo krest'yanina* (Moskva, 1920); V. Lenin, *Bor'ba za khleb* (Moskva, 1918); F. K. Stefanovskiy, *Materialy dlya izucheniya svoystv golognogo khleba* (Kazan', 1893); L. Tolstoi, *La Famine* (Paris, 1893); also H. H. Fisher, *The Famine in Soviet Russia, 1919-1923* (Stanford, 1927); and N. S. Khrushchev, *Pravda*, Dec. 10, 1963 (in report to the Central Committee CPSU).

[2] P. I. Kushner, ed., *Selo viryatino v proshlom i nastoyashchem* (Moskva, 1958), read in detail Chapter I and scan the entire monograph; P. I. Lyaschenko, *History of the National Economy of Russia, to the 1917 Revolution* (New York, 1949), pp. 179-181, 317-318, 729-735, 744-745; G. T. Robinson, *Rural Russia Under the Old Regime* (New York, 1932), pp. 97, 244-245; all of R. E. F. Smith, *The Origin of Farming in Russia* (Paris, 1959); V. P. Timoshenko, *Agricultural Russia and the Wheat Problem* (Stanford, 1932); and also E. Truog and D. Pronin, "A Great Myth: The Russian Granary," *Land Economics*, Vol. XXIX, No. 3, (1953), pp. 200-207.

[3] A. Borisov, *Klimaty SSSR* (Moskva, 1959), pp. 193-202; M. I. Davidova, A. N. Kamenskiy, N. P. Nekyukova and G. K. Tyshinskiy, *Fizicheskaya Geografiya SSSR* (Moskva, 1966), pp. 57-82; and all of I. A. Kiriyenko, *Zasukha i bor'ba s ney* (Nal'chik, 1948).

[4] "Golodaniye," *Bol'shaya Meditsinskaya Entsiklopediya, Tom 7* (Moskva, 1958), pp. 950-966; "Golodaniye," *Bol'shaya Sovetskaya Entsiklopediya, Tom 11* (Moskva, 1952), pp. 626-627; J. M. Ingersoll, *Historical Examples of Ecological Disaster: Famine in Russia, 1921-22; Famine in Bechuanaland, 1965* (New York, 1965); Secretariat, League of Nations: *Report on Economic Conditions in Russia, with Special Reference to the Famine of 1921-22 and the State of Agriculture* (Nancy-Paris-Strasbourg, 1922); and all of A. Alland, *Adaptation in Cultural Evolution: An Approach to Medical Anthropology* (New York, 1970).

[5] *Regulations Governing Supplies to the Ukhta-Pechora Reformatory Labor Camp of the NKVD* (approved by Ya. Moroz, Chief of the Management of the Ukhta-Pechora Camp of the NVKD, Senior Major of State Security), May 27, 1937, pp. 1-25, translation in the Hoover Library Special Collection; B. de Gef'e, *Chernaya godina. Sbornik o golode v Tsaritsynskoy gubernii i obzor deyatel'nosti Gubkompoigola za 1921-22 god* (Tsaritsyn, 1922); A. Ivanovsky, "Physical Modifications of the Population of Russia Under Famine,"

American Journal of Physical Anthropology, Vol. 6, (Oct., 1923), pp. 331–353; A. Keys, J. Brozek, A. Henschel, O. Mickelsen and H. L. Taylor, *The Biology of Human Starvation. Vols. I & II* (Minneapolis, 1950), described in over 1250 pages of clinical reports, experiments, and actual case studies; B. Slovtzov, "Nutrition Problems during Famine Conditions in Russia," *Nature*, Vol. 112, (Sept. 1, 1923), pp. 328–330.

[6]N. W. Desrosier, *Attack on Starvation* (Westport, Conn., 1961), pp. 6–20; M. Kleiber, *The Fire of Life: An Introduction to Animal Energetics* (New York, 1961), pp. 11–59; H. Mitchell, H. Rynbergen, L. Anderson and M. Dibble, *Nutrition in Health and Disease* (Philadelphia, 1968), pp. 35–45.

[7]I. Buchinskiy, "O zasukhakh na russkoy ravnine za posledneye tysyacheletiye," from B. Dzerdzeyevskiy, ed., *Sukhovei ikh proishkozhdeniye, i bor'ba s nimi* (Moskva, 1957), pp. 23–28; and A. Alpat'yev and V. Ivanova, "Kharaktika i geograficheskoye rasprostraneniye zasukh," in A. I. Rudenko, ed., *Zasukhi v SSSR* (Leningrad, 1958), pp. 31–45 and also appended material on pp. 162–165.

[8]For more information regarding droughts and the effects of droughts on agricultural productivity, see: M. Y. Nuttonson, "USSR: Some Physical and Agricultural Characteristics of the Drought Area and Its Climatic Analogues in the United States," *Land Economics*, Vol. XXV, No. 4, (1949), pp. 347–351; P. E. Lydolph, "The Russian Sukhovey," *Annals of the Association of American Geographers*, Vol. 54, No. 3, (1964), pp. 291–309; W. A. Dando, *Grain or Dust: A Study of the Soviet New Lands Program 1954-1963* (unpublished Ph.D. thesis, University of Minnesota, 1969); G. Z. Ventskevich, *Agrometeorology* (trans. of the Russian book, published in Leningrad, 1958, by the Israel Program for Scientific Translations, Jerusalem, 1961), pp. 153–155.

[9]M. Tikhomirov, *The Towns of Ancient Rus* (Moscow, 1959), pp. 101–102 (famine of 1215 in Novgorod). "The harvest was destroyed by frost in the volost', while it remained intact in the area around Torzhok. A famine set in the town because the Prince detained the transport of grain in Torzhok"; A. Rambaud, *The History of Russia: From the Earliest Times to 1877 (Vol. 1)* (New York, 1890), p. 85. In 1170, Novgorodians defeated a besieging army because of "their dependence on Souzdal for corn soon forced them to make peace"; and "Goloda i neurozhai v Rossii 1024 goda," *Dosug i Delo*, (1868), found in the Gosudarstvennaya Biblioteka SSSR imeni V. I. Lenina, Moskva.

[10]J. Koslow, *Ivan the Terrible* (New York, 1961), p. 192. (Famine of 1570) "The Oprichniki had cut down the amount of acreage under cultivation by driving large numbers of landowners and their peasants into exile and burning the fields of boyars suspected or implicated in treasonable activities. Still others, both nobles and commoners, had fled to faraway places to escape the terror, leaving large fertile areas unplanted, or in some cases, already planted to crops that rotted in the fields"; H. von Staden, *The Land and Government in Muscovy* (Stanford, 1967), p. 29 (Famine of 1570). "It was also a period of great famine, when one man killed another for a crust of bread. In the Podkletnye sela of the court, the Grand Prince had many thousands ricks of unthreshed grain in straw, which belonged to the household, but he would not sell them to his subjects, thus many thousands of people died in the country and were eaten by dogs."

[11]E. A. Morokhovets, *Krest'yanskoe dvizheniye 1827-1869* (Moskva, 1931); B. von Haxhausen, *The Russian Empire* (written by an astute first-hand observer of the Russian scene in the middle of this time period, trans. and reprinted in London, 1968), pp. 68 and 439; N. A. Maksimov, *Otchego byuayut zasuki* (Moskva, 1948); and J. D. Clarkson, *A History of Russia* (New York, 1969), p. 256.

[12]As noted repeatedly in A. Emel'yanov, *Golod v otrashenii russkoy literatury* (Kazan', 1921); *Golod i bor'ba nimi* (Ekaterinburg, 1921); V. A. Arnautov, *Golod i leti na Ukraine* (Kharkov, 1922); A. Sergiyev, C. Obradovich and L. Sosnovskiy, *Golod* (Irkutsk, 1921); and

N. M. Tulaikov, "Agriculture in the Dry Region of the U.S.S.R.," *Economic Geography*, Vol. 6, No. 1, (1930), pp. 54–80.

[13]S. S. Balzak, V. F. Vasyutin and Ya. G. Feigin, *Economic Geography of the USSR* (New York, 1949), p. 345. "According to the agricultural census of 1917, Samara Guberniya had 97.1% of its cultivated area in grain crops; Orenburg Guberniya, 97.3%; Ufa Guberniya, 94.2%; Don Oblast, 91.6%; and Saratov Guberniya, 93%.

[14]G. S. Queen, "American Relief in the Russian Famine of 1891–1892," *The Russian Review*, Vol. 14, No. 1, (1955), pp. 140–150; M. S. Miller, *The Economic Development of Russia, 1905–1914* (London, 1926), p. 49; C. H. Way, American Consul-General at St. Petersburg, *Consular Report 106* (Washington, D.C., 1889), p. 278; R. Philippot, "L'aggravation des Famines et la Legislation des Subsistence en Russia, 1891–1914," *Revue Historique*, No. 209, (1953), pp. 58–64.

[15]This theme is noted in the following works: *Golod i pomoshchi* (Kharkov, 1922); L. E. Shishko, *Golod i samoderzhaviye ili po ch'ey vine golodayet Russkiy Narod* (London, 1902); *Zasukha i mery borby s ney* (Berlin, BINT, 1924); and also in N. Samarin, *Zasukha Chasto li povtoryautsya zasukhi v Nizhnem Povolzh'ye?* (Saratov, 1925).

[16]V. Matskevich, *Sel'skoye khozyaystvo* (Moskva, 1971), pp. 11–21; plus peruse V. V. Sinel'shchikova, *Zasukha 1946 goda* (Moskva, 1949); V. V. Dokuchayev, *Nashy stepi prezhde i teper'* (Moskva, 1953); V. K. Ivanov, *Zasukha i bor'ba s ney* (Kuybyshev, 1947); and A. A. Verbin, *Zasukha i bor'ba s ney v stepi Ukrainy* (Odessa, 1948).

[17]S. and B. Webb, *Soviet Communism: A New Civilization (Vol. II)* (New York, 1936), pp. 258–272; G. Vernadsky, *Political and Diplomatic History of Russia* (Boston, 1936), p. 440; M. Fainsod, *Smolensk Under Soviet Rule* (New York, 1963), pp. 240–241; F. Belov, *The History of a Soviet Collective Farm* (New York, 1955), p. 12; D. G. Dalrymple, "The Soviet Famine of 1932–1934," *Soviet Studies*, Vol. XV, No. 3, (1964), pp. 250–284; D. G. Dalrymple, "The Soviet Famine of 1932–1934; Some Further References," *Soviet Studies*, Vol. XVI, No. 4, (1965), pp. 471–474; M. Lewin, "The Immediate Background of Soviet Collectivization," *Soviet Studies*, Vol. XVIII, No. 2, (1965), pp. 162–197.

[18]T. Mills, "Soviet Collective Farm Decree," *Foreign Agriculture*, Vol. II, (1947), pp. 64–69; N. Jasny, "The Plight of the Collective Farms," *Journal of Farm Economics*, Vol. XXX, (1948), pp. 304–321; K. Hutchinson, "Russia's Food Crisis," *Nation*, Vol. 163, (1946), p. 381.

Part IV

Food, population, policies and strategies

Chapter 10

Food availability and distribution

A PERSPECTIVE ON THE WORLD RURAL SCENE

The rural world of nostalgic memory or concise description no longer exists. Adoption and use of modern technology have destroyed the idea that societies fall into more or less spatially restricted, subsistence agricultural based systems or spatially interdependent, commercial agricultural based systems. Closed systems, traditional throughout most of human history, and open, interconnected worldwide systems, nurtured by improvements in communications, transportation and technology, overlap and/or exist together within geographic regions. Contemporary urban lifestyles are remarkably similar and many cosmopolitan central places are located within traditional cultural areas. These central points of innovation and diffusion impact strongly upon their hinterland. As a result, a new renewed rural world is emerging, reshaped in character, outlook and way of life. Technology diffused internationally is the tool rebuilding the rural world. It is a force no always welcomed by those not touched by its impact and is often employed without realizing its far-reaching consequences. Massive changes within the rural world, stemming from advances and partial or complete acceptance of selected aspects of modern technology, are revolutionary in impact. Problems existing and emerging reflect a clash between different sets of values and expectations. Though neither as visible nor as audible as are the crises in many urban centers, these changes are crucial for world food availability and distribution. Applied scientific and technological policies are a concensus mix of historical forces modified by economic and political actions.[1] Any change in

Fig. 30. The rural world of nostalgic memory no longer exists. Technology diffused internationally is the tool remolding the rural world (Photo by Ken Jorgensen, North Dakota Travel Division).

rural and nonrural systems brings problems to individuals, families, villages, towns, cities, institutions, agencies, governments, food production, food distribution and food needs. Abrupt change brings problems in land use and management, pricing and marketing, production and distribution, capital expenditures and investments and competing farm organization schemes.[2] Massive rural change raises issues of poverty and affluence, hunger and dieting, powerless and powerful, voluntary or state action, peace and war and also ways of directing rural change toward a peaceful world without acute hunger and famine (Figure 30).

NUTRITION AND VULNERABLE CULTURAL GROUPS

Currently it is estimated that at least one out of every six people who live in our world is undernourished. Most of these hungry people live in developing, spatially restricted, subsistence agricultural based economic systems where food production has not kept pace with food needs. Daily caloric intake in spatially restricted, subsistence societies averages only about 2,000 calories, compared to 3,000 for spatially interdependent, commercial agricultural based economic systems. The *FAO Food Balances 1964-66* report, listing calories per person per

Table 4. 1964–66 Average Calories per Person per Day
from Eleven Food Groups

Country	Calories per person per day
Developed spatially interdependent commercial agricultural societies	
United States	3,156
Canada	3,142
Australia and N. Zealand	3,192
USSR	3,182
EC-9	3,111
Eastern Europe	3,080
Japan	2,416
South Africa	2,734
Other Western Europe	2,897
Average	3,043
Less developed spatially restricted subsistence agricultural societies	
Argentina	2,885
Mexico and Central America	2,425
Other South America	2,276
West Asia	2,316
China (PRC)	2,045
Brazil	2,541
East Asia and Pacific	1,969
North Africa	2,290
South Asia	1,975
Southeast Asia	2,121
Africa South of Sahara	2,154
Average	2,097
World	2,386

Source: FAO Food Balances 1964–66.

day from eleven food groups, ranks Australia and New Zealand high with 3,192 and portions of East Asia and Pacific region low with 1,969 (Table 4). This average has risen in the late 1970s to over 2200 calories in developing countries and to approximately 3400 in developed countries. People in less economically developed countries are highly dependent on cereal grains, in most years more than 60 percent of their calories are derived from direct consumption of cereals. Those who dwell in economically developed countries consume three times as much sugar, four times as much meat and six times as much milk and eggs. Production and consumption of cereals per capita in developing countries are low when compared with developed countries. Direct consumption of cereal grains in both Canada and the United States, for example, is less than 10 percent of all used as food—90 percent is fed to livestock and poultry. Low personal incomes in developing countries limit diets to cereals or other inexpensive foods. As low personal incomes increase, consumption of grain also increases until a threshhold is reached. In almost all societies, the quantity of cereals consumed directly for food decreases when incomes rise above a certain level.

Malnutrition, at this stage of the world's development, is a direct function of poverty and ignorance. Most of the malnourished live in spatially restricted, subsistence agricultural societies in Asia and Africa. To be more specific, the estimated number of people with insufficient protein/energy supply in 1970 ranged from less than 3 percent in developed regions of the world to 25 percent in the Asian countries with centrally planned economies, 13 percent in Latin America, 30 percent in the Far East, 18 percent in the Near East and 25 percent in Africa (Table 5). The top ten food importing countries of the developing world in 1975, according to John B. Parker, a USDA Agricultural economist, were: India, Egypt, South Korea, Iran, Brazil, Mexico, Taiwan, Iraq, Saudi Arabia and Indonesia.[3] Parker noted that these agricultural commodity importing countries had common food problems, including: (1) a high proportion of the food imported went to rapidly growing urban centers (over 90 percent of the bread in Cairo and Alexandria, Egypt; Seoul and Pusan, Korea and at times Bombay, India is made from imported wheat); (2) agricultural imports are primarily cereals (80 percent for India, 68 percent for Egypt and 59 percent for Korea); (3) current programs to feed the peoples of these top ten importing countries rely upon larger imports of agricultural raw materials and food; (4) large grain imports are viewed favorably in most importing countries for they are

Table 5. Estimated Number of People with Insufficient Protein/Energy Supply, 1970

Region	Population (billion)	Number below lower limit (million)	Percent below lower limit
Developed	1.07	28	3
Developing, excluding Asian centrally planned economies	1.75	434	25
Latin America	0.28	36	13
Far East	1.02	301	30
Near East	0.17	30	18
Africa	0.28	67	25
World (excluding Asian centrally planned economies)	2.83	462	16

Source: U.N., *Preliminary Assessment of the World Food Situation* (Rome: 1974).

believed to lower domestic inflation rates and maintain low domestic food prices and (5) trade policies implemented indicate little concern for food self-sufficiency.

Food habits of cultural groups are, in essence, the product of a group's present natural environment and past history. Resistance to changing food patterns are particularly strong in nations where food commonly accounts for more than one-half of a food consumer's income. People normally tend to be conservative in what they eat and children are taught what is considered socially acceptable behavior in relation to food. Foods imported are usually the same types of food traditionally consumed. When individuals or groups leave their native area or country, they take with them their concepts of diet. Forces of tradition can be slowly overcome in this modern world if the proper approach and if the need is presented clearly and succinctly. Cultural groups which strongly maintain traditional food habits reside where communication and transportation nets are not highly developed or where religion reinforces traditional dietary habits. Urban life and travel outside a particular cultural area exert a strong influence for modification of food patterns. The two most vulnerable cultural groups to food shortages, malnutrition, undernutrition and famine are those unwilling to modify traditional diets and those who unknowingly disrupt a balanced, nutritious diet that had evolved in an area through time.

TRENDS IN WORLD FOOD PRODUCTION

Growth in the average annual rates of agricultural production and food supply has been greater than increases in world population since the 1960s, but estimated food production per capita is less. Nations with developed market economies in the 1961–70 period recorded a 2.2 percent annual increase in food production, and increased this figure in the 1970–76 period to 2.4 percent. Average annual increases in food production per capita stabilized in developed countries at 1.4 percent during the past sixteen or so years. Increments in total food production were less in developed countries than developing countries in the 1961–70 and 1970–76 periods. Growth of total food productivity in developing countries was 3.1 percent through the 1960s, then declined to 2.7 percent in the seventies. Unfortunately, food production per capita dropped precipitously in developing countries during the same time period (Table 6). Computed average annual rates of increases in food production when related to population reveal that food production per capita is consistently less in developing countries than in developed countries. Food production per capita during the 1970–76 period in developing countries has been lowered to a critical level. The already large difference in annual per capita food production between developed and developing countries is becoming greater each year.

Long-term trends in world food production do not reveal the short-term fluctuations nor the spatial dynamics of food imbalances that cause serious temporary food crises. Annual index numbers and variations in food production

Table 6. Average Annual Rates of Growth of Food Production in Relation to Population: World and Regions, 1961–65 to 1970 and 1970–1976

Region	Population (% per year)		Food production (% per year)			
			Total		Per capita	
	1961–1970	1970–1976	1961–1970	1970–1976	1961–1970	1970–1976
Developed market economies	1.0	0.9	2.2	2.4	1.2	1.5
North America	1.2	0.9	1.9	3.1	0.7	2.1
Western Europe	0.7	0.6	2.3	1.6	1.6	1.0
Oceania	1.8	1.7	2.9	3.1	1.1	1.3
Other	1.4	1.6	3.3	2.1	1.8	0.6
Eastern Europe and USSR	1.0	0.9	2.9	1.9	1.9	1.0
All developed countries	1.0	0.9	2.4	2.3	1.4	1.4
Developing market economies	2.6	2.6	3.3	2.8	0.7	0.2
MSA[a] countries	2.4	2.5	3.1	2.1	0.7	-0.4
Non-MSA countries	2.7	2.7	3.3	3.4	0.6	0.7
Africa	2.5	2.7	2.7	1.2	0.1	-1.4
Latin America	2.7	2.8	3.5	3.3	0.8	0.5
Near East	2.7	2.8	3.0	4.2	0.3	1.4
Far East	2.5	2.5	3.5	2.8	0.9	0.2
Other	2.5	2.5	2.1	1.5	-0.4	-1.0
Asian centrally planned economies	1.8	1.7	2.7	2.4	0.9	0.6
All developing countries	2.3	2.3	3.1	2.7	0.7	0.3
World	1.9	1.9	2.7	2.4	0.8	0.5

[a]MSA—most seriously affected.
Source: World Food Survey (Rome: Food and Agriculture Organization of the United Nations, 1977), p. 4.

within developed and developing countries from 1961–65 to 1976 are graphed on Figure 31. Bad weather reduced the growth rate of food production per capita (per caput) within developing countries in 1966. Food production increased in the 1967–70 period in response to better weather and the acceptance of high-yielding "green revolution" cereals and technology. World food production declined in 1972 in absolute terms and was attributed to bad weather in many developing and developed countries. Since 1972, there has been a significant recovery in developing countries and an erratic recovery in developed countries. Grouping all nations in the world into developed or developing categories masks the increasing disparities in growth of food production among individual nations. For instance, those nations most seriously affected by recurring food problems comprise approximately 56 percent of the developing countries' population. A widening disparity exists between the least and the most developed of the developing countries. Regional diversity between developing nations should also

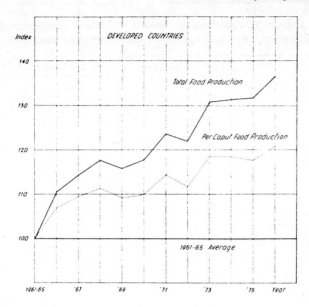

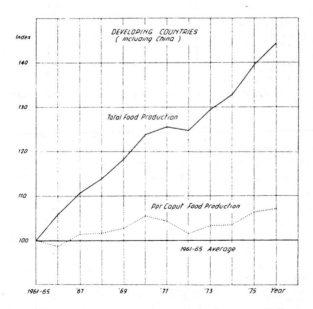

Fig. 31. Total and per capita food production in developed and developing countries, 1961–65 to 1976.
Source: World Food Survey (Rome: Food and Agriculture Organization of the United Nations, 1977), p. 5.

Table 7. Average Annual Rates of Growth of Cereal Production in Relation to Population: World and Regions, 1961–1965 to 1970 and 1970–1976

Region	Population (% per year)		Cereal production (% per year)			
			Total		Per capita	
	1961–65 to 1970	1970–1976	1961–65 to 1970	1970–1976	1961–65 to 1970	1970–1976
Developed market economies	1.0	0.9	2.1	3.0	1.1	2.1
North America	1.2	0.9	1.9	4.1	0.7	3.2
Western Europe	0.7	0.6	2.8	1.3	2.1	0.7
Oceania	1.8	1.7	3.1	6.5	1.2	4.7
Other	1.4	1.6	0.4	0.9	-1.0	-0.7
Eastern Europe and USSR	1.0	0.9	4.1	1.6	3.1	0.7
All developed countries	1.0	0.9	2.8	2.5	1.8	1.6
Developing market economies	2.6	2.6	3.7	3.0	1.1	0.3
MSA countries	2.4	2.5	3.9	2.0	1.4	-0.4
Non-MSA countries	2.7	2.7	3.4	4.0	0.7	1.3
Africa	2.5	2.7	2.9	1.9	0.4	-0.8
Latin America	2.7	2.8	3.5	3.8	0.7	1.0
Near East	2.7	2.8	2.0	5.0	-0.6	2.1
Far East	2.5	2.5	4.2	2.5	1.6	0.0
Other	2.5	2.5	4.3	2.3	1.7	-0.2
Asian centrally planned economies	1.8	1.7	2.9	2.5	1.1	0.7
All developing countries	2.3	2.3	3.4	2.8	1.1	0.4
World	1.9	1.9	3.1	2.7	1.2	0.7

Source: World Food Survey (Rome: Food and Agriculture Organization of the United Nations, 1977), p. 7.

be noted, for decline in food production growth rates was most alarming in Africa and the Far East. African food production problems from 1970 to 1976 are a harbinger of future hunger and starvation (Table 7). Food production per capita declined, as a result of high population growth rates in the 1960s, within 56 out of 128 developing nations. Population growth rates continued to be higher than food production growth rates within these 56 countries in the 1970s, and the number of political entities in this dangerous situation increased to 69.

World food security is based upon cereal production, especially in developing countries, since cereals account for more than 50 percent of total world food energy supplies. Cereal production in developed market economies increased in the 1961–65 to 1970 and the 1970–76 periods (Table 7); only the countries of Western Europe, Eastern Europe and the Soviet Union showed decline. Cereal production growth rates within developing market economies diminished in the same time period. In the countries with the most serious current food problems (MSA's), annual growth rates of cereal production declined from 3.9 percent in

Table 8. Use of Cereals as Food and Feed: World and Regions, 1961–1963,
1969–1971 and 1972–1974

Region	Food (mill. metric tons)			Feed (mill. metric tons)			Share of feed in consumption (food and feed) (%)		
	1961–1963	1969–1971	1972–1974	1961–1963	1969–1971	1972–1974	1961–1963	1969–1971	1972–1974
Developed market economies	90.1	89.6	90.8	197.3	265.4	272.2	69	75	75
North America	19.2	20.2	20.6	120.2	154.7	149.0	86	88	88
Western Europe	45.4	43.4	43.4	69.3	93.8	103.9	60	68	71·
Oceania	1.5	1.6	1.8	1.9	3.3	2.8	56	67	61
Other	24.0	24.4	25.0	5.9	13.6	16.5	20	36	40
Eastern Europe and USSR	68.9	69.7	69.4	60.0	124.2	143.9	47	64	67
All developed countries	159.0	159.3	160.2	257.3	389.6	416.1	62	71	72
Developing market economies	226.6	289.3	312.9	24.1	36.0	41.4	10	11	12
Africa	28.4	36.2	39.0	1.3	2.0	2.2	4	5	5
Latin America	27.7	35.3	39.7	13.0	21.7	26.1	32	38	40
Near East	24.9	31.2	34.1	7.2	8.6	8.8	22	22	21
Far East	145.5	186.4	199.9	2.6	3.7	4.3	2	2	2
Other	0.1	0.2	0.2	–	–	–	–	–	–
Asian centrally planned economies	131.6	171.1	185.6	23.2	30.9	33.4	15	15	15
All developing countries	358.2	460.4	498.5	47.3	66.9	74.8	12	13	13
World	517.2	619.7	658.7	304.6	456.5	490.9	37	42	43

Source: World Food Survey (Rome: Food and Agriculture Organization of the United Nations, 1977), p. 10.

the 1960s to only 2.0 percent during the early 1970s. Cereal production during the past 15 years has declined in Africa, the Far East and the Near East. Per capita production dropped to a dangerous level in Africa, and in all developing nations per capita average annual cereal production was reduced from 1.1 to 0.4 percent in the 1970-76 period. World cereal production also declined in the 1970-76 period from a 1.2 percent rate of growth per capita to a critical 0.7 percent annual average. Concomitant with reduced cereal production, the share of cereals used as animal feed rose from 62 percent during the 1961-63 period to 72 percent in 1972-74 within all developed countries. North America's use of cereals for animal feed is the highest in the world (Table 8). Feed use of cereals in Eastern Europe and the USSR rose from 47 percent in the early 1960s to 67 percent in the early 1970s. Use of grain as animal feed rather than direct human consumption has never been significant in developing world countries—averaging between 10 and 15 percent per year

FACTORS AFFECTING WORLD FOOD PRODUCTION

Food producers' ability to provide sustenance for the world's inhabitants depends upon their use of land and other resources, weather and climate, yield-increasing technologies and agricultural efficiency and socioeconomic incentives. Constraints placed upon food production by land have been a concern of many humanitarians and economists for centuries. Malthus presented the concept of "limited quantity of land–unlimited growth of population" in 1798. Malthus' discouraging implications were repeatedly proven incorrect when new sources of land and new ways of increasing food production materialized after each succeeding wave of anxiety. Food producers currently use only one-half the world's potentially suitable land for crop production. One of the most comprehensive studies undertaken to determine world food production potentials concluded that land suitable for crops in developing regions totaled 1,145 million hectares, and land used to produce crops totaled 512 million hectares—only 45 percent of available cultivable land in regions with severe food problems was used for crops.[4] Iowa State University researchers estimate 3.2 billion hectares of the total world land could be used to produce food, but only 1.4 billion hectares were utilized.[5] All students of factors affecting world food production recognize, however, that there are very serious regional problems in land available for traditional crops in many densely populated, developing countries. Egypt, India and Bangladesh, for example, are nations with limited opportunities for expanding cultivated area. Each of these countries and many others have opportunities to increase food production on land now in use by employing intensive, land conserving agrotechniques. Land becomes less significant in the food-famine equation as food producers become aware of new methods to increase output and as food producers can afford to implement these new methods. Spatially interdependent, commercial agricultural systems rely more on technology for improving yields per hectare and increasing production than continuous expansion of cropland. Limited agricultural land is not the prime factor affecting food production in most spatially restricted, subsistence agricultural systems, but yields per unit of land. Land does become especially critical in food production when the primary resources available are human labor and farm produced capital (Figure 32).[6]

Most of the world's food production is dependent upon favorable local weather and climate. Weather and climate control the rates of photosynthesis and other physical factors which influence crop production. The major cause of season-to-season variations in crop yields is fluctuations in weather and climate. Persistent droughts, heavy flooding, severe winter weather and shifts in the monsoon have induced crop failure or destroyed crops, and have forced people to tap food reserves from non-affected, food producing areas. Great variations in what some claim to be normal weather patterns play havoc at times upon food production in the Soviet Union, the Great Plains Physiographic Region of the United States and Canada, the African Sahel, monsoon Asia and Oceania. Western Europe, most of the United States and Latin America, Africa south of the Sahel and non-monsoon Asia experience relatively constant agroclimatic patterns. Examination of yield variations in the world's major cereal producing areas reveals that when adverse weather reduces yields in one part of the world, adverse weather will also reduce yields in other parts of the world. Good weather and high yields also tend to be experienced at the same time in the world's

Fig. 32. Spatially interdependent, commercial agricultural systems, such as in the Red River Valley of North Dakota and Minnesota, rely on technology for improving yields per hectare and increasing production (North Dakota State Soil Conservation Service photo).

major grain producing areas. Oscillations in crop weather from year to year within regions are normal happenings, and the overall pattern of weather is random. Climate, the synthesis of weather elements and controls over a considerable number of years at a place, has been thought to be much more stable than short-term fluctuations in weather—almost a permanent meteorological situation that could never change in an individual's lifetime. Concerns for climatic region shifts or climatic change have focused upon the gradual cooling of the Northern Hemisphere since the mid-1940s. Whether related to this cooling incident or other factors, there have been shifts in climatic belts, disrupted planetary wind patterns and modifications in many-year precipitation regimes. Recent weather aberrations, such as the persistent drought in the Sahel and monsoon failures in India, have been attributed to changing world climates. Reid Bryson, Director of the Institute for Environmental Studies at the University of Wisconsin, stated, in the February 1974 issue of *Fortune* magazine, that "if it continues, it will affect the whole human occupation of the earth—like a billion people starving." Changes in world climates that would affect world food production cause justifiable anxiety among those who study food-famine topics and those who value every life on earth.[7] All projections of future world food production are based upon normal (?) weather affecting crops in a particular agricultural region.

In developed market economies, rapid increases in food production are directly attributed to increases in nonland inputs, favorable agricultural weather, a benevolent world climate and a strong incentive to produce more agricultural products. With favorable weather and climate, world food production could be increased greatly by doubling the amount of land currently utilized. This approach is improbable, and yield increasing technologies, plus agricultural efficiency, will be the primary source of future additional food stocks. Improved seed, better cultivation practices, new herbicides and pesticides and greater use of fertilizer increased yields dramatically in Western Europe and North America after World War II. Great successes in increasing yields have been recorded in developing-world nations when similar modern agrotechniques were employed. Adoption of high yielding wheat and rice varieties along with the technologies necessary to grow them is referred to as the Green Revolution. Inputs necessary to implement this revolution include fertilizers, improved crop management, insecticides, pesticides and water control. The Green Revolution originated in Mexico in the mid-1940s and yields doubled. Selected agricultural areas in India, Pakistan, the Philippines, Indonesia and Bangladesh were supplied similar seed and technological assistance in the mid-1960s. Agricultural production increased where land, water, capital and attitudes were favorable for this combination of transplanted modern agrotechniques. However, this revolution has not solved the food-deficit problems in the tropics. In many areas, constraints placed upon innovation by cultural bias, farm size, capital availability, land tenure, risk, fertilizer requirements and water needs reduced its full impact. Fertilizers, combined with an associated package of inputs, are a key factor in yield increases everywhere. World fertilizer production and use have increased rapidly in the past few decades. Relatively low energy costs, increases in demand, fertilizer aid shipments by the United States and fears of a famine in the 1963–66 period spurred the use of chemical fertilizers. Recent oil price increases have raised fertilizer cost substantially, but this is only one of many price raising factors. The current world shortage restricts developing nations from using more fertilizers. There is a strong relationship between the amount of fertilizer effectively used in developing countries and food deficits.[8]

To expend time, labor and limited capital for land improvement, irrigation, weather modification (?), new seed, field equipment, herbicides, pesticides and fertilizers, an agriculturalist must be rewarded. Any change in a traditional way of producing food must clearly show potential for increased profit; the food producer must have a socioeconomic incentive. If the total cost of producing and transporting an old or new product is high relative to the prospective net profit, the farmer will not adopt or produce the product. If that which is paid a food producer for an agricultural product has limited purchasing power, and if there is nothing of value to buy, a food producer will not plant or sell more than is necessary for survival. Incentive problems are different in subsistence agricultural systems than those in commercial agricultural systems, for the basic socioeconomic goals are different. This problem is magnified where the agricultural production research effort is successful and technological development is rapid; then the production system of an agricultural enterprise may need to change annually. Socioeconomic incentives sufficiently strong to override the risks must be established at the farm level and induce farm decision makers to innovate, adopt new techniques and establish new and more efficient food yielding systems.[9] An agriculturalist who believes a new crop, product or technology can be blended into an existing system and increase real income will do so. The ultimate decision point in the food chain is the individual food producer and if the producer does not choose to innovate, the elaborate and complex process of agricultural modernization designed to provide more food for a hungry world is retarded or grinds to a halt.

WORLD FOOD SUPPLY BALANCE SHEET: DIVERSITY BETWEEN THE DEVELOPED AND DEVELOPING MARKET ECONOMIES

Average annual rates of growth in food production, total and per capita food production and average annual rates of growth in cereal production need not be the same or equate to food supplies available in a region or nation. Per capita daily food supply in terms of calories, absolute and as a percentage of requirements (Table 9), was obtained by dividing the food available for human consumption by the population of a country. This figure represents only an average calorie supply for the population as a whole and does not indicate what is actually consumed by individuals. Average daily calories, available per person in various world regions and their supply as a percent of daily requirements, as given in Table 9, vary greatly between developed market economies, developing market economies and the most seriously affected nations (MSA) within the developing market economies group. These data indicate that calories available per person have increased worldwide from 1961–63 to 1972–74. Calories available per capita in all developed and developing countries in the study period increased steadily. Daily per capita calorie supplies were highest in North America, 3,530 calories in the 1972–74 period, and lowest in the Far East, 2,070 calories. There was great disparity among calorie supply trends among developing market regions. The increase was slight during the 1970s in the Near East and Latin America, and decreased in Africa and the Far East. Particularly disturbing was the deteriorating situation in the most seriously affected (MSA) countries of the developing market economies group. Calorie supply as a percent of requirements declined from 91 to 90 percent in the 1961–63 to 1972–74 period. It must also be noted that the per capita availability of protein and fat disparity between developed and developing countries was larger than calorie supply. Daily per capita protein supply in developing countries was only 58 percent of that in developed countries. This percentage remained unchanged in the 1960s and 1970s. Differences are related to the availability of animal protein for levels of vegetable origin protein were similar in both developed and developing countries.

Table 9. Per Capita Daily Food Supply in Terms of Calories, Absolute and as Percentage of Requirements

Region	Calorie supply (kilocalories per capita)				Supply as percent of requirement			
	1961–1963	1964–1966	1969–1971	1972–1974	1961–1963	1964–1966	1969–1971	1972–1974
Developed market economies	3,130	3,170	3,280	3,340	123	124	129	131
North America	3,320	3,360	3,500	3,530	126	127	133	134
Western Europe	3,200	3,230	3,330	3,390	125	126	130	132
Oceania	3,300	3,320	3,320	3,370	124	125	125	127
Other	2,570	2,650	2,760	2,850	109	112	117	121
Eastern Europe and USSR	3,240	3,270	3,420	3,460	126	127	133	135
All developed countries	3,170	3,200	3,330	3,380	124	125	132	132
Developing market economies	2,110	2,130	2,190	2,180	92	93	96	95
MSA countries	2,040	2,030	2,080	2,030	91	90	92	90
Non-MSA countries	2,210	2,250	2,330	2,360	95	96	100	101
Africa	2,070	2,100	2,150	2,110	89	90	92	91
Latin America	2,400	2,470	2,530	2,540	101	104	106	107
Near East	2,290	2,340	2,410	2,440	93	95	98	100
Far East	2,010	2,000	2,070	2,040	91	90	94	92
Other	2,130	2,200	2,290	2,340	93	96	100	103
Asian centrally planned economies	1,960	2,110	2,220	2,290	83	90	94	97
All developing countries	2,060	2,120	2,200	2,210	89	92	95	96
World	2,410	2,460	2,540	2,550	101	103	106	107

Source: World Food Survey (Rome: Food and Agriculture Organization of the United Nations, 1977), p. 16.

Also, developed countries had more fat available for their citizens than developing countries, three to almost four times as much in the 1961-63 to 1972-74 period.

Food balance sheets show only average supplies per person and these averages conceal great differences among socioeconomic groups within a country or region. Food consumption patterns vary widely due to locality, social customs, income and many other factors. The only truly accurate method of quantifying supplies, consumption and nutritional quality of a country is to make detailed family and household food surveys.

PATTERNS OF INTERNATIONAL FOOD TRADE: A BRIEF REGIONAL ANALYSIS

After food has been produced, whether from plants or animals, it must be stored, transported and distributed over great distances, then stored again prior to consumption. Great quantities of food are lost in harvesting, destroyed by pests and microbes, lost in storage by deterioration and made inedible by vermin, insects, molds, etc. Still more food is lost in transporting it to distribution points, and again food is lost in preparation and the consumptive processes. Food production, storage, transportation, preparation and consumption patterns vary widely. Some of the reasons for this are related to regional physical characteristics and people's habits. During the last few centuries, most of the useful food plants and food producing animals originating in one region have been spread to other regions of the world. Food distribution and commodity flow on a continental and worldwide basis are a recent development. Refrigerated ships, gas storage and rapid transport (truck and air) are all modern inventions. Developments in food preservation and transportation have greatly reduced people's dependency upon locally-produced foods. In this age when great masses of people live in large urban centers, food must be stored and transported long distances if there is to be a continuous urban food supply throughout the year. Affluent countries are able to secure food from all ends of the earth and provide their citizens a diet with great variety. Seasons are ignored and food is abundant year round in developed, urban-industrial countries, while people anxiously await the next harvest in less developed, less affluent countries. People in developing countries still live mainly on foods produced locally and their diet is more monotonous than the diets of people in developed nations. Universally, diets become more varied and nutritious as income rises. In low-income, spatially restricted, subsistence agricultural systems, most farms are self-sufficient in the sense that only a third of so of total production is sold. Cash earned is used to pay rents, taxes and interests, plus finance some consumptive expenditures through commercial channels. Crop and animal products, that pass into town and urban markets, tend to be the higher quality foodstuffs and inedible raw materials. The majority of world staple and comfort-type foods produced are traded or sold, but only a tenth or so internationally.

Food is a commodity and the same forces that determine the supply and demand for other commodities also give impetus to how much food is produced and how much is consumed. The demand and supply of food have special properties and increase fairly uniformly and predictably with population growth, education and income. Food supply can be unstable because of weather, natural phenomena, human actions and governmental decisions.[10] When supplies fall below a certain limit, people will sacrifice a great deal for food and food prices will rise sharply. However, when food supplies rise above this limit, people will not need the additional food and are not willing to pay for the surplus. Poor people spend much of their limited income on basic foods. Basic foods, such as cereals and pulses, exhibit the least flexibility in demand, and experience the greatest fluctuations in prices.

Canada and the United States are the current major suppliers of cereals, oilseeds and selected livestock products to the world food market, often one-half of the annual world trade in cereals and oilseeds. North American agriculture is flexible and can quickly adapt to changing demands of the world food market. A large proportion of the world's productive agricultrual land is here and there is considerable scope for further expansion in the future. Exports of cereals and oilseeds have been at record highs as the result of favorable world demand and prices. Livestock production could be expanded but North American demands

Table 10. Rates of Growth of Agricultural Production in Relation to
Population: World Regions, 1961–1965 to 1970 and 1970–1976

Region	Total population		Agricultural production			
			Total		Per capita	
	1961–1965 to 1970	1970–1976	1961–1965 to 1970	1970–1976	1961–1965 to 1970	1970–1976
Developed market economies	1.0	0.9	1.9	2.2	0.9	1.3
North America	1.2	0.9	1.4	2.8	0.2	1.9
Western Europe	0.7	0.6	2.2	1.6	1.5	1.0
Oceania	1.8	1.7	2.8	1.3	1.0	-0.4
Other	1.4	1.6	3.1	2.0	1.7	0.4
Eastern Europe and USSR	1.0	0.9	2.8	2.0	1.8	1.1
All developed countries	1.0	0.9	2.2	2.1	1.2	1.2
Developing market economies	2.6	2.6	3.1	2.6	0.5	0.0
MSA countries	2.4	2.5	3.1	1.9	0.6	-0.5
Non-MSA countries	2.7	2.7	3.1	3.1	0.4	0.4
Africa	2.5	2.7	2.7	1.1	0.2	-1.5
Latin America	2.7	2.8	2.9	2.0	0.2	0.1
Near East	2.7	2.8	3.1	3.9	0.4	1.1
Far East	2.5	2.5	3.3	2.6	0.8	0.1
Other	2.5	2.5	2.3	1.6	-0.2	-0.8
Asian centrally planned economies	1.8	1.7	2.8	2.5	1.0	0.7
All developing countries	2.3	2.3	3.0	2.6	0.7	0.2
World	1.9	1.9	2.5	2.3	0.6	0.4

Source: World Food Survey (Rome: Food and Agriculture Organization of the United Nations,
1977), p. 11.

for imported meats and specialty animal products make it likely that this region
will continue to be an importer.

Western Europe, a region of small and medium size agricultural holdings, has
increased food production steadily by enlarging yields per hectare. Historically a
major food importing region, Western Europe has been reducing its dependence
upon major exporting nations through sound agricultural management, and the
potential for increased food production is considerable (Table 10). Dairy
products may be in surplus, grain production could easily be increased and meats
will need to be imported into Western Europe. On the whole, Western Europe is
handicapped by high production costs and sheltered by protective and support
policies.

Australia, New Zealand and other countries in Oceania are major producers of
only a few agricultural commodities, but contribute to the food needs of the

world vast quantities of grains, meat and dairy products. At times Oceania supplies one-quarter of the world's commodity exports of grains, meat and dairy products. Potentials to increase high-quality protein livestock products so needed by a hungry world appear to be limited only by economic factors, accessibility to markets and forage base. On the other hand, potential for increased cereal and oilseed production appears to be restricted.

Japan, a country with a highly developed market economy, has experienced profound changes in food habits since World War II. Japan has become one of the world's largest net importers of agricultural products and accounts annually for ten percent or so of total world agricultural imports. Possibilities for increasing domestic production of rice, barley, soybeans and beef exist, but will require governmental price incentives. Rice production continues to suffer from pressures to produce high quality specialty foods on limited agricultural land. Japan will continue to be a net agricultural importer and food available to the Japanese people will be greatly affected by general world commodity market situations.

Eastern Europe, characterized since World War II by marked changes in land ownership and socialization of agriculture, has suffered from the agricultural sector of the economy being denied adequate finances and agriculturalists being poorly remunerated for their labor. All six countries experience an agricultural framework noted for detailed state supervision, a drive for internal self-sufficiency and strong state pressures to provide low-cost staple food to the urban proletariat.[11] There was popular dissatisfaction with the low levels of food available in the 1950s and early 1960s and with the over-all quality of foods. State policies introduced in the late 1960s, designed to increase production and internal consumption of livestock products, have been successful. Meat is now being exported, but grain and oilseed meal imports are substantial.

USSR has attempted to modify the Stalin model for agricultural development in recent years, and has enhanced agricultural output. An all-out campaign is being waged by the state to raise the dietary standards of Soviet citizens to those of other developed countries. Intensification of agricultural activities has contributed to the successes recorded in the Ninth Five Year Plan (1971–75) and the beginning of the Tenth (1976–81). Setbacks in grain production in 1972 and 1975 reduced the anticipated grain output and led to large grain imports.[12] Growth in livestock herds has exceeded feed production and great quantities of animal feed will be imported. Soviet feed imports have been so large in recent years that the world's cereal market has been disrupted. Bread and feed grain imports have been massive, ranging up to 25 million tons in one year. Large purchases of soybeans and other oilseeds have also been made by the Soviet government. A recent US/USSR agreement commits the Soviet Union to purchase each year (1976–81) 6 million tons of wheat and corn, plus an option for an additional two million tons if needed.

Africa and the Near East. The rural population of that region is basically self-supporting in food products and demands for food imports are generated primarily by urban dwellers. Wheat and rice are the important food grains on most countries' import lists. Bread wheat imports, totaling between 10 and 15 percent of the world's commodity grain, are purchased for urban markets each year. Although Africa and the Near East contain only 10 percent of the world's population, Nigeria and Egypt with annual population growth rates near 3 percent have special problems in providing food for urban dwellers. Increased imports of wheat, rice and meat (predominantly mutton and lamb) will be related to foreign exchange generated by higher oil prices or foreign aid.

Latin America, a vast geographical area containing only 8 percent of the world's population, exports nearly 20 percent of the world's agricultural products annually. Argentina, Brazil and Mexico account for about 60 percent of gross farm production and population. Inequalities in land tenure and slow adoption of modern farming techniques have kept farm productivity low. The majority of rural dwellers in Latin America engages in subsistence farming on small land holdings. Commercial food products are secured mainly from extensively farmed large estates. Daily and annual food consumption levels, although generally satisfactory throughout Latin America, are very low in a few countries. Coffee, sugar, beef, corn, bananas and soybeans are major exports. Several countries in Latin America, unfortunately, have large annual deficits in wheat and dairy products. Cereal and meat exports will probably decline in the future and disparity within Latin America between food surplus and food deficit countries will widen.

Far East. Here delimited to include Iran on the west and South Korea on the east but excluding Asian centrally planned economies, the Far East is a region with many food problems and over one quarter of the world's population. Half of the region's population lives in India; and India, Pakistan, Bangladesh and Indonesia account for a large part of the Far East's food production and international food trade. The Philippines, Malaysia and Sri Lanka are significant importers of basic foods. South Korea, Taiwan and Iran have more or less strong internal economies and affluence has stimulated imports of selected cereals and foods of animal origins. Burma and Thailand are traditional food exporting countries. Population growth, changes in personal incomes and poverty are important determinants of food import demands in the Far East. The majority of the people in the world with very small annual incomes lives in this region. Unless some fundamental changes are made within agriculture and life styles, grain import needs may exceed 40 million tons annually by 1985. To prevent a reduction in basic diets and to avoid a famine, an additional 30 to 40 million tons may be needed.

China's food supply prospects are governed by its large population (about one-fifth of the world's total population) and territory, its developing economy and its modified western socialist-Asian pattern of agricultural production. For decades, the main goal of Chinese agriculture has been to provide adequate food supplies for an increasing internal population. Rice, the mainstay of Chinese diets, has been increased in total production and its growing area expanded. Production of wheat, the most important basic cereal after rice, has doubled in the past twenty or so years. Changes in food consumption patterns in China will be gradual, but there is a growing demand for more rice and wheat, plus sophisticated supplemental foods. China is likely to continue to follow a principle of food self-sufficiency, but will import rice and wheat when prices are favorable.

FOOD AVAILABILITY IN A ONE-WORLD CONTEXT

A precarious food situation exists in many developing countries. Increasing populations, desires for higher quality and greater varieties of food and commitments to use force if dietary expectations are not met, make it imperative for governments to insure stable supplies of quality foods for internal consumption. Recent cereal production figures and consumption trends in the poor countries of the world have been disheartening and a major effort to boost production is necessary. There exist excellent possibilities for expanding agricultural production in the most seriously affected (MSA) countries and external aid can assist in this process. Simultaneous, coordinated efforts by all countries, combined with a desire for developing countries to help themselves, can solve this serious problem facing the world's food economy. Developing countries differ from one another greatly and any development program must take this into consideration. Self-sufficiency in all foods should not be the basis of all programs. An international division of economic activities implies the maintenance and expansion of food trade flows. The physical nature of all basic food production processes dictates that there will be times of surplus and times of deficiencies on this earth; countries must have food available at all times to help other countries or areas where there are temporary food shortages. Many developed and developing countries will continue to be large-scale importers of cereals, but current exporting nations' food policies and responses of surplus food producers should not be conceived as permanent. Experiences of the past six centuries indicate it would be foolish and dangerous to base any country's food plan or regional policy on assumptions of a permanent surplus trend or permanent food deficit.

NOTES

[1]W. Carey, "Concerning the Technology Base," *Science*, Vol. 203 (Feb. 2, 1979), p. 403.

[2]W. Dando and G. Johnson, *Innovations in Land Use Management* (Grand Forks, N.D.: University of North Dakota Press, 1976), pp. 1–3.

[3]J. Parker, "Agricultural Imports by Major Developing Countries—Their Growth in the Last Decade and Prospects for 1976," paper presented at the American Agricultural Economics Association Annual Meeting, Penn State University, (August, 1976), pp. 1–2.

[4]*Provisional Indicative World Plan for Agricultural Development* (Rome: Food and Agriculture Organization of the United Nations, 1969), 2 vols.

[5]L. Blakeslee, E. Heady and C. Framingham, *World Food Production, Demand and Trade* (Ames, Iowa: Iowa State University Press, 1973).

[6]L. Brown, *The Worldwide Loss of Cropland* (Washington, D.C.: Worldwatch Institute, 1978), pp. 33–38.

[7]*Climate and Food* (Washington, D.C.: National Academy of Science, 1976), pp. 9–11.

[8]W. Slater, *Man Must Eat* (Chicago: University of Chicago Press, 1964), pp. 69–88.

[9]R. Whyte, *Rural Nutrition in Monsoon Asia* (Oxford: Oxford University Press, 1974), pp. 3–4.

[10]*The World Agricultural Situation* (Washington, D.C.: U.S. Department of Agriculture Report No. 98, 1978).

[11]W. Dando, "Wheat in Romania," *Annals of the Association of American Geographers*, Vol. 64 (June 1974), pp. 241–257.

[12]D. Shapley, "Soviet Grain Harvests: CIA Study Pessimistic on Effects of Weather," *Science*, Vol. 195, pp. 377–378.

Chapter 11

World food/population balance

INTRODUCTION

The world demand for food is directly proportional to population and closely connected to income elasticity. Uncertainty about future famines and future demands for food can be related to three questions—how fast population will grow, where growth will take place and how much income will be available for staple foods. World population now exceeds four billion and it took only 16 years to increase from three billion. The time span required to add one billion people to the earth's population has declined from 100 years, then 30 years, then about 16 years. Rapid population increases are a recent phenomenon; throughout most of human history the rate of population growth averaged only slightly above replacement levels (Figure 33). Increases in the growth rate began primarily as a result of declining mortality during the last few centuries. This decline in mortality has accelerated significantly during recent decades. Resistance in social structure modification and failure to make cultural adjustments to new life style opportunities are major reasons the decline in mortality has not been accompanied by a parallel decline in fertility within the majority of developing countries. The world population growth rate has risen to about 2 percent per year and if sustained the world's population could double in 35 years (Table 11). Rates of natural increase do range widely among countries and within areas of countries from a negative rate to well over three percent per year. On the average, less than one in 40 children dies before reaching the age of 12 months in developed countries, one in 15 dies before

181

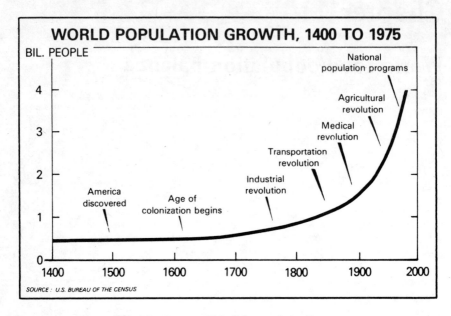

Fig. 33. *Source:* U.S. Bureau of the Census.

reaching that age in Latin America, one in 10 in Asia and one in seven in Africa. In some less developed countries one child in four dies before the age of one year. Life expectancy must be considered in any food/population balance study and there are great global variations in life expectancy. At present, average expectation of life duration at birth is 63 years in Latin America, 57 years in Asia and approximately 46 years in Africa. Life expectancy in the more developed regions of the world exceed 71 years. In many less developed countries governments are explicitly attempting to reduce family size and

Table 11. World Population, 1975 and 2000

Region	1975		2000		Increase	
	Population (mill.)	Share of total (%)	Population (mill.)	Share of total (%)	Total (mill.)	Share of total (%)
World	3,967	100	6,253	100	2,277	100
Developing countries	2,835	71	4,893	78	2,058	90
Developed countries	1,132	29	1,360	22	228	10

Source: U.N. medium variant projection. United Nations Working Paper No. 55, May 1975.

increase longevity, while in a few countries (both developed and developing) governments are attempting to increase family size while adding additional years to already high life expectancy rates.

Throughout the world urban centers are experiencing phenomenal population growth, and urban populations are increasing in numbers considerably faster than rural populations. The majority of the world's population will live in urban areas by the end of this century. Urbanization is equated to modernization and in most countries it now is accompanied by overcrowding in certain districts, urban unemployment, slums, crime, deterioration of environments and social dislocation. Only in a select few countries has the urbanization process been efficiently managed and afforded its citizens the maximum use of the positive attributes associated with urbanization. In most developing countries the high rate of urban population growth has been accompanied by an increase in rural population, although not of the same magnitude. Massive urban emigration, in both more developed and less developed countries, has depleted rural areas of skilled and unskilled young people and left rural areas with populations whose age distribution and skills are not most favorable to economic development. The rural to urban migration in countries is compounded by intra-urban migration between major world cities and has resulted in removal of skilled workers and professionals from the less developed to more developed countries.

Birth rates in rural and urban areas are greatly affected by the population's age structure. Declining age-fertility ratios are the main factor underlying the declining proportion of children in a population. The number of children in the world less than 15 years of age will decline 5 to 10 percent from our current ratio by the year 2000. Because birth rates have declined in developed countries, the population over 65 years of age has increased to at least 10 percent of the total; average population aged 65 years and over in developing countries constitutes only 3 percent. The aging of populations in developing countries has begun and will increase in the future. However, because of relatively high proportions of children and young people in less developed countries, declines in fertility levels reflected in lower population growth rates will not be noted for some time. Countries concerned about increasing the quality of each citizen's life and decreasing the possibility of famine must anticipate future demographic trends and take appropriate action.[1]

DEMOGRAPHIC PROJECTIONS

There has been unprecedented world population growth in this century and the principal impetus has been a rapid decline in death rates (Figure 34) and an uneven but slow decline in birth rates. In 1905, the death rate was estimated to be about 30 per thousand and the birth rate 40 per thousand. World population growth rate was less than 1 percent in 1905. World War I, the influenza epidemic and famines lowered the population growth rate in the 1915 to 1925 period. Birth rates increased in the 1920s and there was a sharp decline in death rates; world population growth rates rose to the 1 percent level and remained

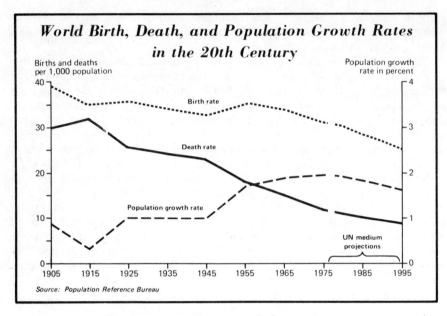

**World Birth, Death, and Population Growth Rates
in the 20th Century**

Births and deaths
per 1,000 population

Population growth
rate in percent

Birth rate

Death rate

Population growth rate

UN medium
projections

1905 1915 1925 1935 1945 1955 1965 1975 1985 1995

Source: Population Reference Bureau

Fig. 34. *Source*: Population Reference Bureau.

rather stationary until World War II. Birth rates rose again in the 1950s, while death rates dropped sharply. This induced the rapid rise in world population that continued till leveling off in the mid-1970s. The peak 1.9 percent annual growth rate in 1975–80 is projected to decline to 1.64 percent in the last five-year period of this century. Anticipated decline in world population growth rates is encouraging when attempting to assess the world's production and distribution of food, and determining famine potential.

United Nations projections for world population in the year 2000 range from a low of 5.8 billion to a high of 6.6 billion. The population estimates for developing countries, including the Peoples Republic of China, vary between 3.5 and 4.0 billion (Table 12). It must be understood that there are great uncertainties inherent in population forecasts. Lester Brown has interpreted population statistics differently and has written that the world's population growth rate declined between 1970 and 1975. He concluded that world population growth lowered from a 1.90 percent annual rate in 1970 to 1.64 percent in 1975. Yearly world population increase, according to Brown, declined from 69 million in 1970 to 64 million in 1975.[2] Regardless of the interpretation, there will be a greater percentage of the world's population in developing countries than developed countries in the year 2000 as shown in Table 12. The United Nations estimated in 1975 that the developing countries, including the Peoples Republic of China, had 71 percent of the world's population. The same countries are projected by the United Nations to have 78 percent of the world's

Table 12. World Population, 1950–2000

Region	1950	1960	1970	1980	1990	2000
World	2,501	2,986	3,610	4,373	5,279	6,253
Developed countries	857	976	1,084	1,181	1,278	1,361
Developing countries	1,644	2,010	2,526	3,192	4,001	4,893
People's Rep. of China	588	654	772	908	1,031	1,148
World excluding China	1,086	1,356	1,754	2,284	2,970	3,745

Source: U.N. medium variant projection. United Nations Working Paper No. 55, May 1975.

population by 2000. Developing countries will need to insure food and sustenance for 90 percent of the world's population growth during the last quarter of this century. Population growth in developing countries is projected to drop below 2.0 percent, but the total population for developing countries may approach 5.0 billion.

WORLD'S CARRYING CAPACITY

Four out of five people who live on the earth in the year 2000 are anticipated to reside in developing countries. Of the estimated demand for food in food-deficit countries, 80 percent will be a direct result of increased population.[3] Developed countries have largely completed the demographic transition and now record low birth rates, low death rates and low population growth (Figure 35). Developing countries are passing through the demographic transition model slowly and are presently recording high birth rates, low death rates and relatively high population growth. The medical revolution has steadily reduced the death rate in most countries of the world and specifically in the less developed countries since 1950. Unfortunately, births recorded in less developed countries declined much slower than deaths in this time period. Birth rates, death rates and natural increase vary by area, country and world region. Growth rates have sharply leveled off in places because the growth reached or exceeded the actual, perceived or desired "carrying capacity."[4] The physical and cultural environments of places can support or carry a maximum number of individuals and when the carrying capacity is exceeded a physical and social breakdown occurs. Famines are manifestations of these breakdowns, but they are only one of many physical and cultural hazards. *Carrying capacity is a term used to describe the ability of a place's resources to support a given way of life.*[5]

Leo F. Laporte, in his informative book, *Encounter with the Earth Resources*, wrote:[6]

> ... the average world food requirement per person per day is 2354 calories, and right now 2420 calories are available .... The world's carrying capacity in

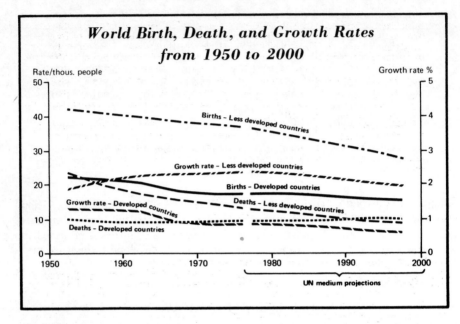

World Birth, Death, and Growth Rates from 1950 to 2000

Fig. 35. *Source:* L. Atkinson, *World Population Growth: Analysis and New Projections of the United Nations* (Washington, D.C.: U.S. Government Printing Agency, Foreign Agricultural Economic Report No. 129, 1977), p. 8.

terms of food resources can, at best, increase eightfold: the amount of farmland can double, the productivity of farmland can double with existing agricultural technologies, and technological innovations can achieve still another doubling in productivity itself. These three doublings can at most, expand food resources eight times what they are now .... At present rates of world population growth, with total population doubling every 35 years, we will reach this predicted carrying capacity in 105 years—when the earth's population is around 30 billion people, eight times the present amount.

Laporte emphasized the three most often cited means of expanding world food production: cultivating new land, intensifying agriculture on land already under cultivation by conventional means and developing new technologies and new sources of food production. Ned Greenwood and J. M. B. Edwards assessed the world's carrying capacity in purely quantitative terms based upon production of grain and starchy tuber food:[7]

One acre of land, producing 44 bushels of wheat per year with energy value of 89,800 calories per bushel, will more than satisfy the caloric needs of four people. Ireland averages 25 metric tons of potatoes per hectare which is equivalent to 7 SNUs per acre. Millet yields as high as 1,069 pounds of grain per acre have been reported in Tanzania when precautions were taken to prevent severe leaching of soil nutrients and chemical fertilizers by heavy precipitation. But it is hard to give any but tentative answers when so many variables are involved. One thing, however, is certain: balanced nutrition draws from a wide range of foods. These include milk, meats, and a variety of fresh fruits and vegetables, all of which have high land requirements. Even under the most favorable cropping, a little more than an acre is needed to produce 1 SNU in milk. Meat is still more expensive in terms of land use: a pound of meat requires about 10 pounds of grain, so that even at the high rate of 44 bushels per acre the meat produced by this technique yields only .4 SNU per acre. Fruits and vegetables vary widely in land requirements, but the high-quality crops typically average 1 SNU per acre.

Thus even under optimum conditions it takes from 1 to 3 acres to produce 1 SNU, if the calories are supplied by foods of quality and variety adequate for normal health. The 3.5 billion acres of arable land now under crop cultivation are not enough to provide the world population of 3.6 billion with adequate nutrition.

Maarten J. Chrispeels and David Sadava analyzed the world's population carrying capacity by considering plant productivity and energy transfer:[8]

How many hectares are needed to support one person? A person who requires 2,700 calories per day (an average figure) needs about one million calories per year. The productivity of many well-managed wheat-producing areas is around 4,000 kilograms per hectare. This corresponds to a net primary productivity of about 1,500 grams of dry matter per square meter per year. The grain yield is less than the primary productivity, because only 25 to 33 percent of the whole plant is grain. One kilogram of grain has a caloric content of 3,500 Calories and the wheat harvest mentioned above thus yields about 14 million calories per hectare. As a result, one hectare can support fourteen people on a strictly vegetarian diet.

They also noted that in many developed countries animal products are a basic component of the normal diet. These animal products are produced largely by using grains (which could be eaten directly by humans), and the efficiency of converting plant products to animal products is about 20 percent. In countries where animal products are consumed, one hectare of land will support only four or five people. Taking this into consideration, Chrispeels and Sadava modified their figure for the number of people who could be supported by one hectare:

Using an average figure of one hectare of farmland in nonfarm use for every 12 people, we calculate that the world can support about 15 billion people on a vegetarian diet or 5 billion people on a mixed diet. Since the world population passed 4 billion in 1976, and will probably double within less than 35 years, the need for population control is apparent. Since these estimates of food production assume that maximal use is being made of the arable land, the need for widespread use of modern agricultural techniques and of high-yielding crop strains is also apparent.

The carrying capacity of our planet can be estimated by its maximum sustainable food yield.[9] This varies widely for humid-fertile areas have greater natural carrying capacities than semiarid, arid or mountain areas. K. Malin, in *How Many Will the Earth Feed* (originally, *Zhiznennye resursy chelovechestva*), computed the carrying capacity of the world from the energy viewpoint. He postulated:[10]

Available estimates reveal that 63.8 million LHPS of solar energy reach the surface of the earth per year. Of this amount, 200,000 LHPS are assimilated by vegetation—15-20 percent of it, or 30,000–40,000 LHPS, by ground plants. Hence, if all the solar energy now assimilated by the ground plants were consumed only by food and fodder crops, there would be sufficient means of substance for 44 to 58 billion people. And if all the marine flora consisted only of food and fodder crops there would be enough alimentation for 290 billion people.

There is no doubt, too, that mankind will eventually master the synthesis of all the components of food and will obtain any foodstuff without the photosynthesis of plants. Potential food reserves will then be determined solely by the energy resources of mankind. In other words, they will practically be boundless.

Malin and Sterling Wortman, President of the International Agricultural Development Service IADS) and Vice-President of The Rockefeller Foundation stress in their publications that the world's food problem today and tomorrow does and will not rise from any physical limitation for food production or potential world food output. Limitations on carrying capacity are to be found, in their estimation, within the social, economic and political structures of countries and in the economic relations among countries. Sterling Wortman and Ralph W. Cummings, Jr., in their excellent book, *To Feed this World: The Challenge and the Strategy*, concluded:[11]

The evidence clearly indicates that the overall physical potential exists on earth to food a vastly larger population than now lives here. Estimates of the carrying capacity of the earth have ranged as high as 76 billion people, based on a minimum subsistence diet of 2,500 kilocalories per person per day. Providing an "adequate" diet, including high-quality protein (protein with the balanced content of amino acids required by human beings and all other warm-blooded animals except cattle and related ruminants) and "protective" foods such as fruits and vegetables, or the equivalent of 4,000–5,000 kilocalories per person per day, the potential gross cropped area of the world is estimated (by Revelle) to be sufficient for 38 to 48 billion people—over 10 times the present human population of the earth.

If Laporte, Chrispeels and Sadava, Malin and Wortman, and Cummings are correct in their assumptions and if the world can provide food for vastly larger populations than now live—why are there famines? A world with a carrying capacity of 5, 10, 15, 30 or 76 billion people should never have recorded one famine. Figure 11 which shows world population growth from 1400 to 1975, provides a clue to the world's carrying capacity enigma. For thousands of years, human numbers reflected closely the carrying capacity of their environments. Various revolutions, such as the Industrial, Transportation, Medical, Agricultural, etc., have permitted populations to exceed the natural carrying capacity of places and when the population/food imbalance became critical a famine or famine-induced migration restored some balance. The food problems of the world are directly attributable to populations exceeding the carrying capacity at places and political-economic systems which nurture and sustain such problems.

The phenomenal increase in world population in the last 100 or so years can be traced to more food being produced each year and to the general improvement in sanitary and medical conditions which have reduced the factor of disease-death throughout the world. Also, the general improvement in the quality of food and the quality of human life on earth was an extremely important factor in increasing human longevity. Increases in the carrying capacity generation after generation were dependent upon cultural and political matters in the acceptance of innovation and change. Estimates of the ability of this planet to support populations vary widely for there have been differences in assessing the physical base (land, water and energy) and differences in assessing the cultural base, specifically levels of acceptable standards of living. Most researchers who study carrying capacity have relegated the existence of nation-states, problems in transportation, production or yield differences, capital disparity, etc., to very minor roles. The world is divided into different cultural realms and political entities, separated by oceans and land space, and its physical resources used in different ways for different purposes.

Humans in each cultural realm are physical mechanisms, biological specimens and intelligent cultural beings. No real discussion of carrying capacity can neglect the fact that man is more than an animal with more than animal needs. Problems arise because needs of individuals come into conflict when all draw from a common store of food. The quality of human life in its many aspects conflicts at times with the quantity of human life. Humans are social beings, but they become distinctly antisocial at times. Individuals belong to a society but tend to be suspicious, hostile and indifferent to individuals in other societies. Most well fed human groups show little visible concern for other human groups suffering from malnutrition or undernutrition, little concern for famine and are unified in large part by opposition to or fears of other societies. The world is not one society with one economy and one universal language. Although the production of food can determine the number of people who might live in a given place, the number who actually exist is determined by numerous social factors. Without changing in any way the amount of arable land, agricultural techniques or energy sources, any one of a number of population equilibria can be established. Until humans become aware of their fellow humans and the correspondence between their well-being and all other humans, until the environment is regarded as a responsibility rather than an economic opportunity, famines will signify that people have exceeded the carrying capacity of an environment at a place, area or region.

NOTES

[1] *United Nations World Population Conference, Bucharest, August 19-30, 1974* (Washington, D.C.: U.S. Government Printing Office, Department of State Bulletin, 1974), pp. 12-14.

[2] L. Brown, *World Population Trends: Signs of Hope, Signs of Stress* (Washington, D.C.: Worldwatch Institute, Paper No. 8, 1976), p. 33.

[3] *Meeting Food Needs in the Developing World* (Washington, D.C.: International Food Policy Research Institute, Report No. 1, 1976), p. 18.

[4] J. Becht and L. Belzung, *World Resource Management* (Englewood Cliffs, N.J.: Prentice-Hall, 1975), pp. 67–68.

[5] L. Brown, *The Twenty-Ninth Day* (New York: W. W. Norton, 1978); R. Durrenberger, *Dictionary of the Environmental Sciences* (Palo Alto: National Press Books, 1973), p. 37; and A. Schmieder, P. Griffin, R. Chathan and S. Natoli, *A Dictionary of Basic Geography* (Boston: Allyn & Bacon, 1970), p. 31.

[6] Leo F. Laporte, *Encounter with the Earth Resources* (San Francisco: Canfield Press, 1975), pp. 157–58.

[7] N. Greenwood and J. Edwards, *Human Environments and Natural Systems* (North Scituate, Mass.: Duxbury Press, 1973), p. 107.

[8] M. Chrispeels and D. Sadava, *Plants, Food and People* (San Francisco: W. H. Freeman, 1977), pp. 76–77.

[9] L. Brown, "Carrying Capacity," *Agenda*, Vol. 1, No. 6 (June, 1978), p. 9.

[10] K. Malin, *How Many Will the Earth Feed* (Moscow: Progress Publishers), pp. 19–20.

[11] S. Wortman and R. Cummings, Jr., *To Feed This World: The Challenge and the Strategy* (Baltimore: The Johns Hopkins University Press, 1978), p. 80.

Chapter 12

Policies and strategies

CROSSING THE RUBICON

The problem of providing food for an expanding world population is not simply a matter of regional food deficiencies, inadequate nutrition, poor transportation networks, cultural inertia—it is a matter of politics, policies and strategies. Most developing nations are not self-sufficient in food production. Along with internal distribution and efficient land use problems, rapid urbanization has placed stress on governments to provide sustenance for burgeoning, concentrated, food-consuming populations. These growing urban centers are growing at the expense of rural areas, giving little return in taxes and hindering efforts to improve agricultural efficiency. Rural problems and rural development are ignored because of the pressing need to feed urban dwellers. Urban food shortages are particularly feared by new governments because of the concentration of people, the potential for famine and the possibility for revolution. Urban food problems are immediate, so governments concentrate on short-ranged strategies to increase urban food supplies by importing staple foods and by lowering prices paid for food, produced in rural areas. Little thought is given to solving the urban food problem by policies directed to improve and enhance internal food production in the hinterlands of urban areas. Frequently, capital investments in urban-industrial complexes are to the detriment of agriculture and rural incentive, but developing countries equate national development with industrialization. Profits from industrial ventures are negated by the need to import food to feed the industrial workers who reside in urban

191

areas. Food shortages, if chronic in the rural and urban areas, lead to political instability, internal chaos and hinder a country's overall socioeconomic progress. Political causes, effects and solutions to hunger and famine are varied and complex. Decisions to distribute a limited resource, food, and provide technical assistance to negate the food/population imbalance in countries are political. The problem of food, population and famine has many physical facets and touches many sensitive cultural areas.

THE FOOD-FAMINE CONTINUUM

The story of famine has been precisely the transformation, or a great movement toward transformation, of communities of people from the Evolutionary Stage, to Spatially Restricted Societies, then Spatially Interdependent Societies and finally to Spatially Restricted Interdependent Societies. In this transformation, people modified the Natural Physical Environment into a Nature-Man Cultural Environment, a Man-Nature Cultural Environment and finally a Man Modifed Physical Environment tending toward a Human Created Artificial Physical Environment (Figure 36). As humans transformed their environments and passed through the Hunting and Gathering, Primitive Agriculture, Intensive Subsistence, Commercial Agriculture, Agro-Biz and the Industrial Agriculture stage, there emerged many centers where food was stored, processed and traded. Agricultural surplus and trade demands generated by

THE FOOD - FAMINE CONTINUUM

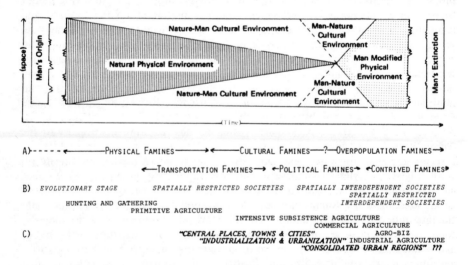

Fig. 36.

individual desires to improve the quality of life led to central places becoming towns, cities, urban areas and consolidated urban regions. Diffusion of foods, specifically grains that could be stored and consumed by people under stress, permitted the carrying capacity of the world to increase. Famines initially were created from natural hazards and could by classified as physical famines. People's ability to modify the physical environment for increased food production soon eliminated, in most parts of the world, the potential for a physical famine. Inadvertent or advertent man-made famines classified as transportation famines, cultural famines, political famines, overpopulation famines and contrived famines replaced physical famines, and famines springing from natural hazards are a risk of a very small fraction of the enormous world population today. The only portion of the world where famines, due to natural hazards, are a risk, is in extremely isolated interior areas of continents or islands which are shut off from the world by lack of transportation and by lack of economic reserves. Members of the world community are no longer dependent upon local food production; they have economic reserves and credit, plus mechanisms of food transport to tide them over with little impact on food consumption if there was a serious crop failure. Technological and economic advances have virtually eliminated the prospect of famine from chancy weather or faulty agricultural practices. The risk of famine from purely natural causes has greatly diminished and the explanation lies in the many-faceted phenomenon, human socioeconomic advancement.

MALTHUS

Thomas Robert Malthus, an ordained Anglican clergyman and professor of history and political economy at the East India College, is most famous for his theory on population. He contended that population increases take place in geometric progression, i.e., population growth tends to exceed increases in food production. His speculations on the relations between human reproduction, food supply and the happiness or misery of nations have had a powerful impact upon food/famine policies and strategies since first postulated in 1798. Malthus' theory on population has been used by many policy makers to justify laissez-faire or noninterference in famine relief and opposition to socioeconomic reforms. In *An Essay on the Principle of Population, as It Affects the Future Improvement of Society, with Remarks on the Speculations of Mr. Godwin, M. Condorcet, and Other Writers*, Malthus postulated that population expands to the limit of carrying capacity, then is stabilized by famine, war and disease. He concluded from his research that population growth reduced the standard of living, was not an economic asset and caused societies to degenerate. Malthus was concerned about the quality of English society and his forcefulness and writing style led to the incorporation of his theory into the theoretical economic systems of the time. He worked to transform what he believed to be correct into state policy and immediate practice, and was so effective he dampened economic optimism and discouraged traditional forms of charity. Malthusian theory of population had an immediate influence on English social policy and the social policy implemented by the cadets he taught who went out to rule British India. Malthus focused much of his attention on the English Poor Laws for he maintained the practices of the Poor Law authorities had much to do with the increase in population. These laws, adopted to meet the distress created by the low wages of farm laborers, provided public relief in proportion to the size of a family and the cost of living, as measured by the price of bread. Malthus contended that the Poor Laws should be abolished and workhouses should be extremely austere. He also opposed birth control for he believed it immoral, would retard economic progress and reduce incentive to work.

The immediate effect of Malthus' theory or principle of population was to prejudice the British upper- and middle-classes' attitudes towards social policies or strategies designed to aid the poor and hungry. Malthusian population theory, when transformed into practice, was very ineffective; it dampened actions to reduce the birth rate or eliminate hunger, inequality and famine. To Charles Darwin, the theory suggested the relationship between progress and the survival of the fittest. Too many educated Englishmen retained the habit of regarding the contemporary history of Great Britain and the United Kingdom as a race between population and food supply until the second half of the 19th century. Malthus' predictions failed to come true but his ideas influenced many policy and decisionmakers to this day.[1]

LIFEBOAT ETHICS

The questions of "who shall live?", "who shall die?" and "who is worth sacrificing for?", applied to international food policy, acknowledge the idea that large-scale famines are inevitable. A decision will need to be made to carefully select countries and peoples for whom aid will make a significant difference. What is the obligation of those who live in affluent developed countries to the poor, hungry and starving people in less-affluent developing countries? Garrett Harden, Professor of Biology and Human Ecology at the University of California, Santa Barbara, proposed the "lifeboat" approach to world food/population problems in the mid-seventies and expanded upon the lifeboat ethic in a paper presented and discussed at The Third Annual Midwestern Conference on Food and Social Policy, Sioux City, Iowa, November 14–16, 1978. Harden's argument against famine relief may be summarized metaphorically as two lifeboats on a survival course, one lifeboat full of affluent well-fed people and the other lifeboat crowded with starving passengers. Those who can, swim towards the lifeboat with food, but what should the passengers in the lifeboat with food do?[2] Harden presents a case against helping the poor and for using famine as a population control tool. He recognizes an emergency situation created by an exploding world population and contends that every life saved by aid provided from surplus food producing countries diminishes the quality of life on earth for subsequent generations. Harden and those who have accepted the lifeboat food policy advocate that the rich nations of the earth must not provide food aid, no financial help to develop national economies, limit immigration from food-deficit to food-surplus countries and reduce other assistance until the overpopulated poor countries have lowered their population within the carrying capacity of their countries. The lifeboat ethic is simple, those who support it are sincere in their concern for the future of the earth, but the ethic is somewhat misleading. A lifeboat is designed to be self-sufficient but countries are dependent upon each other for market and materials; a lifeboat has a definite carrying capacity while the carrying capacity of countries is not known and can be increased; and tempests in the sea on which the lifeboats float or the physical-cultural environment of the world can be so destructive (a world food war) that all boats sink or all countries will be destroyed.

TRIAGE

During the trench-warfare slaughters of World War I, medical units at the front lines separated the wounded into three categories: (1) those likely to die regardless of the treatment they received; (2) those who would probably recover even if untreated and (3) those who could survive only if cared for immediately. With limited manpower, supplies and time the third group *only* received medical attention. Classifying the wounded into groups for treatment was called "triage," from the French verb, trier, to sort. Triage is a standard field hospital procedure for saving the most lives, and for the most efficient use of scarce medical resources. With many concerned population specialists, ecologists and planners troubled about severe food shortages in many parts of the world today and possibly tomorrow, some have advocated the practice of field doctors in dealing with aid to countries suffering from severe hunger problems or famine. Triage, as a food policy, has been discussed and debated in most symposiums or meetings focused upon mounting global food shortages and the maldistribution of food reserves. It was proposed in 1967 by William and Paul Paddock in a book entitled, *Famine—1975: America's Decision: Who Will Survive*. Triage was prescribed as an efficient method of food allocation or food aid in time of widespread famine.[3] The Paddock brothers feared that exploding populations and static food production in food-deficient, developing nations would make famines inevitable, and that the United States will be required to make *the* decision which countries are likely to never solve their food/population problem, which countries will probably solve their food/population problem even if aid is not provided and which countries could solve their food/population problems and contribute to the advancement of a world society if food aid was provided. International triage would require the United States, according to the Paddock brothers, to sort out countries according to those which have a future and should have food aid, and those without a future whose people must be sacrificed for the well being of the world community. Triage has found favor in some circles, but predictably, triage has not been well received by most scientific and academic humanists. The population/food imbalances in parts of the world have accelerated the search for policies and strategies beyond the framework of traditional values, and the specter of triage may be a useful moral prod (Figure 37).[4]

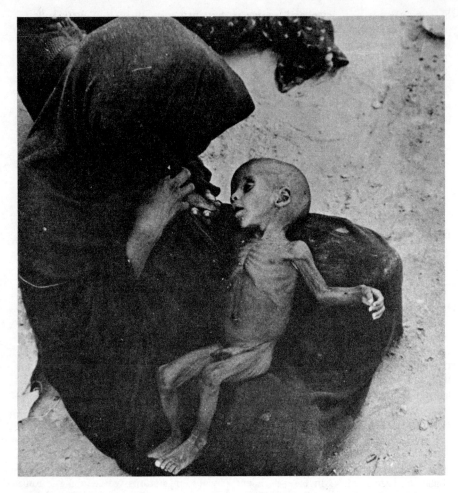

Fig. 37. An emaciated mother tries futilely to nurse her starving son in Mauritana. The boy, though near death, was saved through feedings of a high-protein food mixture supplied by emergency aid (UNICEF photo, ICEF 6944).

CURRENT UNITED STATES FOOD POLICY

In the past decade, fluctuating foreign food needs, regional food shortages, rising food prices and the moral dilemma raised by policy questions such as those presented in the lifeboat and triage ethics have forced the decisionmakers of the United States to re-examine the national food economy and the national food policy. Our internal farm policy, designed to foster and protect American farmers, food processors and distribution, has generated an unofficial national food policy. For decades, food distribution and emergency aid programs were implemented to support farm income by ridding America of surplus commodities. Milton C. Hallberg, an agricultural economist, speaking at a food symposium at The Pennsylvania State University, traced the history of United States agricultural policy and tried to assess its impact; he stated:[5]

> For most crops, prices were supported at high levels with the aid of the Commodity Credit Corporation, acreage controls were imposed to restrict production and export subsidies were used in an attempt to encourage the development of foreign markets. For feed grains (corn, oats, barley, grain sorghum), wheat and cotton, these policies were not successful in reducing surpluses at a reasonable cost. Thus, in time (and specifically during the Kennedy administration), growers of the latter crops were offered payments for leaving land idle in return for lower price supports. By leaving this land idle, not only were surpluses of these three crops reduced to manageable proportions, but also farmers were not encouraged to create additional surpluses in other crops. At the same time additional outlets for farm surpluses were sought through such programs as food aid to less developed countries (PL 480), and the domestic Food Stamp Program. Programs such as the latter were initially sought as a means of disposing of excess production rather than for humanitarian reasons.

Hallberg noted that food surpluses were controlled, farm income supported, markets expanded, consumers kept more or less satisfied and farm efficiency improved to such a degree that by 1972 one farmworker produced enough food to supply himself and more than 51 other persons.

International developments since 1972, precipitated by rising world food demands, devaluation of the dollar, bad agricultural weather around the world and changing consumer food preferences in many foreign countries, necessitated a revamping of federal agricultural legislation. A compromise between domestic consumer food prices, farm income, commercial interests, budget constraints, the needs of the hungry people of the world, plus protection of the environment so future food needs can be met, was needed in a new comprehensive food policy. Robert O. Herrmann, an agricultural economist speaking at the same food symposium, identified a number of considerations he felt needed quantified and balanced against each other:[6]

> (1) the needs and interests of all segments of our own domestic economy—farmers, processors, food retailers and consumers; (2) the needs of our foreign food export customers; (3) the needs of those both at home and abroad who cannot afford to pay for the food they require and must have food aid; (4) the limitations imposed by energy supplies and the energy requirements of food production; (5) the need to balance the use of pesticides, fertilizers, weed-killers and other agricultural chemicals against the desire to protect the environment from their effects.

Herrmann emphasized that the American food consumer must be considered as well as other segments of the food industry. The Agricultural and Consumer Protection Act of 1973 heralded a shift towards a national policy of essentially no government-held grain reserves and no grain reserve policy. Problems arose because reserve grain stocks were necessary for the United States government to meet food emergencies at home and abroad. The bulk of American food transactions became commercial transactions and government policymakers were limited in their ability to directly allocate substantial food contributions to countries seriously affected by temporary food shortages.[7] To rectify this problem in part, a change was made in the 1954 Public Law 480, Title 1, in 1975 and at least 75 percent of P.L. 480, Title 1, programming was directed to be assigned to those countries with per capita income of $300 or less annually.

The Carter administration has repeatedly expressed support for both food price stabilization and an American emergency food relief reserve. Congress drafted in 1977 the "Food and Agricultural Act of 1977," Public Law 95-133, to provide price and income protection to farmers and to assure consumers an abundance of food and fiber at reasonable prices, plus development of a wheat and feed grain reserve.[8] A domestic reserve, consisting of wheat and feed grain, was legislated to be held on farms and controlled by the producers. Target levels for wheat and feed grains were 24 and 29 million tons, but in early 1978 the Carter administration announced that the farmer-held reserve could exceed the 29-million-ton limit originally projected. A second reserve, a United States international emergency reserve, composed of 6 million tons of government-owned wheat, would provide long-term food security for developing countries, benefit farmers in the United States by eliminating a part of their grain surplus and afford the United States an opportunity for cooperation with other countries in establishment of an internationally coordinated famine relief system. Brennon Jones, in the June/July 1978 issue of *Ag World*, urged this two-level reserved system be fully implemented, fully funded, stocked and expanded for grain was available at a depressed price.[9] An unfavorable combination of physical and cultural factors could induce a crop failure draining grain reserves in the United States, and the world could face another period of grain shortages, skyrocketing prices and possibly a famine.

The United States has devised and carried out many food policies and strategies in the past forty years, including using food as a weapon during World War II, as a humanitarian gesture for assisting world economic recovery in the postwar years, as a political weapon to minimize political unrest in the 1950s and 1960s, as a means to dispose of surpluses and as a tool to support internal economic stability while expanding foreign markets and strengthening the dollar. A new era of American food policies and strategies is being entered and issues debated. It is founded on multifaceted economic realities, moral commitments, modern ethics, realization of the importance of the American farming unit as the rock upon which future famine aid is based and the potential for famines. There is an official farm policy, but what are the current United States government's policy and strategies towards famine? Is it abandonment of some poor countries and millions of lives to the silent death or complete food assistance with no strings attached, i.e., a Malthusian, lifeboat, triage or Golden Rule approach?

THE GOLDEN RULE

Although the United States supplies more than one-half of all feed grains that move in world trade, at least one-half of the wheat and about three-quarters of the soybeans in a given year, and could increase its contributions to world food trade, the United States cannot feed the world. The Malthusian, lifeboat and triage approaches to famine relief are morally unacceptable to a great segment of American society for they are perceived as violating the most elementary demands of human justice. At the other end of a famine aid continuum is an ethic familiar to American culture, the Golden Rule. The basic premise of this approach is "give food and aid to other countries in times of acute food shortages or famines as you would want other countries to give food and aid to America in similar circumstances." As a food policy, the Golden Rule is only attainable if the United States can produce and generate the food and insure international tranquility. Earl Butz and many others believe it can be done:[10]

—if we continue to incorporate the latest and best technological advances into our agriculture;
—if we continue with a program of intensive and far-reaching agricultural research;
—if we continue to develop new sources of fertilizers and use them wisely;
—if we continue to develop new types of pesticides and use them wisely;
—if we maintain a viable system of credit to provide the massive capitalization required for intensive agricultural production;
—if we continue to hold together a system of individual freedom and incentives that reach each and every farmer willing to strive for them.

Frances Lappe' and Joseph Collins strongly believe that with American help the people in the food-deficit regions of the world can feed themselves. They have proposed six food-first principles:[11]

(1) There is no country in the world in which the people could not feed themselves from their own resources. But hunger can only be overcome by the transformation of social relationships and only be made worse by the narrow focus on technical inputs to increase production.
(2) Inequality is the greatest stumbling block to development.
(3) Safeguarding the world's agricultural environment and people feeding themselves are complementary goals.
(4) Our food security is not threatened by the hungry masses but by elites that span all market economies profiting by the concentration and internationalization of control of food resources.
(5) Agriculture must not be used as the means to export income but as the way for people to produce food first for themselves.
(6) Escape from hunger comes not through the redistribution of food but through the redistribution of control over food-producing resources.

Melvin H. Middents of Cargill, Inc., agreed with Lappe' and Collins that there is little evidence to indicate the world lacks the ability to feed itself—but differed in the problem of food burden sharing and food distribution. Middents observed that the practical dimensions of the world food problem and the practical limitations on what progress can be achieved often appear overwhelming. One

Fig. 38. Hungry workers on a road in the Andes mountains north of Lima, Peru receiving food aid while working to improve their quality of life (WFP photo by C. Sanchez, 1971).

way of reconciling a sense of moral commitment with a search for practical solutions is policy decisions and policy actions. More liberalized agricultural production and trading policies in both developed and developing countries, plus addressing the problem of population growth in developing countries, are the cornerstone of enhanced world food security.[12] Both conservatives and liberals on how to distribute existing resources, food and technical assistance agree that the solution to the problem is a political one. All note that those who have the power and resources also have the power to allocate those resources. A great deal of cooperation and sensitivity among all nations is necessary for the Golden Rule to be applied to the world food problems. No reasonable individual countenances hunger or famine. Direct attempts to suppress hunger and famine by relief and charity are dealing with symptoms, not causes. Society must respond to the searching question of worldwide food needs and relate policies and strategies to the desired quality of life (Figure 38).

NOTES

[1] A. Flew, "The Structures of Malthus' Population Theory," *Australasian Journal of Philosophy*, Vol. 35 (1957), pp. 1–20; R. Wagner, *Environment and Man* (New York: W. W.

Norton, 1974), p. 473; and M. Micklin, *Population, Environment, and Social Organization: Current Issues in Human Ecology* (Hinsdale, Ill.: Dryden Press, 1973), p. 106.

[2] Read carefully all of the following publications by Garrett Harden: "Lifeboat Ethics—The Case Against Helping the Poor," *Psychology Today*, (Sept 1974); "Living on a Lifeboat," *Bioscience*, (Oct. 1974); "Lifeboat Ethics: Food and Population," in I. Barbour, ed., ed., *Finite Resources and the Human Future* (Minneapolis: Augsburg Press, 1976); and "Carrying Capacity as an Ethical Concept," in G. Lucas and T. Ogletree, eds., *Lifeboat Ethics* (New York: Harper & Row, 1976).

[3] W. Paddock and P. Paddock, *Famine—1975: America's Decision: Who Will Survive* (Boston: Little, Brown & Co., 1967).

[4] J. Mayer, "What We Must Do to Feed the World," *Reader's Digest*, (Sept. 1975), pp. 75–78.

[5] M. Hallberg, "U.S. Agricultural Policy and the Consumer," in *Food and Our Future* (University Park, Pa.: Pennsylvania State University, 1975), p. 148.

[6] R. Herrmann, "Needed: A National Food Policy," in *Food and Our Future* (University Park, Pa.: Pennsylvania State University, 1975), p. 153.

[7] C. Christensen, "Food: American Power and Metapower," unpublished paper presented at the meetings of the American Association for the Advancement of Science and the International Studies Association, (Feb. 1976), pp. 15–16.

[8] "Food and Agriculture Act of 1977," Public Law 95-113, Senate and House of Representatives of the U.S. Congress (Washington, D.C.: U.S. Government Printing Office, 1977).

[9] B. Jones, "Needed: An Emergency Food Reserve," *Ag World*, Vol. 4, No. 6 (June/July, 1978), pp. 12–13.

[10] E. Butz, "Butz Scores Restraints on Incentives," *Milling & Baking News*, (March 9, 1976), p. 70.

[11] F. Lappe' and J. Collins, "Food First!," in T. Emmel, ed., *Global Perspectives on Ecology* (Palo Alto: Mayfield Publishing Co., 1977), p. 464.

[12] M. Middents, "Analyzes ability to meet food needs," *Milling & Baking News*, (June 3, 1975), p. 18.

Epilogue

This study of the spatial, temporal and regional dynamics of famine traces our species bond with the earth, focusing on the physical and cultural parameters of food production, the evolution in food sources and preferences and malnutrition and undernutrition. Many scholars have applied the word *famine* to any great shortage, but a more concise working definition, "a protracted total shortage of food in a restricted geographical area, causing widespread disease and death from starvation," was used to delimit five major world famine regions. These regions were Northeast Africa and the Middle East, 4000–500 B.C.; Mediterranean Europe, 501 B.C.–A.D. 500; Western Europe, A.D. 501–1500; Eastern Europe, A.D. 1501–1700; and Asia, A.D. 1710–1978. Famines, as cultural hazards with spatial and temporal dimensions, are multifactored in origin, but can be classified by the dominant factor at a particular time in human historical geography. Using a data bank of over 8000 famines spanning more than 6,000 years, projections indicate a high probability for famines in the future. However, a review of the literature also reveals there are many conflicting views and interpretations of contemporary world food problems. Prominent researchers with specific points of view provided guidelines into the socioeconomic characteristics of countries which would best provide insights or the right physical-cultural mix for meaningful famine case studies. These case studies were developed with the thought that the past might serve as a key to the future and with the hope that they would help readers better understand the full ramifications of a famine. Countries selected for case study review were ones that provided a balanced view of what could occur in the future, in distinct political-social-economic systems.

England/United Kingdom was chosen for this island kingdom epitomized western culture and capitalism; Russia/USSR for it epitomized a mixed-cultural, mixed-racial base and Marxist socialism; and India for it epitomized eastern culture, colonialism and a hybrid political system. People through time in each study area have molded different climatic, soil and vegetal resources into distinctive cultural landscapes—and each case study area has experienced many famines. These case studies substantiate and reinforce the theme that famines are not confined to a single racial group, a distinct cultural region, a particular country, a specific natural zone or a certain time in human history.

A world famine could begin tomorrow but it could not remain unrecognized long for there is unity in the diversity of this one-world. Diversity in foods produced and food waste, seasons when foods are planted and harvested, storage and preservation practices, transportation and packaging techniques and modes of distribution to consumers and human needs have led to diversity in views regarding the world's food/population balance. The world's carrying capacity for humans (the number of people who can be properly fed in a given year) is very difficult to quantify with certainty for there are too many unknowns. Millions of people on earth are currently suffering from undernutrition and malnutrition, and this strengthens the contention that food policies and strategies, not carrying capacity figures, determine who will eat and who will not eat in the future. The food-famine continuum illustrates the role humans play in molding their physical and social environment and places famines in their proper cultural, decision making perspective. Malthusian population theory and social policies, the lifeboat ethic, the triage ethic, the current United States food policy and the Golden Rule are possible policies and strategies that will be used by those who have food and power. There are many critical food issues for the future and this geography of famine is only one of many studies that will be written for many geographers have recognized famine as a cultural hazard with discernible geographic dimensions.

Index

205